Praise for Just

FIRST EDITION

"Non-lawyers will be challenged to understand and endorse the work of legal representation ... once they finish the book, they'll understand why the law demands that even the most unsavory persons are entitled to zealous advocacy."

       DONALD C. BROSS, Professor Emeritus,
       University of Colorado School of Medicine

"David Savitz offers a unique view of the case, the characters and the multiple personality defense that made the Carlson case front page news in Colorado- and across the country- for years."

       BRIAN MAASS, Investigative Reporter for CBS4 Denver

"This book is a poignant forensic case study of a young man accused of murdering his parents. Through the eyes of the criminal defense attorney, we learn much about the enduring emotional damages from the horrid abuse, the unmentionable cruelties and suffering inflicted, and emotionally barren and loveless childhoods endured by the youngest of children."

       A.E. OBOLSKY, Medical Director and Forensic Psychiatrist,
       Health & Law Resource, Inc., Chicago, IL

"The crime, not a whodunit but why it occurred, is an absorbing mystery of claimed mental illness and parricide from the perspective of a passionate defense attorney. . . . Among others who will enjoy this true crime book, there is much to learn here for criminal defense attorneys and forensic mental health professionals."

       PHILIP S. TROMPETTER, Police and Forensic Psychologist

"*Just in the Nick of Time* is one of the most profound cases of Multiple Personality Disorder (MPD), all told from the perspective of the person who interacted most with the personalities, his criminal defense lawyer David Savitz. It is a book about what happens when a mental disease far outpaces the understanding of the courts, the psychiatric community, and the public."

       LARRY POZNER, NACDL Past President

"A must read of two lawyers whose empathy pushed them to persist beyond the call of duty to defend an accused double murderer with a bizarre mental disorder in the face of a state's active resistance to comply with two judges' orders! What shines from every page is their humanity despite the horror of the story."

        MARC SAGEMAN, M.D., Ph.D., Scholar on
        Forensic Psychiatry and Terrorism.

"Unflinching and insightful, a masterful read about the difficulties of mental health issues, empathy and compassion for the client, and the frustrations encountered in our present day criminal legal system. *Just in the Nick of Time* has all the makings of a classic true crime novel but what sets it apart is the relationship that unfolds between defense lawyer and client."

        LISA M. WAYNE, President of the NACDL Foundation
        for Criminal Justice and Past President of NACDL

Just in the Nick of Time

By David B. Savitz

NACDL PRESS

For Customer Service, Call 1-202-465-7661

Copyright ©2021 David B. Savitz

All rights reserved. No portion of this book may be reproduced or transmitted in any form whatsoever, including electronic, mechanical or any information storage or retrieval system, except as may be expressly permitted in the 1976 Copyright Act or in writing from the publisher.

Requests for permission should be addressed to:
NACDLPress
1660 L Street NW, 12th Floor
Washington, DC 20036

Library of Congress Control Number: 2021943847

ISBN: 978-0-9994728-4-2

Just in the Nick of Time (1st Ed.)
Published by NACDLPress
Washington, DC

Manufactured in the USA

Contents:

Chapter 1: November 2, 1989 1

Chapter 2: From Baguettes to Murder 4

Chapter 3: Our First Meeting – October 17, 1983 8

Chapter 4: Funding the Defense 12

Chapter 5: The Beginnings of the Making of a Lawyer 15

Chapter 6: Helping Others 21

Chapter 7: The Final Shaping of a Trial Lawyer 26

Chapter 8: A $25 Fee & a Nunchaku 31

Chapter 9: The Psych Hold 38

Chapter 10: Another Sybil? 45

Chapter 11: Three Girls & the Doppel Ganger 59

Chapter 12: One Black Suitcase & Nine Personalities 66

Chapter 13: Sans Eyebrows 73

Chapter 14: Justin, Steve & Norman 78

Chapter 15: Black & Blue & Finally Ross, Too 88

Chapter 16: Birthday Cake, Matzo Balls, & a Fig Newton 97

Chapter 17: Born into Sin..................................105

Chapter 18: Spark Plugs & Judge Day.....................111

Chapter 19: Before the Homicides.........................115

Chapter 20: The Lawyers Take the Stand..................121

Chapter 21: The Defense Experts Take Center Stage 130

Chapter 22: The Prosecution's Experts Follow.............135

Chapter 23: Our Ace in the Hole..........................140

Pictures..143

Chapter 24: Judge Day's Decision 173

Chapter 25: The Nightmare Begins 176

Chapter 26: A Gentle and Perfect Beginning 184

Chapter 27: Connecting as One............................189

Chapter 28: Their Love Has Endured......................194

Chapter 29: The Nightmare Becomes Worse...............197

Chapter 30: The Changing of the Guard 204

Chapter 31: The Soul of an Angel 210

Chapter 32: Hospital Friends 213

Chapter 33: Understanding the Many Sides of Ross Carlson . . . 219

Chapter 34: The Interminable State Diagnoses 226

Chapter 35: Enough is Enough 234

Chapter 36: Cyborgs & Dr. Martin Orne 240

Chapter 37: A Chair-Rocking Marathon 246

Chapter 38: Kingsley's Solution 254

Chapter 39: Psychotic Machines and the Firing of Walter . . . 262

Chapter 40: Adolescent Pen Pals 271

Chapter 41: Ottsie's Disappointment & the Decision 275

Chapter 42: What's a Little Nosebleed? 284

Chapter 43: The Demons of Life-Saving Treatment 290

Chapter 44: Dancing with Ginger and a Colt 45 301

Chapter 45: Goodbye, My Friend.........................311

Chapter 46: Remembering Special People................323

Chapter 47: Bring Him Home 327

Epilogue: 336

Appendix A: From Paracelsus to the Hillside Strangler......342

PART 1

CHAPTER 1

November 2, 1989

While holding a yellow legal pad in his right hand, The Honorable Robert T. Kingsley emerged from the courtroom's rear door after the luncheon break, signaling the resumption of the day's hearing. "All rise," the bailiff instructed. Not one for much formality, the judge quickly told everyone to please be seated, as he climbed the few steps to the bench. The lanky jurist dropped his notepad on his desk, took his seat, and poured himself a glass of water. He looked at his court reporter and asked her if she was ready; she replied that she was. The reporters and courtroom artists who had laid claim to the first two rows of the courtroom, sat poised with their spiral notepads and sketch books. A handful of Ross's friends, a few executives from the hospital, and a number of curious residents of Castle Rock sat scattered throughout the balance of the courtroom's half-dozen rows. Walter waited eagerly for the judge's invitation for the DA to begin his closing argument; Walter would follow for the defense.

If history were any indicator, His Honor would probably take a brief recess after the closings, revise or add to any findings he had already sketched out, and then return to announce his ruling. The pool television cameraman readied in the back corner of the courtroom. When Walter and I entered the courthouse after the lunch break, we had already seen the TV stations' news trucks revved up in anticipation of the afternoon's live feed. If the reporters had their way, the judge would quicken the pace so the hearing's results could make the afternoon's first news telecast at 4:00. That was doable.

Walter's closing, which he and I fine-tuned both before the hearing began that day and then during the noon break, would probably take 30 to 40 minutes, and DA Bob Chappell would probably take about the same time. Would Ross be returned to the state hospital, or would his two counts of first-degree murder finally move forward after the case's protracted delay? Chappell would press for the latter, arguing that the State had shown Ross was now capable of standing trial. Chappell was hoping that this third time would be a charm. Walter would emphasize that Ross's outlandish behavior and the hospital's antipathy toward treatment and skepticism about the diagnosis had not changed since our last competency hearing more than two years ago. Judge Kingsley leaned forward in his chair, clasped his hands in front of him, as was his custom, and began speaking.

"I don't intend to slight any attorney," Judge Kingsley said respectfully to a quiet audience. "However, in my opinion, it will not serve any purpose to have closing arguments."

I continued looking straight ahead at the judge while seeing from the corner of my eye Walter pushing aside the pages of his closing statement. After working with Walter for nearly two decades and on this case alone for six years, each of us knew the other would be surprised at Kingsley's election to forego closing arguments. During the time of the judge's presiding over the protracted competency aspect of one of Colorado's most unusual murder cases, he had always welcomed closing arguments after our numerous hearings. To abandon that protocol now, especially after this particular hearing that had lasted more than two weeks, was unprecedented. I had an uneasy feeling. I wrote the word "Order" in the middle of the first line of my legal pad. Ross, who was seated to my left, didn't flinch at the judge's opening comments.

"Things have changed since my ruling of October 1987," Judge Kingsley explained. "The most significant event being Dr. Orne's interview of Mr. Carlson. That was when Mr. Carlson rocked backed and forth in his chair for nearly 45 minutes without uttering a word while Dr. Orne tried to engage him in conversation in order to conduct his examination. I had never seen anything like that before in all my years on the bench. However, after Dr. Orne concluded the

Chapter 1: November 2, 1989

interview and Mr. Carlson returned to his ward, he immediately called his attorney and spoke to him for almost 30 minutes."

I wrote in the left margin, "Kingsley has mixed up two different sessions; didn't pay attention to how bizarre that call was." The judge continued to speak for at least another ten minutes, but once it became clear where the judge was headed, I put down my pen. The five-year interruption of Ross's murder case had come to an end today, November 2, 1989. Now, we would begin the Herculean fight to keep Ross out of prison for the rest of his life.

After providing the press with sound bites of our disappointment in the judge's ruling but nevertheless expressing optimism about the next phase of our court battle, Walter and I left the Castle Rock courthouse for our return trip to Denver. During the 40-mile drive, we mapped out our next legal strategy for the sanity phase of the case; that trial date would be set before Judge Turelli. After arriving at my office and unloading my oversized brief case and returning the two large expandable witness folders to the "Carlson Competency" shelves of my bookcase, I leaned back in my chair and looked out the window. Across the street, the City of Glendale softball field was active with an after-school pickup game. The recently completed World Series sweep of the Oakland A's over the San Francisco Giants, dubbed the "Earthquake Series," was obviously still fresh in the minds of baseball's diehards. A few blocks further to the west, late afternoon traffic streamed north and south along Colorado Boulevard. The snow-packed Rockies rippled along the horizon, and the Denver metro's chinook winds blew away the area's smog, affording me a vivid view of the mountains' postcard scene. I was about to organize a "things to do" list for the preparation of Ross's sanity case until my mind diverted. I began thinking about the events of the last six years.

CHAPTER 2

From Baguettes to Murder

For me, Friday evening of September 23, 1983, proved a fairly typical introduction to the weekend. I had just finished a six-mile run and was prepared to spend an uneventful night watching television in my garden-level family room. This spacious area was where I spent most of my free time in my tri-level house.

My friend Janey Lozow redecorated this entertainment area after my divorce of about ten years earlier. She commissioned an artist to draw a colorful mural of a variety of horizontal and vertical lines, and geometric shapes on the white wall that led from the white-tiled entryway foyer down the half-dozen, carpeted stairs into the family room. Straight ahead was the laundry room, and to the right were the storage, full bath, and office rooms. To the left was the grand family and entertainment room with its dominant green plaid carpet, accented by blue and yellow lines. To the immediate left of the stairs was a built-in bar with its black stone top and three high-bar stools with chrome bases and yellow soft cushions on the seats. Janey's flair for decoration assured that the cushions were a perfect accent to the yellow lines of the plaid carpet.

Located a few feet from the end of the bar and in the far-left corner of the room was a glass table with a white marble, octagonal-shaped base; the table was surrounded by four green cushioned and stainless-steel-sided armchairs. This was the perfect venue for a cozy dinner for four when I eschewed my more formal dining room on the second level. Situated to the immediate right of the table and against

Chapter 2: From Baguettes to Murder

the wood-paneled wall was my favorite blue velvet L-shaped sectional couch, which provided the main seating area of this entertainment room. A heavy-white square table sat in front of and was the width of the couch while two individual blue-velvet sections were on the opposite side of the table. This area could comfortably accommodate at least seven people.

Overall, the room provided great relaxation and comfort. Choices included watching burning embers fly randomly from the fireplace embedded within the floor-to-ceiling rocked wall and hearth, which ran from the left of the couch to the width of the room. There, four or more could sit. Or, one could also choose from a large variety of classics or best sellers that filled the built-in bookcase that consumed three-fourths of the wall across from the sectional. The balance of that wall was occupied by a 27-inch RCA perched atop a swiveled platform on two finished vertical cabinets, which housed my chess and backgammon sets. The games saw occasional action on the couch's white table. When I had my MASH soiree, nearly twenty of us fit nicely into this entertainment room to watch the final episode.

Tonight, however, my plan was to enjoy a turkey sandwich on a warmed French baguette, while relaxing on my couch and watching TV. Regrettably, these were my evening substitutes after the auburn-haired and curvaceously stunning Tanya had broken another of our dates earlier that day. I wondered if an evening with such an elusive beauty could ever be as memorable as I had often fantasized it would be.

At least, I rationalized, I wouldn't be tired tomorrow from a long and spicy night out, again continuing my fantasy. After all, Saturday was usually a productive workday. There would be few phone calls, no client appointments; just preparing for the next week's court matters and finalizing some pleadings whose deadlines were fast approaching. On second thought, a mild case of "good" tired would not have been so bad. The phone interrupted my daydreaming about Tanya.

"David, Walter."

"How you doing, Walter?" A call from my long time mentor and lawyer extraordinaire, Walter Gerash, on a Friday night usually meant I referral of a new case was likely coming my way.

"Listen, David, this kid, Ross Carlson, the police think he killed his parents. It's been all over the papers."

"Yeah, I've read about it. I thought the public defender was representing him."

"That's true, but he wants me. His parents left a trust; it supposedly has assets, including cash. Under Colorado law, he can't inherit his parents' estate if he caused their deaths by killing them. But he hasn't been convicted of anything yet. I need you to represent him in the trust matter. Convince the bank — United Bank is the trustee ... some guy named Talbert is in charge. In fact, call Dick Hughes, he's the bank's attorney, or maybe he drafted the will. I don't know. But call him; he can fill you in. Call me tomorrow for his number. Hold on, David! Wait a minute! 'Rose, did you find the paper with the lawyer's number?' David, you there? She can't find it."

"I haven't left, Walter." I was imagining his wife Rose frantically looking for something that he had set aside without telling her where.

"Whatever you do, convince the bank to pay my fees to represent Carlson. Do that and I'll get you in the case."

Talking to Walter about a case familiar to him but not to me was like arriving late to a Hitchcock movie, seeing the audience riveted to the screen, and not knowing what you'd missed. Walter normally got to the gist of a matter without much delay ... just rat, tat, tat. If you didn't listen carefully, you'd be lost. He took a breath, so I jumped in.

"How'd he kill his parents?"

Walter provided a short but chilling explanation.

"Jesus! Why?" I asked.

"I don't know. It's a heavy case. Call the trustee. Call the attorneys for the bank. We'll need a lot of money for doctors and investigators. We need to get Carlson examined right away. The public defenders have already hired MacDonald and Sundell to examine him. Smart move! This way the DA can't hire them. If these doctors find something wrong with Carlson, that would be the end of the case; the DA wouldn't question their findings. But that's not likely to happen, especially with MacDonald. Can't remember the last person he found insane, if ever. Doesn't matter. I'll get other doctors to see Carlson."

Chapter 2: From Baguettes to Murder

    I peppered Walter with more questions, thanked him for the referral, and agreed to call him tomorrow. After I hung up, I tried my damnedest to remember some of what I had learned in law school about wills and trusts. It was a futile exercise. It quickly became apparent that I would need to call a couple of specialists for primers on the subject and that I was probably in store for a few long sessions in the law library. After that, I could make a "things-to-do list" for the eventual hearing in the probate court.

CHAPTER 3

Our First Meeting — October 17, 1983

On October 17, 1983, I arrived at the Denver courthouse an hour before the 9:00 a.m. scheduled hearing and went directly to the sheriff's office on the fourth floor. Once there, I was buzzed into the prisoners' holding area. I walked past the three large, crowded cells of people in custody and entered the small attorney's room where I sat down and waited for the sheriffs to bring in Ross. Two folding-metal chairs and a worn wooden desk furnished what must have been a broom closet in its prior life. I closed the door for privacy in anticipation of my upcoming visit and to muffle the requests of the sheriffs by the other defendant as to when their case was going to be called and was their lawyer coming to see them. I figured most of these detainees were represented by the Public Defender's Office, which meant those overwrought lawyers would not likely have had the time to visit any of these clients until they walked into court that day.

Within a few moments, Ross entered and closed the door behind him. As I stood, he greeted me with a firm handshake and a simultaneous "Hello, Mr. Savitz. Thank you for visiting with me beforehand."

"Ross, please call me David," I reminded him from our earlier phone conversation. His eyes quickly diverted from mine while he checked me out head to toe. As a 40-year-old, I didn't want clients, even this 19-year-old, to call me Mister, especially because I wanted them to feel relaxed. And, I didn't mind Ross's body scan because I had given myself a huge thumbs up before leaving the house that morning: a dark gray suit, crisp white shirt, and a gray, black, and

Chapter 3: Our First Meeting — October 17, 1983

white striped tie was an excellent ensemble, I thought (actually, I knew this combination worked because my practice was to buy my suits in New York from family friends, who were manufactures of men's clothing; then I would take my suits to the Shirt Broker in Denver, which was owned by my buddy, Alan Berg, a former practicing criminal lawyer from Chicago, who moved to Denver a few years ago to go into the custom shirt business; Alan would select the shirts and ties that would go perfectly with my new purchases, and I would arrange the grouping in my closet in their neat individual packages, so there would be no question what went with what when I dressed for work on any particular morning. This, in my mind, was the perfect solution to my color blindness and desire to replicate the pictures that captured my eye from time to time in the men's clothing magazine Gentlemen's Quarterly).

"Thanks, I'll try to remember that," he said, smiling. We both sat down.

What a handsome young man, I thought. He looked like a Calvin Klein model with his thick-blond hair and Scandinavian good looks. Even with his drab orange, one-size-fits-all, county-issued, jump suit, he was neat as a pin. The short sleeves of his loose-fitting, jail-issued outfit revealed a taut physique and the muscular arms of a middle-weight bodybuilder.

As I sat across from this 19-year-old, I thought of my own son, Curtis, who although more angular and a bit taller than Ross, was a year younger and about to enter his first year of college. I was thankful, knowing that Curt's future was much brighter than that of the young man in front of me.

Before I could begin with my explanation of the upcoming court proceedings, Ross caught me off guard.

"I apologize for this God-awful orange thing" he said, looking down at his jump suit. "I asked to be able to dress in my own clothes, but I was told I couldn't. Is there anything you can do about this? I'm not thrilled about appearing before the judge like this."

I was taken aback as Ross continued to apologize for his appearance. This was the first time in 15 years of practice that a client in jail had ever made such a stink over how he looked, let alone a

19-year-old. I told him that during some hearings and certainly during any trial he'd be permitted to wear his own clothing; he appreciated the explanation but was not pleased with it.

I then delved straight into the crux of the morning's hearing in the probate court. "Ross, plain and simple — Colorado law prohibits one convicted of murder from inheriting his victim's estate. However, you haven't been convicted of anything; you've only been charged. Therefore, I'm going to argue that your presumption of innocence would be violated if the trustee refuses to pay for your defense from your parents' estate."

I further explained that the bank was concerned that it could be sued no matter how it decided. If the bank refused to pay for the defense, it feared a suit against it by Ross. If the bank opted to pay, it feared a possible suit by Ross's grandparents, who were the contingent beneficiaries under the terms of the trust. To insulate itself from this dual-sided attack, the bank wanted the protection of a court ruling. In my view, the bank was unnecessarily cautious since I had already obtained written waivers and consents from the grandparents, which shielded the bank from suit and authorized the hiring of Walter Gerash and me.

I then outlined the parents' assets as revealed to me by the trust officer, John Talbert. Ross leaned forward in his chair and paid close attention. "The family house and contents are worth around $115,000, but would probably net only about $50,000 because of the mortgages against it. Life insurance proceeds on your parents' lives total about $200,000. The police are keeping your folks' Cadillac for evidence, but the Oldsmobile can be sold for around $4,000. As far as I know, there are no stocks or bonds, little cash, and a few small debts. Banks invest pretty conservatively so the joint estate of approximately $270,000 may only grow about 5% or more annually."

My last comment about the growth of the estate prompted Ross to engage in a lengthy dissertation about a variety of investments, including commodities, short and long-term CDs, and high-yield blue chip stocks. I was unprepared for that kind of sophisticated knowledge since teenagers were usually preoccupied with subjects much more titillating than the rise of the Dow-Jones average. My son Curt and

Chapter 3: Our First Meeting — October 17, 1983

his friends had ongoing discussions about what was available on "the market," but those conversations had little to do with the best stocks and bonds. Ross then took me by surprise again.

"David, I've been thinking a great deal about the hiring of Walter as opposed to staying with Craig Truman."

During our initial phone conversations, Ross was adamant about hiring Walter. He thought he had no chance with the public defenders, especially after his first couple of meetings with Truman who, according to Ross, "looked like he had just spent two hours at a truck stop buffet." After those initial meetings, however, Craig had done a great job at the preliminary hearing, creating second thoughts with Ross about needing to hire an expensive lawyer like Walter. Craig had more experience defending murder cases than any number of private attorneys put together, with the exception, however, of Walter. And Ross had heard about Walter's stellar reputation but nevertheless insisted that Walter visit him in jail before making a final decision. After that jailhouse visit, Ross was sold on Walter, especially after learning from Walter personally about his vast experience in handling grisly and high-profile murder cases. And, I had confirmed that information about Walter's experience when Ross and I had spoken, so I was thus confused by yet another seeming change of heart by Ross.

"What is it, Ross?" I asked, trying not to appear impatient.

"David, the best way for me to go is to hire Walter, even though it will be expensive."

I didn't know why he felt he had to repeat what he had told me just a few days ago. "Fine. Let's go and see Judge Benton," I replied. As I walked with the sheriff and a handcuffed Ross Carlson to the courtroom, I pondered the forthcoming irony. I was about to ask a judge to order the funding of a criminal defense from the estate of my client's parents whom he was charged with killing.

CHAPTER 4

Funding the Defense

Once inside Judge Benton's courtroom, Ross introduced me to his maternal grandfather, the Reverend Harvey Hill. Reverend Hill had traveled from Minnesota as the representative of Ross's four grandparents. Dressed in a conservative gray suit, the Reverend Hill appeared to be in his early 60s. He was polite, formal, and ready to tell the court that the grandparents had agreed that Ross's defense should be paid from the trust even though before this trip, the Reverend and his wife Linnea had expressed some misgivings about signing the consents I had prepared. The Hills were concerned there would be insufficient money left for Ross's future needs once the criminal case concluded. Their apprehension was allayed when they learned that the trusts were valued at approximately $270,000, believing that once Ross's simple case was over, there would be plenty of money left for him.

There I stood, conversing with the father of the deceased Marilyn Carlson. The Reverend and I were talking about the wishes of his grandson, who was charged with the brutal murder of his mother, the Reverend's daughter. Our discussion in front of Ross centered on using the assets in Marilyn Carlson's estate to hire one of Colorado's best criminal defense lawyers to represent Ross. Despite having lost his daughter to such a cold-blooded death, the Reverend Hill focused exclusively on Ross's future. This macabre juxtaposition was right up Alfred Hitchcock's alley. I tried to appear composed, wondering if I was the only one uncomfortable with this scene. Both

Chapter 4: Funding the Defense

the Reverend and Ross seemed utterly unfazed by the conversation. Saved by the gavel!

Judge Benton entered the courtroom. The court proceedings finally began with the judge's analysis of the trust's provisions. The judge meant well, but his initial explanations of the provisions of the Carlson trusts did not seem to portend a very sanguine outcome. Nonetheless, I continued to pay careful attention, ready to pounce on any judicial utterance that would allow the trustee to go my way. Suddenly, my interest was piqued.

Judge Benton said that because the trustee had been granted such broad powers and discretion, the judge had no authority to tell the bank what it could or could not do. The bank had to make its own decisions. The judge said it would be perfectly proper for the trustee to make payments for Ross's defense, or it could elect not to do so. Of course, I feigned deafness to that last comment.

After the hearing, John Talbert advised me he needed a few days to confer with the bank's officers and their lawyers. Finally, on October 28, Mr. Talbert informed me that the bank had agreed to fund Ross's defense on three conditions. First, a formal written agreement had to be signed by Ross, the bank, and the grandparents, and then approved by Judge Benton. Secondly, the grandparents had to hire independent counsel to advise them with respect to the terms and ramifications of the agreement. Finally, Ross had to select a court-approved conservator who would be responsible for the administration of the defense costs, which I had advised would run the gamut from attorney fees to expert witness fees and everything in between.

Armed with the news, I called Walter and Ross; both were equally elated. Ross then seconded Walter's invitation to have me join in the defense of the criminal case. I naturally accepted and proceeded to satisfy all of the bank's conditions.

The grandparents followed my recommendation and hired my friend and very able attorney, Paul Vranesic. For the position of conservator, Ross requested Jack Keller, who, with his wife Maryann, had been instrumental in helping me obtain the grandparents' consents.

Jack and Maryann Keller's teenage daughter Suzanne had long been a close friend of Ross whose politeness had always made him welcome in the Keller home. Last August when the Keller family heard of the news of Rod and Marilyn Carlsons' deaths, they attended the memorial service for the Carlsons. Although Ross was under a psychiatric hold at the time, he nevertheless received a pass from the hospital to attend the service. At the time, no criminal charges had been brought against him. Upon observing Ross's inconsolable grief at the service over the loss of his parents, the Kellers decided to stop by the hospital later that day and pay their respects.

A day or so later, Ross called the Keller home and apologized for imposing but said he needed Pearl Drops toothpaste, a toothbrush, and a comb. The hospital wouldn't buy any of the items. Dumbfounded by the hospital's refusal to spring for the meager outlay, Maryann called her husband, who said he would purchase the toiletries and run them over to Ross.

During Jack's visit, two Arapahoe County deputy sheriffs walked into Ross's room and, without any explanation, requested he sign some papers. The 50-year-old, burly Jack Keller resorted to his ex-Marine persona, rose from his chair, and instinctively instructed Ross not to sign anything unless he had an attorney review the documents. Frustrated in their mission, the two deputies promptly escorted Jack from the room for interfering with their duties.

The next day, Jack called the ACLU and asked them to represent Ross. "No one was going to push that kid around and violate his rights!" Jack would later tell me. Hiring of the ACLU became moot once we obtained the trust moneys for Ross's defense and a few months later drafted Jack to act as Ross's conservator.

The agreement between the bank, Ross, and his grandparents was entered into on November 14. Judge Benton approved it on November 25, 1983.

Two months before, I had been retained to tackle this unusual assignment regarding the trust. With that accomplishment, however, came the realization that the most difficult tasks were still ahead. Now, the stakes were higher — a client's life — but I wasn't shaken. After all, I had been groomed for the practice of criminal law since I was a youngster.

CHAPTER 5

The Beginnings of the Making of a Lawyer

On June 6, 1943, at approximately 2:30 a.m., weighing about eight and one-half pounds, I entered the world of Sam Savitz, age 28, and Isabelle Webber Savitz, age 25. Waiting excitedly at home for her baby brother was my two-year-old sister, Carol Ann. She was the spitting image of a smiling Shirley Temple complete with her golden, curly locks and soft, pink skin.

At the time, we lived at 45 Amherst Avenue, Wilkes-Barre, Pennsylvania; population approximately 60,000. Located in the northeastern part of the state and at the foothills of the Pocono Mountains, Wilkes-Barre was considered the soul of the anthracite coal region. While the cold, vast labyrinth of coal mines was situated underground, rich farmland, gentle rolling hills, and beautiful green landscapes covered most of the region's topsoil. The lengthy Susquehanna River separated Wilkes-Barre from the town of Kingston, its smaller neighbor located on the opposite side of the bridge, and meandered several hundred miles to the central part of the state and its capital city, Harrisburg.

As a toddler, I was oblivious to the events of World War II though I had celebrated my first birthday on D-Day, which marked the Allied invasion of Normandy. (This occasion was etched indelibly into my memory because my very special Uncle Joe would send me a birthday check every year and always noted on the card, understandably since he was a veteran and served in the Army at the time, "One year old on D-Day!") In any event, the war ended not too soon afterwards, and I lived quite a frolicsome life from ages 1 through 4. I responded to the name of Butchie, a nickname bestowed by my father and apparently befitting my physical appearance: chubby, freckle-faced, and curly-red hair. We didn't have television during those early years to entertain our family, so I shouldered the responsibility as a toddler to bring excitement to our household, including a number of adventures, or rather misadventures, the boldest of which was an ingenious peccadillo perpetrated at the age of four. The victims of the misappropriation were our downstairs neighbors, the Joneses. The innocent carrier of the soon-to-be-pilfered item was our Purvin Dairy milkman.

This proud employee's work ensemble was all white: white truck, white trousers, white shirt, and white cap. When he stepped off his truck, he carried an open metal container that contained eight metal slots each of which had room for one bottle of milk. For our particular stop, six slots rattled with bottles of Purvin Dairy's finest as they were transported to our duplex.

We and the Jones family each received two bottles of white milk and one bottle of chocolate. The Joneses had only one child, a daughter, while we, of course, had two thirsty youngsters — my sister and me.

One morning when I was preparing to enjoy a refreshing glass of chocolate milk, I realized that our bottle of chocolate had less than a satisfying swig remaining. I was parched, having run for a considerable time throughout our two-level apartment, annoying my sister Carol and ducking from her back-handed swipes. In an effort to quench my thirst, I walked next door and saw that the Jones' milk had not yet been retrieved from their back porch. I heard no sounds coming from their apartment. Their garage bay was empty. I deduced that the Joneses were tending to their respective daily responsibilities away from their home. I could see into the window of our back door. No one from our apartment was visible. I knew my sister had locked the door to her room to prevent my re-entry and had just earlier seen my mother tending to her household chores in the front of our home. Hearing no footsteps or voices, I stealthy descended upon the Jones' back porch, absconded cat-like with their bottle of chocolate milk and secreted myself in our garage.

Chapter 5: The Beginnings of the Making of a Lawyer

After honoring the notion of "good to the last drop," which I had often heard my dad exclaim as he drank bone dry a glass of some yellowish liquid that fizzed and created a white foam when he poured it from a can, which my mother had retrieved from our refrigerator, I filled the empty bottle of chocolate milk with stones from our driveway. Later that morning when Mrs. Jones had returned from her grocery shopping at the A & P, she informed my mother of the unusual state of their bottle of chocolate milk. To my surprise, I was questioned about the Jones discovery. I naturally denied any culpability and suggested that the focus of the investigation should be upon my older sister. Surely, such an act required a more mature mind and some sophisticated planning and execution, I argued.

By this time, my six-year-old sister had been anointed by my dad as his "dollygirl." Admittedly, she was a pretty girl with her blond hair, omnipresent smile, and pleasant disposition, which, I suppose, earned her that appellation. And clearly she was the apple of my dad's eye, not to suggest, however, that I considered myself any less loved. In any event, dollygirl Carol vehemently denied any involvement and began to cry hysterically at the accusation, no doubt fearing that even the accusation would diminish her standing in our father's eyes. I didn't think that far ahead, but, nevertheless, the investigation quickly focused back upon me. A novice at stealth and not yet ready for prime-time advocacy, the brown color line above my upper lip most likely gave away my indiscretion. A plump Butchie with a telltale piece of physical evidence did not bode well for a finding of not guilty. Thus, compelling circumstantial evidence and a dollygirl's professed innocence proved the undoing of my first petty offense and a resultant red tush.

Although I had been caught, the event marked the beginning of my understanding of the need for eloquent oratory, the value of a good defense, and the desirability of the plea bargain. If I had been conversant in the arts of contrition, negotiation, and mitigation of punishment, I could have suffered a harsh rebuke instead of the unpleasant spanking I received for my thievery and refusal to accept responsibility. As a youngster of four, I was unaware of what my life's profession would ultimately be, but in order to avoid a repeat of the recriminations suffered from the chocolate milk caper, I deemed it essential that I learn the skills of persuasion and negotiation and the need for empathy. I would learn many of these attributes from the master, my father.

In 1939, by the time he had reached his mid-20s, my father was the VP of and buyer for my Uncle Abe Savitz's business, the American Furniture and Jewelry Corporation. Although the company's main office was in Wilkes-Barre, it had another eight branch stores located in small communities throughout Pennsylvania and New York. The business sold blankets and pillowcases, toasters, irons, toys, clothing, sofas, watches, and numerous items in between. A household could stock its kitchen, living room, bedroom, and kids' toy chests with items acquired from the American. And the customer didn't even have to leave the home to make the purchases. Instead, one of the American's salesmen drove his car to the customer's home, which he stocked with an inventory of smaller articles and a catalog describing larger ones. From the comfort of her home, the lady of the house would make her purchase, pay a few dollars down, and continue paying down her balance every week when the salesman returned to collect the weekly payment. Of course, the goal was to ensure that each household made continual acquisitions to ensure perpetual weekly visits by the American.

Throughout my adolescent and teenage years, I would accompany my dad on his buying trips to New York City where I would meet the American Furniture's suppliers and observe the marathon buying sessions between them and my father. A casual observer might wonder what interest a teenager had in sitting through bargaining sessions about pots and pans, but I knew what the carrot was as the end of the stick. It was dinner at Mama Leone's and the next day's baseball game at Yankee Stadium. What kid wouldn't jump at the opportunity of a plate of pasta and veal parmigiana and three hours of Mantle, Berra, and Skowron in return for watching a couple of middle-aged men haggling over the price of some cooking paraphernalia!

By the time I reached 16 and was more knowledgeable about the ways of the world and brilliance of my father, it became apparent that most sales managers knew my dad was going to get the best of them. They just didn't know how. He was the preeminent negotiator;

Chapter 5: The Beginnings of the Making of a Lawyer

the maestro of persuasion, the kingpin of determination, the standard by which other aspiring "Hall-of-Fame" soft goods merchants were measured. One buying trip was an example. It occurred while I was a junior in high school.

My dad, setting out to buy watches, scheduled meetings with three different watch manufacturers whose main offices were in Manhattan. Bulova and Benrus were two of the manufacturers. He printed the name of each of the companies on a different piece of scratch paper and folded the three pieces of paper in the palm of his hand. As he spoke with the owner or sales manager of each company, he made meticulous notes on their respective piece of paper. Each of them saw that he was writing prices they had quoted him, but none of them, of course, knew what the other manufacturer had quoted. After the first day, he had a comparison of each manufacturer's prices and terms. After two days of negotiating with all three, he finally settled on the Benrus watch company but, of course, didn't let on that he had come to a decision. He returned to Benrus for one last session. The sales manager confidently thought it was to wrap up the terms of the final order. My dad felt differently.

"Now, Sam, I just gave you the best deal I've ever given anyone. I have no problem in sending 200 watches to Wilkes-Barre and 100 to Binghamton, but I can't send just five watches to Shamokin, three to Pottsville, and two to Shickshinney. Hell, I don't even know where those other cities are. In fact, I can't even find Pottsville on the map. I'll send the watches for the Pennsylvania stores to Wilkes-Barre, and you're people from Chickininey, or whatever it's called, can pick them up there."

"It's Shickshinney, Harry, and Pottsville is not too far from Forty Fort and Maukanaukwa"

"Of course, Sam, but listen . . . .."

"Harry, now wait a minute, did you hear the story about ... " A few minutes later after the guy had been left teary-eyed from laughter after hearing one of my dad's jokes, which, of course, I had heard hundreds of times before but never let on that I did, he said, "Ok, Sam, just this once. Now tell me again the addresses for Pottsville and the two others, but remember, the postage is going to be extra."

"Harry, now wait a minute, there were these two guys, and one guy said to the other . . ." A few minutes later, Harry's side was hurting again. My dad, sensing his prey was about to relent, started another story. Harry threw up his hands in surrender and finally said,

"Ok, Sam, I'll throw in the postage." The two had completed their deal.

My dad had just refused to give up until he was convinced he got the best deal he could. His success was borne out of humor and tenacity. His legacy, however, revolved around helping others. Enter my lessons about empathy.

CHAPTER 6

Helping Others

When my dad was a youngster, he had a paper route to help out his family (he was the third born of eight children — seven boys and one girl). He often gave his younger sister, Sophie, a nickel from his earnings so she could buy a pack of gum. When World War II ended in 1945, my father was 30 years old. His younger brothers, Morris (we called him Uncle Maishie), Sydney (called Uncle Shy), and Joseph (naturally, Uncle Joe), returned to Wilkes-Barre from the War, after having each served in the armed forces. My dad was the anointed patriarch of his family at the time since my grandfather Julius was in declining health and no longer working. So, my dad gave each of his returning brothers $2,500 to invest in a business or pursue an educational interest. My Uncle Joe used his nest egg plus the financial benefits of the GI Bill to finish college and enroll in 1948 at the University of Pennsylvania Law School. My Uncle Maishie, the freest spirit of the three, stayed in Wilkes-Barre and worked for my dad and Uncle Abe, at least, during those days when he wasn't spiritizing! Uncle Shy, the baby of the family, enrolled in Wilkes College, which not surprisingly was located in Wilkes-Barre. There he met and soon afterwards married Florence Kunen (our Aunt Flossie). Some of our family members called my dad, Shlamie. I later learned that all of these names were derivations from the Yiddish language that many Jews in Europe spoke before immigrating to this country. After I learned that my Uncle Al was called Anchie and my Uncle Hank, Heshie, I elected not to ask my father what the name David was in Yiddish.

Just in the Nick of Time

In 1949, when I was six, life became particularly stressful for my mother. By then, my younger brother, Eddie, had already entered the family and was just two years old. Dollygirl Carol was eight. My father traveled frequently on buying trips, leaving my mother home to take care of her three darlings. My mother's father, my grandfather Jacob Webber, died on Memorial Day that year in his hometown of Binghamton, New York, which was about 200 miles from us. Because my grandmother Emma was blind, she could not live alone. Her two other children, who lived only a few blocks from her, couldn't afford to take care of her. My father unhesitatingly said, of course, Grandma Emma could live with us. By then, we had moved into a larger home in the town of Kingston, which was literally across the bridge from Wilkes-Barre on the other side of the Susquehanna.

Grandma Emma added beautiful melody to our home because she loved to play the piano and sing her favorite songs in her elegant soprano voice. She was a gifted songstress with a memory that stored a library of lyrics. She bothered no one and was a woman of simple pleasures. She never forgot my parents' generosity and kindness, but then again those were integral parts of their character.

When I was nearly 14 years old, my Aunt Sophie's husband, Jake Weinstock died. It was March of 1957. As a widow with four children, ranging in age from 4 to 16, Aunt Sophie felt overwhelmed, especially with her four-year-old son, Bruce, who was quite a handful. He made my adventures as a toddler seem tame in comparison. Bruce wouldn't just drink the neighbor's chocolate milk; he'd pee into the empty bottle and return it to the porch. By then, we had expanded to a family of four children (six-year-old brother Jack was the baby having entered the world in 1951) and Grandma Emma. My folks knew our Aunt Sophie needed help, so, not surprisingly, our house added one more. Bruce would stay with us until my aunt could get back on her feet. Naturally, I had to become a role model for my young cousin since by then, I had matured into a somewhat agreeable teenager. Within a year or two, having lived under my guidance, Bruce eschewed his incorrigible ways and later returned to Aunt Sophie's home.

These and other similar deeds were second nature to my parents — the most loving and giving people in the world. There was always a

Chapter 6: Helping Others

seat available at our dinner table for a relative or friend, my mother's shoulder for anyone to cry on, a place in our family room for our next-door neighbors, the Walshes, to watch the Friday night fights, and an extra bedroom in our house for a family member in need. My parents established a standard of helping others that we children considered second nature. It became part of our fiber.

Having now learned about the art of negotiation while shadowing my dad and having learned from my parents the nobleness of helping others, I was still lacking a couple of key components to becoming a lawyer. One was the necessary educational prerequisites. My accomplishment of the academic objective of pre-law, or something related to it, was temporarily sidetracked by a curve ball thrown by my father.

After my sophomore year at Penn State, I had decided to spend the summer of 1962 in Los Angeles. There, I would work at the branch office of the family business (now bicoastal), catch a few Dodger games, and await my Hollywood discovery as a Jewish Adonis. If I failed in the last endeavor, I was prepared to return to college and elect a major of study toward which I could earn a handsome living.

My father, sensing my intellectual capabilities, had decided upon a worthy profession for me. To enlighten me about his choice, he visited Los Angeles in August. During his stay, he invited me to join him for a car ride along the posh Wilshire Boulevard. After passing the grand homes of Beverly Hills with their gated entrances and manicured lawns, we came upon the business district lined with tall, gleaming office buildings, parking garages filled with Mercedes Benzes and BMWs, and hurrying pedestrians dressed in Italian suits and couture dresses. While pointing out these beautiful sights, my dad spoke of the esteemed medical profession. He mentioned the physicians' importance to mankind, their breakthroughs in research, and skills in healing. And, he emphasized repeatedly, they earned considerable income during the process.

"Yes," I responded. I was aware of all that; however, I thought I'd try psychology. I was fascinated by the human mind and the various personality traits and characteristics that make us all so different. "No doubt," he replied, "but look at those fancy office buildings on Wilshire Boulevard. Wasn't I aware of who owned those buildings?" Of course, I wasn't. "Doctors," he said. "You're such an intelligent kid," he said, flattering me, although I knew where he was headed with this conversation. "When you return to school, take pre-med, not psychology."

I didn't want to disappoint my father by telling him that I hated chemistry, couldn't stand the thought of dissecting a frog, and was too fastidious to work around other people's blood. In spite of my misgivings, I reluctantly agreed to pursue an MD instead of a PhD, believing I could overcome my doubts, especially with a nice real estate portfolio in tandem with helping the sick.

When I returned to Penn State in the fall, I halfheartedly completed the necessary registration papers for my major in the healing sciences. The obligatory interview was then scheduled with the dean of the pre-med department.

I was prompt for our meeting, confident I would have ample time for tardiness once I became a physician. Dressed in one of my new fall Eagle suits purchased from Wilkes-Barre's flashy clothier, Rosenthal's, I easily surpassed the dean in sartorial splendor. Academicians, I surmised, probably did not earn as much as their clinical counterparts.

"Well, Mr. Savitz," the dean said, about to ask the key question that I had anticipated, "why do you want to become a doctor?" I had been rehearsing the answer for several days and was fully prepared to enlighten him.

I told him what an exciting science medicine was, and that I believed dedicating one's life to treating the sick and finding new ways to cure illnesses was a great human service. I then inquired of him.

"Have you ever been to Los Angeles?"

When he said, "No," I seized upon the opening. I informed him about Beverly Hills and Wilshire Boulevard with its gorgeous high-rises, and the impressive real-estate holdings enjoyed by physicians. I became animated as I talked about the substantial wealth that I understood was accumulated by physicians and the kind of lifestyle one would be afforded as a result. To my surprise, a cemetery silence quickly filled the room.

Chapter 6: Helping Others

The look on the dean's face had suddenly changed from mildly interested to that of considerably dismayed. I paused for a few seconds and sat still. I reflected upon my last remarks. They seemed to have reverberated off the dean's bookshelves, striking me upside the head. The dean looked at me and sat motionless. His left thumb and index finger cupped his chin. I had learned about catatonia from my introductory psych class and wondered if he had entered such a sorry state. I spoke.

I said perhaps I needed to reconsider my selection and that I had actually been contemplating a career in clinical psychology. My comments triggered an awakening. The dean suddenly became animated and very talkative. He unhesitatingly encouraged me to pursue the study of the mind. He stood up to shake my hand and instantly guided me to his door.

I quickly exited his office, ran to the psychology department with a wonderful sense of relief. I eventually mustered the courage to tell my father about my substantial coolness toward the practice of medicine. He understood; I tried to assuage his disappointment by promising to buy one of the American Furniture's sofas once I opened my clinical psych practice. Although I was still not certain where a degree in psychology would take me, a different career path came into play after listening to one of the greatest orators of our time.

The civil rights rally occurred during the turbulent time of the mid-60s when campus unrest flared throughout the country. On the international front, President Lyndon Johnson had increased the deployment of American troops in Vietnam, resulting in huge casualties, while in this country Martin Luther King's inroads were met with frequent acts of violence. During my senior year at Penn State, I was mesmerized for an hour and a half by Dr. King when he spoke at a standing room only crowd at our events center. His perpetual struggle to improve the lives of African Americans paralleled the principle with which I had been imbued by my folks of wanting to help others less fortunate than I.

CHAPTER 7

The Final Shaping of a Trial Lawyer

After graduating from Penn State in June 1965, I decided to go to law school; in my dad's view, also a very honorable profession. After all, by now my Uncle Joe had become a partner of Wilkes-Barre's Rosenn, Jenkins, & Greenwald, one of northeastern Pennsylvania's most prestigious law firms. My Uncle Abe and dad had used that firm almost exclusively for their business before my Uncle Joe stepped one foot in a law school class. The firm's senior partner and founder, Max Rosenn, was considered as possessing one of the great legal minds of his era and was a dear friend of the Savitz families. He hired my Uncle Joe as the firm's first law clerk. Knowing how my dad often thought way ahead of anyone else, he undoubtedly figured his oldest son would return to his roots and also join the firm of RJ&G, as it was affectionately known by the local bar. I was not thinking that far ahead.

So, that fall, with my car fully packed and Triple A trip-tik on the passenger seat, I drove the 2,200 miles from Kingston, Pennsylvania to Boulder, Colorado to begin my first year at the University of Colorado's School of Law. I didn't know a soul in Boulder, but I had heard from two of my fraternity brothers at Penn State, who had transferred from Denver University to Penn State during their sophomore years, that the CU campus was one of the prettiest in the west and the centerpiece of the college town of Boulder, which was nestled in a beautiful valley with a backdrop of flatirons and foothills that were visible as one arrived at the peak of Highway 36 (the main

Chapter 7: The Final Shaping of a Trial Lawyer

highway between Denver and Boulder) before descending into the city a few miles away.

I knew law school was in the major leagues of academia and that I would be competing against students who reportedly ripped cases out of law books and hid them in their apartment in order to gain an edge against other students in a course. Supposedly, only the best and brightest of the graduates were offered the plum jobs after graduation with the top law firms. My scholastic rank among the future graduating class of 1968 was made clear during my first visit to CU's Fleming Law Building. It was September 1965 — orientation night.

The joke was that this evening might be the only opportunity to meet all of my first-year classmates because, by the end of the semester, one-third of us would have either dropped out or flunked. When I heard the quip, I didn't think it was very funny. It seemed even less humorous after my only memorable but sobering experience of that orientation night.

"Oh, yes, Mr. Savitz. I remember. Very interesting application," the law school's Assistant Dean, Professor Albert Menard, commented cordially as he greeted me while peering over his bifocals and reading my name tag. I didn't quite know how to respond to this introduction. Showing great restraint, I dispensed with a cute retort and instead replied, "Oh, how so?"

"Well," he answered, "you have some of the lowest LSAT scores and GPAs of any incoming student."

"My God!" I thought. Before I had a chance to reveal my untapped brilliance, the assistant dean was preparing my pink slip. I knew a 550 LSAT (out of a possible 800) and a 2.5 college grade point average (a 4.0 was perfect at Penn State) might not qualify me for the United States Supreme Court. However, who would want to join a club with only nine members? Besides, as a BMOC, including Intra-Fraternity Council President of the 54 fraternities at Penn State, Chairperson of PSU's Freshman Orientation Week, President of my fraternity, Phi Sigma Delta, as well as Phi Sig MVP in three intramural sports and a perfect attendance at sorority mixers, there wasn't enough time in the day to excel at anything else.

"On the other hand," the professor emphasized, suggesting a flicker of hope, "you had more extracurricular collegiate achievements than any other of our applicants. You were president of several campus organizations, a member of *Who's Who* in Colleges; the list was quite impressive. We believe you're highly motivated to succeed in something, but motivation isn't measured by grades alone. We'd like to see if you can channel your energy into academia."

I assured him that no one would work harder than I. As he walked away, the room suddenly became very warm. I began to perspire. I loosened my tie, retrieved my handkerchief from my back pocket, and patted my forehead. I went to the punch bowl for some refreshment. I walked around the room and made small talk with a few other first year students, but I didn't hear a word they said and had no idea if I was cute or boring in my responses. I drove back to my studio apartment that was in a nearby motel and watched some tv in an effort to relax before my first day of classes.

Having accepted Professor Menard's challenge, I immersed myself in my studies during that first year. Briefing all of the assigned cases before the next class, taking copious notes during the lectures, summarizing my notes after class, and spending long days in the law library, late nights in my apartment, and weekends without dates proved a successful formula for scholastic achievement. At the end of the year, I was confident I could earn a law degree. I earned decent grades in all of my first-year courses, including contracts, criminal law, and legal research. By my second year, I even toyed with the idea of becoming a trial lawyer, having also taken torts and learning of the verdicts in some of those cases. Reading about the exciting trials of the great criminal attorney, Louis Nizer, and his equally successful civil counterpart, Melvin Belli, revealed at least three elements that the great trial lawyers possessed in common: a gift of oratory, the art of skillful negotiation, and a passion to help others. I felt I had possessed the foundations to excel in all three. After the happening of two national tragedies during my senior year, I couldn't wait to pursue my career.

On April 4, 1968, I was visiting a girlfriend in San Francisco during spring break. That night, we heard the news that Dr. Martin

Chapter 7: The Final Shaping of a Trial Lawyer

Luther King had been assassinated. Like many Americans, I was devastated by his death. It was similar to the sorrow and emptiness I felt when President John F. Kennedy had been murdered five years earlier. I wondered if America would ever stop killing leaders who championed the end of bigotry and unfairness in this country. After Dr. King's death, I believed that the American dream of equality could still be salvaged by Robert F. Kennedy, who was then mounting a strong campaign for the Democratic nomination for President of the United States.

Senator Kennedy made a campaign stop in Denver about a month after Dr. King's death. My law school roommates and I attended the rally for this charismatic candidate. His presence electrified the room as he worked the crowd, shaking everyone's hand while occasionally whisking away his wavy brown hair that would continually droop onto his forehead. I was determined to shake his hand. As he made his way through the masses of admirers while flanked by secret service agents, I followed his path on a parallel course. When I saw an opening, I nudged my way between two people, extended my hand, and smiling said, "Good luck, Senator." He responded graciously with a firm handshake, looked me in the eye and replied, "Thank you."

On the night of June 8, I cheered at the television as the election returns declared Bobby Kennedy the winner in California. I smiled with adoration as the senator stood at the ballroom podium of the Ambassador Hotel, thanked his supporters, and exclaimed in his Bostonian accent "Onward to the convention." I yelled at the TV, "Way to go, Bobby!" This was a terrific week. I celebrated my 25th birthday two days earlier. My parents were flying into town for my law school graduation. The future looked bright for America.

A few moments later, horror! Someone screamed, "The Senator has been shot! The Senator has been shot!" The ballroom erupted into chaos. Soon, television cameras showed him being attended to while lying on the kitchen floor. He seemed to be conscious. For the next few hours, I remained riveted to the TV and awaited the outcome of his fate. I cursed whoever shot him and wondered, why, why?

The following day, Senator Kennedy's body was returned by train to our nation's capital to lie in state. I remained glued to the television watching as the train slowly passing through a shocked and grief-stricken America. It was a day of sorrow. That afternoon, I picked up my folks at the airport. It was so good to see them. The next day they beamed as I happily accepted my law school diploma. I was proud, but a part of me was also sad.

The slaying of three leaders whom I had so admired reemphasized the importance of our cherished liberties and need to ensure their protection. To help those less fortunate and fight to uphold everyone's rights, I would muster the skills to compete in an arena in which I thought I could succeed — a court of law.

CHAPTER 8

A $25 Fee & a Nunchaku

Before I could begin honing my trial skills, I faced a commitment to the United States military. After graduating from law school, I received a notice from my local draft board to return to Kingston for a physical. It was one exam I knew I would fail.

I suffered from congenital lumbar disease which eventually might require the surgical removal of two disks and a fusion of the spine at the location of the removed disks. The Army was unwilling to take the risk and rejected me for service. In the fall of 1968, I was free to return to Colorado which I had fallen in love with during my three years of law school in Boulder. The dry climate, clean air, majestic mountains, and variety of activities won out over the frigid winters, stifling humid summers, and crowdedness of the east.

I decided I wanted to live in Denver and there found an office sharing arrangement with three established Denver practitioners; one of them was a trial lawyer with a substantial civil and criminal case load. The second lawyer delved primarily in real estate, and the third was the state's foremost securities practitioner whose specialty was taking private companies public. The three needed a young lawyer to help them from time to time. In return for my working a specific number of combined hours per month for them, they would absorb my only two office expenses: rent and phone. I could use their secretaries, and if I worked more than the guaranteed number of hours, they would pay me the handsome wage of $15 per hour. Not hearing any offers from Melvin Belli or Louis Nizer, I accepted the arrangement, especially because of my interest in the trial attorney's practice. Thus, my history as a sole practitioner began.

Within a few weeks of hanging my shingle, a new client called the suite for the trial lawyer. However, he, the receptionist explained, was in court. The caller had an emergency. The receptionist referred the call to me. After a few moments of explanation, I knew this case cried out for my talents.

The client owned an extremely affordable motel on South Santa Fe Drive and faced a dire situation. A female guest had bolted her room from the inside and was distraught. Evidently, her life had "gone into the toilet" over a failed romance. She was threatening suicide. The owner didn't know what to do and was shortly anticipating a flurry of guests. "I'll be over right away," I responded, eager to handle the matter as a result of my having chosen to major in psych and not pre-med.

Upon arriving at the motel, I quickly grasped the situation. A neon sign with the motel's name and underneath the words "free XXX adult movies" was affixed to a three-story high pole. The signage was obviously designed to lure weary motorists, who traveled along the parallel interstate highway and who might otherwise be unaware of this resting place's amenities. Just to the right of the pole and a few feet back from the sidewalk was a small, square-shaped office identified as such with the word "office" stenciled in bold, six-inch letters on the front door. Pacing outside was a heavyset man, wearing a short-sleeved shirt, and looking at his watch every few seconds. About 30 feet from the man were a series of white parking lines striped diagonally in front of each of the approximate dozen garden-level motel rooms. An unoccupied, late-model automobile was in front of one of the units, straddling two sets of white lines, which I assumed was in violation of motel policy. I introduced myself to the client, whom I was able to immediately identify as a result of his earlier description of his colorful Hawaiian shirt and substantial girth during our initial call. He reconfirmed the matter's pressing nature and walked briskly to the troubled guest's room while motioning me to follow. He knocked on the door and told the woman I was a lawyer who could help her in her time of distress.

Chapter 8: A $25 Fee & a Nunchaku

After disclosing my identity, I told the woman I understood how she was feeling. I disclosed how I had been dumped at Penn State by my first college love when we were freshmen and that she had fallen for a junior, who was neither the dancer nor athlete that I was. I convinced the woman she had too much to live for to allow this failed relationship to be her swan song. The woman calmed down and allowed me into her room. After a few moments of my lay therapy, the woman agreed to seek professional counseling. I told my client to call the police whom I convinced to issue a 72-hour mental health hold so the woman could be seen in an inpatient unit where her safety and care could be managed.

"Great job! How much do I owe you?" the grateful owner asked. This was my first billing decision. Although the two attorneys were paying me $15.00 an hour for their work, this was an emergency situation. It required an immediate and decisive response. I spent slightly more than an hour on the matter learning the basic facts during the initial phone call, driving to the motel from my office, and engaging in a successful mental health intervention. A woman's psyche, if not life, was at risk. My client needed this room since space in his facility was in high demand because of the free cinema offered. In my view, all of the foregoing were appropriate factors in determining a reasonable fee.

"$25 will cover it," I said without hesitation. He paid it happily. I placed the wages in my pocket confident that the amount was commensurate with the services provided and well earned. And in my view, I was now experienced enough to take on larger cases.

About a month later, I assisted the trial attorney in a false imprisonment suit brought by one of his African American clients against a local jewelry store. It seems the young woman had been admiring a particular cocktail ring during a number of different visits to the store but ultimately decided against its purchase. During the client's last visit, the store clerk became momentarily distracted by another customer before returning to the jewelry tray to rearrange the merchandise being viewed by the client. The cocktail ring was missing. Suspicion immediately focused on the client, who was the only female African American person in the store; she was detained and searched by store personnel. The search uncovered nothing.

The young lady convinced me and the trial attorney that she was "done this way because I'm Black." We filed suit; I was assigned to prepare the case through the use of depositions and pre-trial motions. A few days before trial was set to begin, I negotiated a significant settlement for the client with the merchant's insurance company. The client received a nice check and said, "Savitz, you haven't heard the last from me or my family. We won't forget what you did for me." Several weeks later, her boyfriend, O.C. McNeal, called.

"Listen, Savitz, this is O.C. McNeal, Jackie's boyfriend."

"Yes, sir. How can I help you?"

"Listen here. I be sittin' in my kitchen with some friends. We be playin' cards and things, and them muther fucker cops kick the door in, flash their guns, those muther fuckers, and scare the shit out of our kids and stuff. Say they find some heroin and shit in the house. Bull shit! They planted that muther fucker dope in the house. That's what I think. What you gonna' do about it? You take my case?"

Of course I did. I proved the search was illegal, and got the case dismissed. Fortunately for me, O.C. came from a large family and was blessed with many close friends. Coincidentally, many of these people also had unfounded drug accusations lodged against them. They, too, hired me. During the next few years, my practice grew nicely, emphasizing criminal defense and civil litigation.

In 1971, having practiced for three years, I met attorney Walter Gerash when he and I represented separate clients accused of running a cocaine ring in nearby Jefferson County. I represented Praxedes Ortega, one of O.C. McNeal's close associates. It seems the county's district attorney had obtained a court-ordered wiretap and was glowing over the results. The prosecutor believed that once a jury heard the audio-taped conversations, guilty verdicts would be returned quicker than their vote to select their foreperson. Our adversary's prediction of a successful prosecution, however, became derailed.

We were dealing with a state wiretap statute that was barely two years old. There was no Colorado case law interpreting any of its provisions. The statute was patterned after its federal predecessor. During my research, I found the United States Senate Judiciary Committee's 284-page Report No. 1097, which formed the basis for

Chapter 8: A $25 Fee & a Nunchaku

the federal legislation. The report provided insight, including existing case law, into the Senate's intent behind the passage of each provision of the federal statute.

The report convinced me that the Jefferson County District Attorney had made a critical error. Instead of personally applying for the wiretap, the prosecutor had delegated the task to his chief deputy. The Senate report was unambiguous — the decision to invade the privacy of a citizen's phone communications had to be made by an identifiable prosecuting official whose job was subject to the political process. In the federal system, that would be *the* Attorney General. Thus, I contended, only *the* local prosecutor in the state scenario, in our case *the* district attorney, was authorized to make the application; his underling could not. If the judge agreed with my analysis, he would have no alternative but to throw out the tap, thus allowing our clients to walk. Except for Walter, none of the other more experienced defense attorneys shared my thinking.

At the conclusion of a full day's hearing, the judge rejected all of the co-defendants' arguments except the one requiring *the* District Attorney to apply for the tap. As a result of the victory and our working together to achieve it, Walter began referring me different cases.

One referral involved several movie projectionists accused of slashing a $20,000 movie screen and exploding firebombs in theater lobbies. The destructive behavior was supposedly in response to the theaters' corporate owner beginning to automate, thereby making the projectionists expendable.

The prosecution's case was built exclusively upon the testimony of a turncoat, John William Ford III. Ford had befriended a few of the projectionists and knew how angry they were about their imminent unemployment. Ford convinced the DA that he could bury all of the defendants, provided he was given total immunity. The DA agreed, realizing he had no case without Ford.

Our defense strategy was simple. We would attack Ford as an egomaniacal exaggerator of the highest order and whose trustworthiness was lower than a slithering rattlesnake. We had evidence that supported our strategy.

Ford had been hospitalized in an army psychiatric facility after completing a tour in Vietnam. Ford professed extraordinary skill in the use of the nunchaku, the ancient Japanese weapon. Ford also was capable of precipitating profuse nose bleeding by sheer concentration.

When it became the defense's turn to cross-examine Ford, Walter was our designated clean-up hitter. Before he came up to bat, the first three of us defense counsel managed to ensnare Ford in a gargantuan web of deceit by highlighting the many different versions of our clients' alleged criminality he told to friends, the police, and grand jury. Ford had no choice but to answer "Yes," to each of the countless instances where his trial testimony had differed from his grand jury statements. A few jurors shook their heads when Ford even shamelessly admitted "Yes" to a category of questions regarding lying to his mother about the most innocuous of matters. We had stripped Ford of nearly all his veracity and dignity by the time we turned him over to Walter.

Walter allowed Ford to spin lengthy tales of his military service in Southeast Asia. After listening to Ford, you would have thought he was the reincarnation of John Wayne, General Douglas MacArthur, and Rambo and that he single-handedly had stopped the Tet offensive. After Ford finished extolling his battlefield heroics, Walter asked him to leave the witness chair to demonstrate his proficiency with the nunchaku. Ford unabashedly accepted the invitation and began displaying his bamboo mastery to a packed courtroom of incredulous spectators. "Okay, Mr. Ford," Walter interrupted. "Stop! Now, show us how you would feign being injured and bleed from your nose."

Suddenly, Ford became still. He remained standing in the middle of the courtroom, paused, and stared straight ahead. Within a few seconds, droplets of blood appeared from his nostrils. Walter announced: "No further questions," and sat down while Ford and the prosecution's case dripped onto the courtroom floor. After the prosecution rested, the judge dismissed the case without requiring the defense to present any evidence.

Most attorneys would not have pursued Walter's strategy, believing it too histrionic with the potential to backfire. Walter, however, did not consider his tactic risky.

Although the unusual was his standard rather than the exception, he made decisions like the chess master he was. He was

Chapter 8: A $25 Fee & a Nunchaku

not a "seat of the pants" lawyer, but one who prided himself on thorough preparation. Walter possessed a sixth sense in knowing what jurors wanted to be proven, and he presented it to them as well as any advocate. Walter's combination of an uncanny intuition and a honed battery of lawyering skills were the hallmarks possessed by all great trial lawyers and were qualities gained only by experience.

Walter was the rare attorney who excelled in both civil and criminal law. One week he could successfully defend someone in a high-profile murder case, and the next week he could be equally eloquent demanding a high award for a severely injured commoner.

Walter did not possess the large physical presence of Perry Mason or the immaculate grooming of an English barrister. With his nearly 5'7" frame, balding head, conservative suits, and omnipresent beret, he looked more like a college professor than a flashy litigator. However, once inside the courtroom he was an adversary nonpareil. He was an unrelenting pit bull who feared no judge or adversary when it came to championing the cause of his client.

Walter and I began to try many cases together during the succeeding years — civil and criminal. It made no difference. He was sixteen years my senior and an extraordinary mentor. In 1983, twelve years after we first met, he invited me to assist in the defense of Ross Carlson for murder. One of our first tasks was to learn more about our client and the fateful night his parents were killed.

CHAPTER 9

The Psych Hold

On August 18, 1983, while making his midday rounds at Presbyterian Hospital, Dr. Gregory Wilets's beeper sounded. "Ross Carlson called around 2:30 p.m. and said it was urgent," his answering service reported. Wilets finished his current round and then walked quickly to the doctors' private workstation where he returned the call. He was forwarded to Captain Klein and listened in disbelief as the police officer described the Carlson murder scene and Ross's expressions of grief during his interview by the police. "We just released him," Klein said. "He wanted to be driven home so one of our officers is transporting him. He probably called you because he was so upset."

Wilets immediately thought of the last two sessions he had with Ross and his parents and now, hearing about their murders, believed that Ross's release from police custody was ill-advised.

"Captain Klein, I think Ross Carlson might be a danger to himself and others. You need to hold him for a mental evaluation," the distraught Wilets pleaded. "Once you get him back, let me know, and I'll make appropriate arrangements as soon as I can."

The doctor, stunned by Klein's call, then sat back in his chair and recalled his recent past history with the Carlson family.

In September 1982, the then 18-year-old Ross placed an ad for explosives in a local mercenary magazine, *Soldier of Fortune*. The ad caught the police's attention. An undercover cop arranged to meet Ross and, after hearing about Ross's search for some dynamite, placed

Chapter 9: The Psych Hold

him under arrest. During a police-station interview, Ross explained that he had wanted the dynamite to blow up his house because it had structural problems. The night after Ross's release from jail, his parents took immediate steps for him to see Dr. Wilets.

After an initial evaluation, Wilets saw Ross twice a week through the middle of January 1983, at which time the dynamite case was plea bargained. The judge ordered probation on the condition that Ross continued his treatment with Wilets.

Ross told the doctor that he considered himself "to be an unwanted child by parents who were unprepared for the complexities of parenthood." Wilets learned from Rod and Marilyn Carlson that they were unwed and seniors in high school when Marilyn discovered she was pregnant. "My pregnancy was uneventful," the 36-year-old, blond-haired, Marilyn Carlson told the doctor, mentioning only that Ross was born with a "spot on top of his head," requiring him to remain in the hospital nine days after birth. As a result, Wilets had considered an early bonding problem between mother and child.

Wilets knew how lonely and depressed Ross had felt from the time he was a child, feeling practically like an outsider compared to the extremely close relationship his parents had with one another. During their nine months of psychotherapy, Wilets believed that Ross had successfully addressed the issues of being unplanned. By June 1983, both Wilets and Ross agreed it was time to terminate therapy, although the doctor left the door open for Ross to return to discuss any unresolved problems. The hiatus was short-lived, leading to the last two family sessions, which Wilets was now pondering as he sat at the Presbyterian Hospital work station, waiting for the sheriff's office to call him back.

During mid-July of that year, the Carlsons returned home from a two- or three-week trip and found about $2,000 worth of expensive clothing in Ross's closet. Mrs. Carlson was angry. She called Wilets, demanding he obtain an explanation from Ross. Two sessions with Ross and his parents were scheduled for successive days. The sessions were intense.

Ross explained that the clothing had been given to him by four or five women who lived in the wealthy Denver suburb of Cherry

Hills Village. These ladies had asked Ross to escort them around town while their husbands were traveling. For his troubles, the ladies bought Ross clothing.

Wilets remembered that the explanation produced an immediate outcry from Rod Carlson and the accusation that Ross was a gigolo. Marilyn Carlson felt humiliated. She said that, of all the possible explanations, Ross's story hurt the most. Dr. Wilets saw something more sinister. He believed that not only was Marilyn Carlson right, but that Ross appeared to enjoy seeing his parents pained by his response. As devout churchgoers, the Carlsons could not have felt worse even if Ross had said he purchased the clothing from the devil. In fact, Marilyn Carlson said that she could have accepted an admission of shoplifting, but not this. Wilets remembered the smirk on Ross's face as his parents squirmed when they heard his story. The doctor wondered if that's all it really was — a story.

Although those sessions were heated, it had never occurred to Dr. Wilets that the Carlsons' lives were in danger. He was devastated when he learned of the Carlsons' fate from Captain Klein's call and asked himself why two schoolteachers, who had apparently never harmed anyone, were lying dead on a remote dirt road?

During nine months of therapy, Ross had been a cooperative, sincere, overly polite, and seemingly hard-working patient. He impressed Wilets as non-violent. Even though the last sessions showed a spiteful and unpredictable side to Ross, this new development of the Carlsons having been executed on a remote dirt road was too bizarre. Wilets suspected Ross had killed his parents, but he did not know why.

The doctor believed he needed to have a plan in place once Ross was returned to the Arapahoe County Sheriff's headquarters. He called various colleagues for advice and assistance. He sought a consensus of opinion regarding the following questions: Whom should he get to examine Ross? Should he do the examination, or would that compromise his therapeutic relationship with Ross? Should he talk to Ross on the phone first and make a preliminary assessment of the situation?

As he spoke to his fellow doctors and then hung up, he repeatedly questioned whether he missed a diagnosis or overlooked some facet of dangerousness in Ross's personality. Up until that last

Chapter 9: The Psych Hold

family session, Wilets believed that Ross was the model patient. If this seemingly polite teenager did kill his parents, how was he able to mask his anger so well during nine months of therapy, the doctor asked himself? And what could the parents possibly have done to evoke so lethal a response from their son?

Finally, after about an hour had passed from Captain Klein's initial call, the police called Wilets back to let him know that their officers had returned Ross to the police station. Ross and Wilets spoke.

"What happened?" Wilets asked.

"Do you remember Justin?" Ross asked. Wilets was startled by the question, remembering that Ross had mentioned the name Justin during a therapy session.

"Yes, continue, Ross. I'm listening."

"Dr. Wilets, please arrange for my release from jail. After I get out, we can take a ride and talk." Taking a ride with someone who may have killed his parents was the last thing Wilets was going to agree to.

"Ross," Wilets said, "the situation is very complicated. First, I need someone, other than me, to evaluate you."

"Doctor Wilets, you don't think I could have done this to my parents, do you?"

"I don't know, Ross," Wilets replied candidly with his hand to his forehead. The doctor was filled with a mixture of emotions as he pondered this most horrific type of event that had ever occurred in his practice. His reply was not the response Ross had anticipated, prompting the teenager to suddenly become quiet.

"I'll try to come by later, Ross," Wilets said.

"Very well," Ross replied matter-of-factly.

Wilets hung up and stared into space for a few seconds. Ross's reference to Justin smacked the doctor up the side of the head like a two by four. Wilets had a hard time believing what he had just heard, although it made sense. Justin, Ross! Violent, nonviolent! Bad, good! "That's it!" Wilets cried out while slamming his hand on the hospital desk and exclaiming "MPD," a diagnosis that he had both studied during residency and experienced later in his clinical practice.

Wilets felt he needed to secure a mental health hold against Ross immediately. He hurriedly called Dr. Irwin Levy, Director of the

Arapahoe County Mental Health Center, to arrange an emergency evaluation of Ross. Wilets briefed Dr. Levy but was careful not to breach Ross's doctor-patient privilege by disclosing too much.

"Greg, I agree that a 72-hour hold may be appropriate," Dr. Levy said assuredly. "Our on-call evaluator is Carol Murphy. Call her!" Wilets did, providing her a quick overview of the circumstances of his call.

"Miss Murphy," Wilets began to wrap up, "I believe when I spoke to Ross this afternoon, he was experiencing a psychotic transference. I think he actually thought I was his father. He wanted to take me for a ride, I believe, to harm me ... the same thing he did to his parents."

Wilets cautioned Murphy that Ross might look good when she first visited with him, but that he might change very rapidly and become suicidal at any time. He shared his suspicion about the diagnosis he believed Ross was suffering and in what kind of mental state Ross may have probably killed his parents.

"I'll visit him as soon as I can," Murphy said, believing she was about to interview an evil doer who would be exhibiting such outlandish behavior that a psych hold would be a slam dunk. She gathered her hold forms, notepad, and pen, left the mental health center building, and hopped in her car. As a social worker with the county mental health center, Murphy had done a number of these evaluations before but admittedly never one of a 19-year-old who may have just killed his parents. And although she had heard about the diagnosis, Wilets suspected she had never before evaluated or diagnosed anyone with such a bizarre disorder. Frankly, she didn't know what to expect.

Murphy arrived at the sheriff's department around midnight and within moments was escorted to a private interview room. Soon she heard a knock. Ross entered.

"How do you do? I'm Ross Carlson," he said as he sat down with disarming calmness and the politeness of a Boy Scout. Murphy returned the greeting.

"Mr. Carlson, I've been asked by your doctor, Dr. Wilets, to evaluate you. Is that alright with you? Do you understand why?"

Chapter 9: The Psych Hold

"That's fine," Ross replied. "I believe Dr. Wilets is concerned. My parents evidently have been killed, and the doctor is worried about me."

Murphy made notes and pursued her evaluation. Throughout the interview, Ross was affable, responsive to Murphy's questions, and oriented to person, place, and time. Murphy observed that although Ross frequently lost his train of thought and tended to ramble, he showed no evidence of suicidal thinking or homicidal ideation.

It did not surprise Murphy terribly that Ross was not in touch with the reality of his parents' death and expressed no grief or sadness over their loss. Although some of his thinking seemed juvenile and superficial, such as, "I suppose I'll have to drop out of school and work to support myself," Murphy attributed those thoughts to someone who acted like, in the words of her report, "a typical sixteen-year-old."

Upon completion of her interview, Murphy felt that Ross seemed pretty together mentally. She spoke with the police to see if they could add anything. Since they were unable to provide any evidence of Ross's bizarre or unusual behavior, Murphy was satisfied with her conclusion. She called Wilets.

"Dr. Wilets, I'm sorry but I can't find anything that would justify holding Mr. Carlson. If you have more information which would support a hold, then you should pursue it."

"I'll be right down!" Wilets said, evidently disappointed but not surprised given his belief of Ross's diagnosis. "Tell the police not to release Ross." Wilets already had plan B in place.

At 2:00 a.m. Wilets arrived at the sheriff's department, this time with a psychiatrist, Dr. Steve Miller. Before Dr. Miller began his assessment, Wilets had also told him of the likely diagnosis. "I'll keep that in mind," Miller replied.

During the course of Dr. Miller's evaluation, Ross again was very polite. He admitted that he had chronic difficulties with self-esteem, had been suicidal on an intermittent basis since the age of five, and had suicidal thoughts that very day.

"Tell me a little bit more about how you felt today," Miller prodded.

"Well," Ross said, "it's been a little unusual. I felt that I was floating and that my eyes were wobbling."

Miller asked, "When did you last touch a gun?"

"A friend purchased a rifle a couple of weeks back," Ross replied.

"When did you last feel like hurting somebody?"

"A month ago, I felt like punching someone at a local restaurant." Ross also revealed that ever since the dynamite incident, he had felt "paranoid." He elaborated, describing himself as having been "bugged" or watched in some way. Finally, he added, "I feel at times that robots have been placed alongside me on this planet looking for the human weakness in me."

After hearing about robots, wobbling eyes, and being bugged, Dr. Miller felt he had heard enough. He concluded that Ross suffered "from a mental illness characterized by chronic personality problems with acute paranoid traits." He felt that Ross was in some danger of hurting himself if he did not receive supportive treatment in an all-day setting. Wilets received his 72-hour hold. He let out a huge sigh of relief.

Later that day of August 19, 1983, Ross was admitted to the psychiatric unit of the University of Colorado Medical Center. By the end of the day, the hospital certified Ross for an extended 90-day hospitalization.

During the next month, the police's investigation of the murders of Rod and Marilyn Carlson finally concluded with the fortuitous discovery of a small black suitcase. The suitcase contained compelling evidence that linked the probable killer to the crimes. The police confidently drove to the hospital and arrested Ross for two counts of first-degree murder.

Wilets was relieved when Ross was held in jail without bond. In late November when Walter and I finally entered our appearances in the criminal case, one of our first tasks was to interview the doctor.

CHAPTER 10

Another Sybil?

On November 29, 1983, the judge in charge of Ross's case, Judge Richard D. Turelli, postponed the arraignment for a month to allow Walter and me sufficient time to investigate the proper plea.

The first item on our agenda was a meeting with Dr. Wilets since he was the doctor who possessed the most recent insight into Ross's pre-homicidal mental state. Wilets had agreed to meet with us, providing his own attorney could also be present. The repercussions of the *Hinckley* case evidently concerned Wilets.

On June 21, 1982, a District of Columbia jury found John W. Hinckley, Jr. of Evergreen, Colorado insane for the attempted assassination of President Ronald Reagan and assaults of the president's press secretary, James Brady, and two secret service agents, Timothy McCarthy and Thomas Delahanty. As a result of their injuries, Brady and the agents sued Hinckley's psychiatrist, Dr. John Hopper, Jr., in Denver federal court.

Brady's theory was that Hopper committed malpractice in deficiently diagnosing Hinckley and should have known that Hinckley was a danger to others. If Hopper had properly treated his patient, the suit contended, Hinckley would never have committed the assaults. Even though Brady's suit had been thrown out of court for lack of a recognizable legal ground, Wilets nevertheless felt he had to proceed cautiously before our meeting. He thought he could possibly be sued by Ross or his grandparents on the theory that the doctor had failed to properly diagnose and treat Ross and that such failures resulted in the

Carlsons' deaths. A suit against Wilets, however, was the furthest thing from our minds. All we wanted was his cooperation. I picked Walter up at his home on Saturday morning, December 3, for our meeting with the doctor.

The Gerashes' two-story, early-twentieth home was located on Humboldt Street between 8th and 9th Streets; the back yard abutted the grand Cheesman Park, which was surrounded by other grand homes and high-rise condos situated in an eight-square-block area. The Cheesman Park area was one of Denver's most stately neighborhoods.

Turn-of-the-century American elm and silver maple trees formed an umbrella-like shade around the Gerash home, which was perched on this elevated side of Humboldt Street. From the sidewalk, visitors had a modest ascent of about a dozen stairs before reaching the home's front porch. After ringing the doorbell, I never had to wait long; Walter was always on time. This morning was no exception.

As I entered the main floor, I could hear the music of one of Walter's favorite symphonies. True to form, Walter named the work like a student preparing for an exam at Julliard. With Walter, it was never simply Rachmaninoff's Piano Concerto No. 2, but rather Vladimir Ashkenazy playing Rachmaninoff's Piano Concerto No. 2, Op. 18 in C minor, with Kyril Kondrashin conducting the Moscow Philharmonic. I never made light of his enriched recitations, but rather eagerly accepted the opportunity to absorb his knowledge.

On this morning, Walter was his customary exuberant self. He broke out into a huge smile and spoke softly as he described the title of the concerto. He gently grabbed my arm, and quietly said "Listen to this. You got to hear this. Isn't it great?" I uttered my usual but genuine, "Yes, Walter, it's great." With that, he smiled again and off we went to Gerald Pratt's office.

Gerald Pratt was an associate of Long & Jaudon, an eight-lawyer firm well known for its defense of physicians of all specialties. In fact, the firm had successfully represented Dr. Hopper in the Brady suit.

Long & Jaudon's success was reflected in its law offices, a converted late 19th-century Denver mansion. The Bailey Mansion, named for George B. Bailey, the successful real estate and silver

Chapter 10: Another Sybil?

speculator of the late 1890s, was located on the periphery of downtown, contained about 10,000 square feet and dwarfed the other residences on the block. The sandstone structure easily accommodated the firm's dozen or so lawyers and staff.

Once inside, one was struck by the mansion's elaborate trim and hard wood finishes of butternut, oak, cherry, bird's-eye maple and ash. The only reason I knew about the wood finishes was because a brochure on the receptionist desk listed them. There was a gracious quietness about the offices that remained undisturbed by those few people who were working this Saturday morning.

The receptionist directed us to the conference room that was situated just off to our right. Walter and I entered through one of the two wide, pocket doors. Gerald Pratt and Dr. Wilets were seated next to one another at the south end of the room's conference table, which could comfortably accommodate all of the lawyers at Long & Jaudon and probably most of their staff.

Wilets wore a look of strained congeniality. Pratt's role as legal protector was reflected by how closely he sat to the doctor. The power of the room's cherry wood doors and high-back, red-cloth chairs, which served the conference table, seemed to add strength to Wilets's apparent fragility.

Among the four of us, Walter was the elder statesman. Wilets appeared at or very close to my age of 40, and Pratt looked a couple of years younger. Pratt and Wilets evidently believed they added formality to the interview by dressing in sport jackets and ties. Conversely, Walter and I opted for the more casual look of slacks and sport shirts, believing a more informal look would ease the tension that Wilets had inserted into this meeting by his insistence upon counsel.

After we exchanged pleasantries, Pratt sought a clear understanding regarding a release Walter had promised that Ross would sign. Bowing to Walter's experience, I played the role of dutiful listener at this juncture. The conversation between the two attorneys was accompanied only by the soft ticking of a grandfather clock standing behind me.

Walter first addressed Wilets's concerns regarding a possible lawsuit. "Because of the potential liability, you have your own attorney present, which is very unusual. I've never seen that kind of caution in twenty-eight years of practice," Walter stated while assuring that Ross would sign a release discharging the doctor from any possible liability for the Carlsons' deaths.

Wilets and Pratt quickly exchanged approving nods with one another. Walter continued, "Dr. Wilets, we don't want you to be inhibited in fully revealing any notes, any tape recordings, or other material that will throw light on Ross Carlson's mental condition. I need your help since you had more contact with Ross than any other doctor," Walter explained.

"Dr. Wilets wants to cooperate," Pratt responded. "However, I'm wondering whether you will still obtain the release if the doctor's information doesn't help you."

"You bet," Walter agreed. "My first wife is a psychiatrist. I'm sympathetic. I'll have Ross sign a release no matter what. Otherwise, the doctor might feel inhibited, especially since this might have been the first time one of his patients had killed somebody."

"You can bet on that!" Wilets interrupted, making sure everyone heard that disclaimer.

"The release is guaranteed, is that right?" Pratt insisted.

"That's right," Walter confirmed.

Once Pratt gave his client the green light to speak freely, Dr. Wilets appeared to finally relax. Although it was evident the doctor felt he could be faulted for this tragedy, I didn't know what mental illness he thought had eluded him. After all, neither Walter nor I had seen any of Wilets's records that described his opinions or any contacts he had with the sheriff's office, Dr. Levy, Carol Murphy, and Dr. Steve Miller the day after the Carlsons were killed.

"You may find this hard to believe," Wilets said, "but except for the patient's very first appointment, I don't take any notes. I keep my cases in my mind. The notes I gave to Craig Truman were reconstructed from my memory. The only other notes I made were when the police informed me about the Carlsons' deaths. That's when I instructed them to return Ross to the police station."

"Why did you think he was a danger?" Walter asked.

"There were several things," Wilets said without hesitation.

Chapter 10: Another Sybil?

"One is, and this is a doctor talking, who in the hell is going to shoot his parents, two nice schoolteachers who never harmed anyone? Why were his parents left dead, on a remote dirt road? Two, the last time I met with Ross and his family, there was yelling and screaming."

The doctor described the "intense" family session in July and the glee with which Ross spoke of escorting wealthy women around town. "He was sitting there telling them this, and I was thinking to myself, what is going on here? I'm not saying I believed it, but if you know Ross, it was possible."

Wilets then emphasized his third reason. "This is important. Ross is obviously not as predictable as I had thought. If he is guilty of the charges, that's not predictable behavior."

Wilets next touched upon a potential motive for the murders. "During therapy," Wilets revealed, "Ross had shown an obsession with money and material things."

When Wilets read the newspaper accounts about the trusts, it was the first time he realized Ross could inherit around $250,000. "Since I didn't know there was money available, I had no inkling that the parents were in danger," he lamented, thinking back to the last family session.

At this point, I broke my silence. "We don't know if Ross was aware he stood to inherit a substantial estate. The trust documents do not describe the value of any assets. The trust acquired value only when it received life insurance proceeds. Also, during their lives the Carlsons allowed certain life insurance policies to lapse. Therefore, Ross could not have known what, if anything, he was going to inherit."

I continued. "When I represented Ross in the probate proceedings, he always asked, 'how much is in there and where is it coming from?' That suggests he was ignorant of the details of any potential inheritance." With that, quietness overtook the conference room. What, then, was the motive for the murders, if not money?

After a few seconds, Wilets broke the silence. "Another explanation for the mysterious clothing is multiple personality disorder. One personality goes out and shoplifts," he explained. "The clothes show up in the closet. The personality shifts. Ross doesn't know where they came from, so he fabricates." Whoa, multiple personality

49

disorder! That was a bomb shell from left field! What's Wilets talking about? I asked myself.

"Multiple personalities have to confabulate because when one personality does something, they find themselves in a mess they can't explain." Wilets continued. "So, what happens is, they start spinning stories. When you confabulate, you then take the essence of your personality into your confabulation — rich, beautiful, wealthy. I'm not convinced that's what he has. I didn't suspect multiple personalities in treatment."

As Wilets continued, I began to think of "Sybil." The idea of multiple personalities sounded fascinating but also extremely off-the-wall. I suppressed a smirk, believing no juror would buy such a bizarre explanation, even if it were true. On the other hand, don't be so dismissive, I cautioned myself. If this is what the evidence showed, we were obligated to investigate it. I wanted to hear more. Walter then added a twist to Wilets's explanation.

"I haven't read the whole DA's file since it was just recently delivered. However, you were aware of the circumstances behind Ross's earlier arrest that led to his treatment with you," he said, looking at the doctor. "Ross's advertisement when he wanted to buy the dynamite. He used the initials JNT when he placed the ad. Stands for 'just in the nick of time.' Independent of that, I talked to a 16-year-old girl. She said that last year Ross, when he was eighteen, stated he was sixteen and had a brother, Justin."

"Ross did?" Wilets asked, unnerved by the revelation.

"Listen to this!" Walter insisted, reading from the notes of his interview with that teenager. "That he had a brother Justin, a twin brother, who is much more handsome, much more successful ... he is 16. And his name is Justin Nicholas Time."

"Lived in Phoenix," I added, having also read Walter's notes of his interview.

Wilets leaned forward in his chair, anxious to hear more.

"I'm serious," Walter said loudly. "The girl was in my office ... Suzanne Keller. This was even before I read the file. When I talked to the girl, I didn't know about the dynamite case and that he advertised and used those initials."

Chapter 10: Another Sybil?

"You should have told me!" Wilets stressed.

"See. I didn't know that!" Walter shrugged his voice still at a high pitch.

I added, "I asked him who is Justin Nicholas Time? And he said, someone who I want to be like."

There was another brief silence. Suddenly, Wilets slammed his fist on the conference table, as if he had just experienced an epiphany. "Let me tell you what happens! Can I?" he asked, eager and excited to speak. No one dared to deny Wilets the stage because that's why we were meeting in the first place — to hear his explanations and learn his insights that could prove invaluable to Ross's defense.

"Go right ahead," Pratt encouraged.

"Because I have worked with multiple personality, there are little subtle things," Wilets cautioned. "I doubt your other doctors would know. And, regrettably, I wasn't aware of this while the case was going on ... to show you how fooled you can be. What happens now is that Ross needs to defend the other personality. The other personality will be saying things to Ross now like, 'shut up, don't say a word about me, don't reveal.' I know this sounds crazy, but this is what happens."

"Ross will be attempting to cooperate with you obviously to save himself, and he will have this incredible internal conflict. If this is the case, they'll be working against you because he doesn't want to be released. The other personality wants to stay. My hunch is Ross is telling you guys, 'I don't know what happened.'"

Walter revealed we had not asked Ross about the murders. I asked, "what if Ross tells the doctors who are evaluating him that he did it?"

Wilets offered alternate theories. "If he tells you that, it's either because one personality observed and watched the other personality; or he did it, and he's just a bad guy." This sociopathic alternative was muddled, however.

Wilets had Ross undergo psychological testing by Dr. Bruce Pennington in October 1982, when Ross was in the early stages of treatment. One of the standard and most reliable tests, the MMPI, did not reveal any gross antisocial features.

Wilets explained that Ross could be a true multiple with one personality as "the most severe sociopath you'll ever see in your life. It got concealed from me in therapy and was not uncovered in the tests. Many of the doctors who are now examining Ross will never pick up his illness," Wilets predicted.

Wilets went on to explain that individuals with this disorder are highly, highly hypnotizable. "A highly hypnotizable individual is like a chameleon. You put them in a legal environment, and they'll talk like a lawyer. You put them in a store, and he can act like a manager. They assume roles real fast. And what I just realized is, this happened to me. You put him in my office, and he acts like a patient, a good patient. This was not a patient who I thought was going to kill somebody."

"How do you distinguish a manipulative person who may be an antisocial personality from this chameleon-type person who is a multiple personality?" I asked.

Wilets replied that Ross did not fit within the psychiatric criteria of an antisocial personality. "Multiple personalities are strange," he added, shaking his head. "They tax the imagination, and one of your problems, if this is the case, is to sell it. Not everyone believes in MPD," he warned. "In 1979, the chairman of my psych department told me and other residents that MPD was 'bullshit'."

I listened attentively to Wilets, who for the last several minutes had released all of his pent-up tension and was talking freely and openly. I kept asking myself if the features of MPD fit this case. The notion which had seemed so preposterous just a few moments ago was now taking shape as a real possibility.

Walter and I had thought the district attorney might use the dynamite case as proof that Ross had been planning his parents' murders for over a year. In therapy, Ross had explained the incident as a combination suicide by him and economic solution for his parents who lived in a home with a defective foundation. Ross knew he had been conceived out of wedlock, felt he had been a burden to his parents since birth, and thought of his self-annihilation as a delayed abortion. "What connection to the case did those feelings have?" I wanted to know.

"There are a number of different ways to look at it," Wilets explained. "The defect in the house symbolizes the defect in his mind.

Chapter 10: Another Sybil?

He knows he has a problem in his head which is unlike what anybody else has. He doesn't know exactly what it's all about. By getting rid of the defect in the house, he also gets rid of the defect in his brain, which started with the child who should never have been born. I bought it lock, stock, and barrel! This was a suicide, a bizarre suicide."

"Well, did you ask him what JNT was?" Walter asked.

"Sure I did," Wilets said. "He said that's the name I used in order to buy the dynamite. I said what does that mean? He said 'just in the nick of time I wasn't going to do it.' Just in the nick of time. Justin Nicholas Time. So, I really wasn't suspicious. I didn't suspect multiple personality because he had an explanation."

Wilets then touched upon his hesitation to wholly commit to the MPD diagnosis. If Ross were found insane, he would be confined to the Colorado State Hospital until restored to sanity. Then, he would be returned to society. Wilets had worked at the hospital; he was well aware of its shortcomings.

"Somebody like this flies right through the system because there is no overt pathology," Wilets observed. "He won't be a behavioral problem. The other personality goes underground. It does not get treated. Effective treatment for multiples requires one therapist for 8, 10, 12 years. At Pueblo, the therapists are residents who rotate every year. Any time Ross might attach to a therapist, the therapist will shortly be gone. He won't get treated."

"If he's found insane, he could be out pretty soon," Walter predicted.

"And I'm not real comfortable with that," Wilets admitted, believing Ross had blamed him for the 72-hour hold at University of Colorado Medical Center.

"He's not dumb," Walter observed.

"He's not dumb, but he's not smart either," Wilets retorted.

I, on the other hand, found Ross to be mature and intelligent. I mentioned Ross's fairly sophisticated knowledge regarding the stock market and other investments. That description differed from Wilets's profile of a younger acting, superficial teenager.

"Different personalities have different IQs," Wilets said. "Ross's IQ is 103 which is normal. That's not stupid, but it's not bright. In sessions with me, he would misuse words. He would come across trying to be smart."

Walter, however, thought Ross displayed real cleverness by being able to lure his parents to the Ramada Renaissance and having them drive to Cottonwood. What still perplexed us though was that the Carlsons were killed without any sign of a struggle. Wilets offered an explanation.

"When the personalities change, everything changes ... facial expression ... tautness in the face. If the parents are in the front seat, and he's in the back seat ... when they turned around and saw somebody looking like a demon, they would be very, very intimidated. No longer would he be their sweet, little boy."

"Will you be comfortable seeing him again?" Walter asked, knowing the doctor's diagnosis of MPD could be a great plus for our case. Wilets was very forthright, repeating his discomfort that Ross might be found insane and committed to Pueblo.

"The doctors down there are administrators," Wilets revealed with disdain. "You have mental health workers attempting to treat patients that skilled psychiatrists would have trouble treating." In Wilets's opinion, a perfect example of what happens with less experienced observers already occurred in this case with Carol Murphy. The social worker visited Ross and found nothing wrong with him. A few hours later, the more experienced Dr. Steve Miller found sufficient evidence to hold Ross for observation. (It wasn't until Walter and I had read the DA's discovery of the evaluations by Murphy and Miller that we actually learned that Wilets had suspected MPD the day of the homicides. Wilets, however, did not share that tidbit with us during this meeting with him).

"How can we lessen your inhibitions?" I asked, sensing Wilets's reluctance to become more involved in the case. "If you feel MPD is meritorious but are more concerned about Ross's premature release from Pueblo, I have problems with that."

Wilets's candid rejoinder was fraught with anxiety. "I would prefer that I hardly exist in terms of your defense. I don't want a lingering image in his mind because it's too scary. Someday he'll get out without getting better."

Chapter 10: Another Sybil?

I temporarily tabled the doctor's angst and instead sought a fuller understanding of MPD. "Could the dynamics of this disorder explain Ross's conduct between the time of the dynamite incident and the murder of his parents?" I asked. I laid out the scenario where one personality in September of 1982 bought dynamite and inquired about a gun. That personality disappeared for several months and popped up again in May 1983 to buy a Rossi firearm, which was determined to be the murder weapon. That same personality disappeared for another several months, and then popped up again on that terrible night in August.

"Right, that's what happens," Wilets answered. "Personalities can pop in and out. They show up for ten minutes and disappear. It's weird."

"Let's assume," I said, "that Ross is a multiple. Let's assume that he killed his parents. Let's assume that certain personalities popped in and out during one year, and eventually committed this crime. What is the significance of his leaving a trail that directly connects him to the crime?"

"Here's what happens," Wilets replied. "The bad personality sets up the good personality to get caught. I treated a patient with four or five personalities. One was a sociopath. One was sweet as can be. Another was a prostitute. But anyway ... one of the personalities began writing bad checks with a trail as easy as hell to track down. They arrested the good personality. The devil, the bad one, sets up the good one."

"Well," I said, "he also takes his best friend, Ken Cortez, to the movie about an hour before the murders, leaves and says I have something to do. He returns a couple of hours later and says everything's cool. My parents were trying to Lone Ranger it. Does that fit within what you're saying?"

"He's setting up Ross," Wilets retorted. "Justin is setting up Ross and punishing him."

Each of Wilets's responses suggested more questions. Since my mind was flooding with so many thoughts, I usurped the next few minutes, fearing I might forget to ask something important.

"Could the docile or meek personality have taken his parents out to the scene and made it appear they were going out for a nice evening ride, and then all of a sudden the enraged personality came out?"

"Could be, I don't know," Wilets admitted. "The switches can be immediate; they're instantaneous."

"Which personality plans the whole thing?"

"The bad one."

"And the bad one can tell the good one 'you got to do these seemingly innocuous things while I do other things'?"

"I don't have any experience with knowing that," Wilets answered.

"How do you distinguish the multiple personality from just a bad guy?"

"You have to find out whether Ross has amnesia between different personalities," Wilets responded.

Amnesia! Now, that was another curve ball. "How does amnesia fit into this illness?" I asked not understanding the connection between the two.

Wilets recalled that for one session, Ross showed up at the doctor's office at their regular standing time of 2:00 p.m. However, because of an agreed change in plans, Ross wasn't supposed to show until 4:00 p.m. According to Wilets, that faux pas could have been either an innocent mistake or indicative of one personality agreeing to the later appointment time. A second personality, who had no knowledge of the change and whose role was to merely arrive at a particular destination, actually showed up two hours earlier.

Wilets explained further. "Another legal thing is, what if Ross is not amnestic? What if he knows what the other personality is doing? What's the legal responsibility then? What if he is observing the other personality and not putting a check on it?"

Walter interjected. "After all, you're trying one body and one brain, and that defense is difficult to sell to a jury. I've already had preliminary discussions with Rewey, and so far he's been indicating a dissociative reaction." I could tell by Walter's comments that he was not enamored with an MPD defense, but instead favored the diagnosis made by another of his psychiatric experts, Dr. Richard Rewey.

Wilets, on the other hand, was less concerned with our legal

Chapter 10: Another Sybil?

dilemmas and more consumed by the personal haunt of whether he misdiagnosed Ross. "I'm a guy who's really quite sensitive to this illness. I've read a lot about it and worked on it, and I didn't know. Steve Miller didn't pick it up. He saw something else; he picked up the paranoia."

"As a parent myself, I wouldn't be too sympathetic if I were a juror," Walter admitted, reaffirming his initial disdain for this defense.

"There will be a lot of disbelief about this diagnosis," Wilets forewarned.

By now we had spent over two hours with Wilets; the Saturday-noon sun was entering through the room's south window. Pratt stood and adjusted the shutters to block the sun from Wilets's face. That blocked illumination was reflective of the end result of this meeting. As a result of certain misgivings, Wilets had clearly expressed his noninterest in becoming further involved in the case.

Noting that reluctance but not dwelling on it, we agreed to conclude this first interview and thanked the doctor and Pratt. Wilets had introduced much food for thought. It was now time for Walter and me to digest everything. As the two of us walked back to my car, we agreed upon the obvious. This was not going to be an easy case. Walter had little interest in pursuing the MPD defense, believing it too bizarre and something a jury would never buy.

"Rewey is leaning toward finding Ross insane on the basis of a dissociative episode," Walter reminded me. "That's a much more common psychiatric explanation for murder and is more easily understood by a jury. Don't you see, like Wilets said, even some psychiatrists don't believe in MPD."

"Walter, don't you think we have to pursue whatever mental illness is dictated by the facts?" I asked. "Why don't we wait to see what your doctors have to say before making any decision now?" Walter agreed, although I knew his collegial smile masked serious doubts.

As I drove Walter back to his home, he and I formulated a game plan. We would read the hundreds of pages of police reports and then view the physical evidence at the sheriff's office. We needed to first learn about the prosecution's case before deciding anything else. The burning question of what illness would be the basis of our ultimate defense was left for another day. Although I concurred with

57

this approach, I nevertheless could not resist in trying to understand MPD and the other dissociative disorders. This, I agreed, was going to be a more interesting study than what I painstakingly endured during my crash course regarding wills and trusts.

After undergoing a brief primer about the various dissociative disorders, I was prepared to meet with our experts to learn from them from what mental disease, if any, Ross suffered, and how, if at all, that illness rendered him legally insane. I would then learn as much as I could about the illnesses endorsed by our experts in order to become an effective advocate on Ross's behalf. That educational process would spring into high gear in early 1984, but not until I first took a brief social detour.

PART 2

CHAPTER 11

Three Girls & the Doppel Ganger

Murder cases have voracious appetites. If permitted, they can consume your every waking moment and result in endless restless nights. I sensed the murder-consumption phenomenon was about to begin after we met with Dr. Wilets in early December. When the holiday-party season was about to kick into high gear the following week, I agreed to escort my friend Marsha Scheer to the Carik Christmas gathering on Sunday, December 11. Marsha's husband, Carl, one of my running buddies, was out of town. Instead of an evening at home watching *60 Minutes* and the Sunday night movie, Marsha lured me out of the house with the prospect of meeting beautiful, single women who sold Carik's upscale clothing and jewelry to Denver's fashionable ladies. I picked up Marsha early.

One of the first women Marsha introduced me to at the party was Robin Childs, an exquisite-looking, 30-year-old with flawless skin, large hazel eyes, and shoulder length brown hair. Looking at a strikingly beautiful woman and no wedding ring easily diverted my attention from the recesses of Ross Carlson's mind to the life of Robin Childs. I spent the next hour or so in her company learning as much about Ms. Childs as I could.

Having only partially succeeded in this educational process, I called Robin the next day. Yes, she'd love to go to a Nuggets game tomorrow night. Boy, was I a romantic; a basketball game for our first date! Well, I thought, at least we'd be in the company of 17,000 of my closest friends.

On December 13, 1983, the Nuggets and Pistons played the

highest-scoring game in NBA history — a triple overtime thriller won by the Pistons, 186 to 184. I figured any woman as lovely as Robin, who could enjoy watching ten guys in shorts run back and forth on a hardwood floor for three hours, was meant for me. By the end of the evening, I was smitten!

Robin and I had become inseparable during the next two and a half months. Occasionally, her two daughters, nine-year-old Rachel and six-year-old Kristin, joined us during our weekend slumber parties. What I had failed to notice after a number of visits was an accumulated assortment of female and children's toiletries and clothing at my home. Before I realized it, I was gradually acquiring three new roommates. I vowed to become more observant once I got a better handle on Ross's case.

Just who was Ross Carlson, from what mental illness, if any, did he suffer, and why did he kill his parents? I had hoped that upcoming interviews with Walter's mental health experts, Drs. John Glismann, Richard Rewey, and Ralph Fisch would provide answers. During February 1984, we met with each doctor.

Glismann, a stately-looking man with a thick head of graying hair, was the first of Walter's doctors to have examined Ross. Because Glismann and Walter had known each other for several years, the psychiatrist began by speaking directly to Walter after he and I sat on the doctor's couch and were ready with notepads and pens. The doctor took his customary "therapist" chair. "My first impression of Ross Carlson was that he was the best dressed young man, or old man for that matter, that I have ever seen in a prison setting," Glismann said, as he leaned forward in his chair. "Yet, he was only dressed in prison garb."

"I thought to myself," Glismann said, "How could a 19-year-old make orange, jail uniforms look not only freshly pressed, but almost regal? He looked great, possessed finely chiseled features ... very, very confident. He had a good command of the language. He obviously prided himself on his good taste in practically everything."

The thoughtful psychiatrist spoke of the sessions he had with Ross, and of the ease with which the two got along. Ross, according to the doctor, spoke freely about a number of topics, exuding both self-assurance and humor.

Chapter 11: Three Girls & the Doppel Ganger

"Ross's description of his life contained recurring themes of perfection, high ideals, and lofty expectations, all of which had been inculcated by his parents," Glismann explained. "Rod and Marilyn Carlson didn't drive just any kind of car; they each drove a Cadillac. Ross's mother didn't just clean the house, but rather 'was the kind of a woman who sat in her living room waiting for the dust to fall,' Ross told me during one session," the doctor continued.

Glismann saw a clear pattern emerge in Ross's upbringing. The Carlsons expected Ross to appreciate the standards they had established and to adhere to them, whatever the cost.

"If you had closed your eyes and did not know Ross's age, how old would you have thought Ross was by just speaking to him?" I asked, interrupting my note taking and breaking my silence.

"I would have thought I was talking to an individual of considerable experience," Glismann answered, looking at me. "I would have thought him much older, maybe 27, 28. There was a youthful exuberance about him, but the values he talked about, the emphasis he placed on things had very little of the adolescent quality. There wasn't a great deal of the adolescent confusion or adolescent moratorium. He knew who he was supposed to be."

According to Glismann, Ross described that when he was around three years old and had a potty accident, his parents' technique of toilet training consisted of rubbing Ross's face in his dirty underpants. Now that's really disgusting, I thought to myself. Kids aren't supposed to be treated like dogs. What the heck was occurring in the Carlson household, I wondered.

In the doctor's view, the toilet training story evidenced not only "the extremes to which the family would go to meet expectations, but also their lack of empathy for one another. It sent a clear message to Ross from an early age," the psychiatrist continued, "that upholding the expected standards were more important than caring about one another." At the conclusion of his sessions with Ross, the doctor believed he suffered from a "severe narcissistic personality disorder" and was insane at the time of the murders, explaining that Ross's interpersonal relationship with his parents was so disturbed and lacking in empathy that he would have considered it perfectly normal and indeed necessary for him to end their lives because of the way they treated him. Glismann's explanation was a head scratcher to me, and I frankly didn't know what to make of it. I was curious to learn Walter's impression.

At the conclusion of our meeting, Walter cordially thanked Glismann. The doctor seemed to force a smile, probably sensing that Walter was not wild about the doctor's diagnosis. Over the years, I had participated in enough joint interviews of experts with Walter to agree with Glismann's likely intuition. Once we got in Walter's car and headed back to his office, he agreed that Glismann's analysis would probably be a difficult sell to a jury. A few days later, we met with Dr. Richard Rewey, the next of Walter's experts to have examined Ross.

The soft-spoken psychiatrist, appearing to be in his early 40s, provided us with a lengthy account of Ross's troubled upbringing, including the fecal smearing as punishment for his lack of progress in toilet training. "As a teenager," Rewey noted, "Ross suffered chronic loneliness, depression, a lack of friends and continuing thoughts of suicide." The doctor cited Rod Carlson's "demands for perfection," and Marilyn Carlson's "unyielding support for her husband's heavy-handed parenting" as contributing significantly to Ross's emotional problems.

Rewey related that "when Ross was around 13 or 14, he began to exhibit signs of forgetfulness and uncharacteristically bizarre behavior, such as cruelty toward animals." Then, reminiscent of what 15-year-old Kelli Olson had told the police during their murder investigation, Rewey informed us that "at the age of 17, Ross created an alternate identity for himself — a twin brother named Justin Nicholas Time." "Justin," Rewey said, "would often save Ross from suicidal attempts 'just in the nick of time.'"

In contrast to Justin, Rewey said, "Ross felt himself to be woefully inadequate, weak, frequently taken advantage of, and totally dependent upon his parents. Soon, Ross began developing yet another identity, one which included the evil attributes of himself." He called this part of himself, the "Anti-Christ," Rewey explained.

This lack of empathy or caring on the part of Ross's parents was a recurring theme throughout Rewey's discussion. The doctor spoke of the intense stress in Ross's life following high school graduation

Chapter 11: Three Girls & the Doppel Ganger

when, because of low SAT scores, he was not accepted into a college of his choice. Instead, he had to go to Metro State College in Denver and work as a janitor in the school where his mother taught. Ross tried, unsuccessfully, to gain his parents' attention by creating fictitious drug and alcohol problems. He eventually succeeded in angering his parents when he confessed to acting as an escort service for some local women. However, "the Carlsons' response was to ask Ross to leave their home and live on his own," Rewey said.

Dr. Rewey's comments regarding the escort service meshed with Dr. Wilets's recollection of his last two family sessions with the Carlsons and the heated exchange between parents and son. This consistency in Ross's reporting to Wilets and several months later to Rewey was a positive point for an eventual insanity defense, I noted to myself. It's a common prosecution strategy to look for inconsistencies in what a defendant says to different doctors as a strike against the defendant's credibility because it shows efforts to manipulate the evaluation process after the defendant has committed a heinous crime.

In recalling the day of the murders, Ross told Rewey that "he felt ... driven toward doing something awful to his parents when he placed his pistol in the car, although he had no thoughts at that time to actually commit the murders." That night, when he was driving his parents to that fateful country road, Ross "felt that his mind was like a roller coaster and that he was being pushed into something bad," Rewey recounted.

According to the doctor, before killing his mother, Ross recalled her saying "Go ahead and shoot me, this is terrible."

Ross admitted to Dr. Rewey that he felt little guilt or remorse. He realized this was the opposite of how he ought to feel and was perplexed about his lack of emotion regarding the killings. Now, I was thinking that perhaps Glismann's diagnosis was not too off the wall because this piece of Rewey's explanation seemed consistent with the narcissism element Glismann discussed. In summarizing, Rewey concluded that Ross committed the homicides during a dissociative episode and was insane at the time. Rewey identified Ross's mental illness as a severe borderline personality disorder with developing features of MPD.

Walter seemed pleased with Dr. Rewey's analysis because it did not emphasize Ross's multiple personalities. "David," Walter began, as we left Rewey's office, "this is much better. Don't you see? Rewey focuses on Ross's severe borderline personality disorder and the phenomenon of dissociation. I'm tellin' you; these concepts are more easily explainable to and understood by lay jurors. We got to go with Rewey."

Admittedly, I knew little about dissociation or borderline personality disorder, but, from my lay perspective, I thought Rewey described a cold-blooded killing. At the same time, however, my fascination with the MPD diagnosis increased substantially because of Rewey's description of Justin and the Anti-Christ. "I understand, Walter. Let's wait until we hear from all of the doctors. Plus, we need to look at the DA's discovery to see where that takes us."

Before reviewing the discovery, we met on February 23, 1984, with Walter's next expert and accomplished psychologist, Dr. Ralph Fisch.

Dr. Fisch's influences as a professor and psychological tester extraordinaire were apparent during our meeting with him. This small dynamo was intense and enthusiastic about his findings, supporting them with citations to the professional literature and other recognized scientific authorities. Dr. Fisch detailed the uncanny similarities of two MMPI tests that Ross had taken more than a year apart. These two profiles showed major features of disorders, such as MPD, involving fragmentation of the ego. The first test was administered nearly ten months before the murders by a Dr. Pennington, who had done the testing for Dr. Wilets, and the second one by Dr. Fisch only a couple of months ago. The existence of the Pennington test was further evidence that MPD existed before the homicides and was not something that Ross had cooked up afterwards in order to appear insane.

Dr. Fisch emphasized a recent telephone conversation he had with Ross. "He called me just a couple of days ago, pleading for help," Fisch said excitedly. "He claimed to be bombarded by other personalities who "phone me ... they just phone me ... they control me..." Ross named these personalities "Steve, Michael, Blue, and Grey," the doctor explained. I couldn't help but feel Fisch's excitement.

Chapter 11: Three Girls & the Doppel Ganger

Walter, on the other hand, looked intrigued, but I could tell he wasn't too thrilled with the notion of trying to sell this to a jury.

Fisch was steadfast in his conclusion that Ross suffered from multiple personality disorder and was insane at the time of the crimes. In support of his insanity opinion, the doctor alluded to a recognized psychological phenomenon known as a "doppelgänger" or "autoscopy" in Ross's account of the murder scene. Ross's description, according to Fisch, was a classic dissociative episode, a classic feature of MPD.

"Ross described having a visual hallucination of himself committing the homicidal act," Fisch said. "It was as though he was a spectator or detached bystander, watching himself commit the murder from an external vantage point."

For the first time since we began conferencing with doctors, Walter and I had more than just clinical interviews and client histories as the basis for the MPD finding. Now, we also had a reliable, objective, and recognized psychological test, the MMPI, to support the finding. As a result, I left Fisch's office with two books he lent me about dissociation and MPD and a much more persuasive view regarding Ross's probable diagnosis. I wasn't sure if Walter shared my enthusiasm. Our further discussion about MPD, however, was temporarily shelved because our next task concerned reviewing the prosecution's evidence.

CHAPTER 12

One Black Suitcase & Nine Personalities

The morning after we had met with Dr. Fisch, Walter and I headed to the sheriff's office to review the results of their investigation. Although Walter realized that the psychiatric data and the supporting literature from Wilets and our three forensic experts pointed toward MPD as our primary insanity defense, deep down I believe he was hoping that the physical evidence would point elsewhere.

Our private investigator, Gene Tardy, met us at the sheriff's department. The county's lead investigator, Gary Robinson, escorted us to a room normally used to interrogate suspects. A two-way mirror covered almost an entire wall. I suspected, and from Walter's bodily language and measured conversation with Robinson, felt he shared my suspicion, that another police officer was sitting on the other side of the mirror chronicling our study of the evidence. To facilitate our review, Robinson proceeded to neatly stack boxes filled with papers, books, and bulging manila envelopes upon a table at which Walter, Gene, and I sat.

On top of this mound of material, Robinson placed a small black suitcase. It was obviously the department's prime piece of evidence. While resting his hand on top of the suitcase, Robinson said, "this is everything gentlemen."

As the three of us went through the evidence, Robinson sat across the table like a Marine sentry. My fears about the two-way mirror became moot; instead, a watch dog was practically seated in

Chapter 12: One Black Suitcase & Nine Personalities

my lap. Robinson stared straight ahead and said nothing unless we spoke to him. Although he was polite, his presence was intrusive. Therefore, Walter, Gene, and I said very little to one another or to Robinson. Initially, we took pictures of certain pieces of evidence, which enabled Robinson to compile a mental list of what had sparked our interest. As a result, before we left the room, I asked Gene to take photos of all the remaining items of evidence.

However, one did not have to be a member of Mensa to know what items were the most significant to proving two counts of first-degree murder. The black suitcase found hidden on the Norgren property was the proverbial "smoking gun." Upon opening the case, the items on top consisted of a plaid shirt, a pair of blue jeans, and a gray and red gym bag. The gym bag contained a blue jacket. The clothing was Ross's size. Below this first layer of items were two blue vinyl and fiber floor mats, each emblazoned with a Cadillac insignia. Two similar floor mats were missing from Rod Carlson's Seville when it was discovered the day after the homicides.

Underneath the first two layers of materials were: a blue nylon, Velcro wallet; a vinyl purse; a leather glove; a pair of rubber surgical-type gloves; and a pair of hiking or work boots. Inside the left boot was a gold cloth bag which contained a .38 caliber Rossi revolver. It was the very weapon that was bought for Ross by a friend, Edward Heatley, three months before the homicides.

When interviewed by the police, Heatley told them that, after the purchase, Ross placed the gun and the bullets bought with it in a black leather suitcase similar to the one in front of us. Ross, according to Heatley, also asked him not to tell anyone about the firearm's and ammo's acquisition.

In the left side pocket of the suitcase was a box of .38 semi-jacketed hollow point bullets. The ballistics report confirmed that the bullet recovered from Rod Carlson's body and the one found where Marilyn Carlson's head had lain were fired from the same weapon, either an FIE Derringer or .38 caliber Rossi.

The vinyl purse contained a Colorado driver's license issued to Marilyn Carlson of South Forest Court, Littleton, Colorado. Inside the blue Velcro wallet was a Colorado driver's license issued to Ross M. Karlson, last name spelled with a "K," with a birth date of 5/28/61 and an address on South Forest Court, Littleton, Colorado. The photograph on the license was that of Ross. The birth date indicated he was 21. The address was that of Ken Cortez. The combination of the gun, bullets, Ross's ID, his clothes, his mother's wallet and ID, the ballistics report, and Heatley's statements screamed for two convictions of first-degree murder.

While the black suitcase and its contents were damning pieces of evidence, the most unsettling part of the morning was viewing the autopsy photos. I was looking at the most private anatomy of a young mother and father, the parents of my client. I couldn't help but feel like a voyeur. After blocking out the discomfort (a more normal kind of dissociation, I had learned from my quick study about dissociation), I arranged the photos in front of me and placed the coroner Dr. Ben Galloway's report to my right. Dr. Galloway's words provided insight into the events of that fateful summer night.

Mrs. Carlson's height was measured at 5'3"; her weight estimated at 115 pounds. A deeply penetrating gunshot wound measuring 5/16" in diameter was present in the left back of the head, 3-1/2" behind the left ear, and 1/4" below the lower margin of the ear. From there, the bullet traveled inward, across the undersurface of the left mastoid bone, penetrating the outer wall of the pharynx and underneath the surface of the tongue. The propulsion caused extensive trauma to the inner aspects of the mouth, resulting in several fractured teeth in the upper and lower jaw. The bullet exited the body from the right lower margin of the mouth. The hands revealed no evidence of trauma.

Rod Carlson was measured at 6'1" and weighed 210 pounds. Although, his gunshot wound was noted to be approximately in the same area as that of his wife's, the path of the bullet was different. Here, the wound entered the left occipital region of the skull, traveling upwards and lacerating the left cerebellar and cerebral hemispheres of the brain. A mushroomed, lead bullet and jacket were retrieved from the external surface of the upper portion of the left parietal lobe. Essentially, the bullet had transected the brain.

Chapter 12: One Black Suitcase & Nine Personalities

Galloway further indicated that he found no evidence of "powder stippling" on either victim. As a result, because no powder residue was found on the body of either victim, in Galloway's opinion, both individuals were shot from a distance of no closer than two feet.

After our review of materials, Gene Tardy went his separate way to continue his investigation. Walter and I walked down the jail's corridor to visit Ross, the autopsy pictures of Rod and Marilyn Carlson still fresh in my mind.

As had become our practice, we visited with Ross in a cell that was in the middle of the jail and directly across from the sheriff command post. Once we finished, Walter and I would pound on the steel door of the cell to have the officers unlock it, so we could be on our way.

On this particular day, Ross was lying on the cell's twin-size bed with his left hand cupped upon his forehead, his face a brooding mask of depression. Walter and I tried to be as upbeat as possible, but we could not seem to lift Ross out of his funk. He knew of our meeting with Wilets, and the doctor's suspicion of MPD. He was further aware that Dr. Fisch came to the same diagnosis, although with more conviction based, in part, upon his learning from Ross the names of four alternate identities: Steve, Michael, Blue, and Gray. We, of course, had also learned of Justin and the Anti-Christ from Dr. Rewey.

For the first time during any of our conversations, Ross discussed another part of himself, namely Steve. He described how Steve liked to draw and mentioned that Steve had sent Dr. Fisch a collage. I seized this opportunity to try a little test of my own.

I stood up from the small table where Walter and I had been sitting and moved my chair closer to Ross. Although it was becoming increasingly clear that the existence of multiple personalities presented Ross's **best defense, I still had some doubts. I handed Ross my legal pad and asked him to list the names of his other personalities on the top page. He** immediately took pad and pen in hand and while lying on his back drew the following diagram:

69

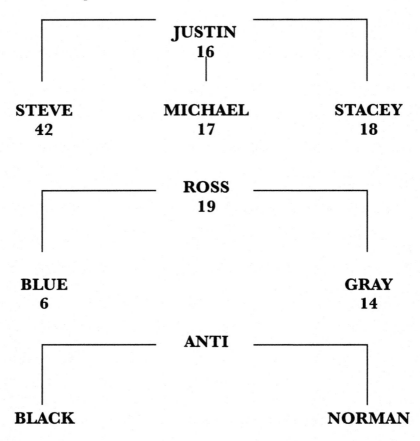

He drew separate straight lines emanating from Justin directly to Steve, Michael, and Stacey, likewise from Ross to Blue and Gray and similarly from the Anti to Black and Norman. The numbers under or by certain names indicated their age. Once Ross finished the drawing, I asked him if he would talk about the night of the murders. He readily agreed, sat up on his bed and turned to face me. Walter dragged his chair closer to us. Sitting between his two attorneys, Ross leaned forward and spoke quietly, practically whispering.

He began with a recitation of the seemingly innocent events leading up to the murders; his account was precisely what his friend, Ken Cortez, had told the police about that night. Ken had picked up Ross at his house around 6:00 p.m. to have dinner at the Canterbury

Chapter 12: One Black Suitcase & Nine Personalities

Inn. After dinner, the two went to Tamarac Square to see the movie "War Games." A few minutes into the movie, Ross got up and told Ken he had to do something and would see him later. Outside the theater, Ross called his folks, who were at home. He asked if they would meet him at the Ramada hotel and from there drive to a new subdivision, Cottonwood, in a nearby county.

"I'm not sure how I got to and from Tamarac and the Ramada," Ross said about the 10- to 15-minute, one-way trip. "I think my father drove us to Cottonwood." (The day after the homicides, the police located Ross's '76 Chevy truck parked across the street from Tamarac. The day after that discovery, the Carlsons' 1980 Cadillac Seville was found in the Ramada's parking lot.) "I had no idea why I chose Cottonwood. I wasn't familiar with the area," Ross explained. "I told my parents I wanted to show them a mailbox I had built for the Norgrens." Neither Walter nor I interrupted Ross's narrative except I would occasionally say something like, "Okay, what happened next?"

As Ross began describing the crime scene, he became more sullen. "My parents didn't even struggle," he said, shaking his head. "One time my father tried to hit me with a hammer, and I grabbed it away from him ... I don't know." His voice trailed off. As he was about to describe the actual murders, my heart began to beat faster.

"It was like I was watching through a camera. I saw the back of a person holding a gun and aiming it at my parents. They were standing, facing the shooter. I could see their faces. That's all I can remember." He paused again.

"Then what happened?" I asked somberly, wondering if he would mention what he had told Dr. Rewey about Marilyn Carlson looking at her son and saying, "Go ahead and shoot me. This is terrible."

Instead, Ross recalled driving by the Norgrens' house and throwing a suitcase onto their property, without knowing why he did it. Ross didn't recall how long he had been away from the theater. Ken Cortez had told the police it was a couple of hours — between 9:30 to 11:30. Ross remembered drinking beer with Ken after the movies and finding that so strange. "I don't even like beer," he said. "In fact, it was more than two years ago that I last drank some."

An hour or so had passed since the beginning of this jail visit. Walter and I felt I had pressed Ross enough. "Ok, David, we should leave," Walter said firmly. However, I still had some unfinished business.

Just as Walter and I were about to ask the guards to open the door, I asked Ross to make the list of his personalities again. He complied without the slightest hesitation, but this time I gave him a different piece of paper. The diagram he drew this second time was identical in every respect to the first one he had drawn.

As we stepped outside to what was now a sunny afternoon, I felt the slight sting of a mentor's mild rebuke. "David, I know what you did. I think the client could construe it as mistrusting him."

"Walter, I had to do it for my own piece of mind." Walter's disapproving look became replaced by a smile. I felt Ross's diagram was the counterpart to Robinson's black suitcase. Any doubts I may have harbored about the MPD diagnosis were now evaporating. However, the establishment of a client's mental disease to advance an insanity defense was not enough. It also had to be shown that the illness so impacted or fragmented the client's mind that he was unable to distinguish between right and wrong. Just how debilitating the illness could become was shown in the weeks ahead.

CHAPTER 13

Sans Eyebrows

During the middle of March 1984, Ross and I were in court for a motions hearing.

During most of the morning, he appeared relaxed. He was polite and composed during the hearing even when the judge ruled against us on certain motions. The last matter heard that day was our request for bond. Judge Turelli treated this issue with the same respect he had accorded our other motions, notwithstanding, the prosecution scoffed at the request. While the judge explained in his even-toned fashion why bail for two first degree murder offenses with strong evidence was inappropriate, my attention suddenly became diverted.

From the corner of my eye, I noticed Ross staring at me. I turned and looked at him. He had an icy gaze and appeared agitated, a demeanor in marked contrast to his earlier pleasantness. The courtroom was quiet except for the sound of Judge Turelli's continuing remarks. Ross spoke softly so only I could hear.

"David, I have a metallic taste in my mouth," he said casually. "I don't believe that's good. I'm going to pick up our table and throw it at the judge."

A metallic taste — this was new to me. I had no idea what that meant, but Ross sounded dead serious. Although the middle of a judicial narrative was not a propitious time to learn about the vagaries of a client's taste buds, I was even more aware of the potential consequences of a defendant throwing large projectiles at a judge.

"Ross," I said, looking directly at him, "*that* would not be a good idea. The hearing will be over in a few minutes. Try to relax."

Ross suddenly became quiet. His eyes shifted to the extreme right and then rolled and darted wildly back and forth. After a few seconds, he looked at me and smiled. He was his typical, congenial self. I was struck by the transformation, curious to learn more about it, but also relieved with the outcome. I made a mental note to ask Fisch about the darting of the eye thing and to understand what triggered Ross's sudden change in demeanor.

Ross's thoughts about heaving an indoor shot put toward the judge would not have been an endearing gesture, especially one week before our change of venue motion was set to be heard. That motion was necessary because of a poll we had commissioned of Douglas County residents concerning their attitudes about the case. The poll's results were alarming.

- 94% felt Ross was guilty;
- 84% felt the defense of insanity was inappropriate; and
- 78% felt Ross was probably sane.

These results strengthened our earlier suspicion that Douglas County's conservative population had developed an even stronger prosecution bent as a result of the case's massive pre-trial publicity. We needed a less biased and more open-minded population, especially since our defense would emphasize the intricacies and complexities of the human mind. It was Ross's irrational and unpredictable behavior that was now becoming more frequent the closer we got to the sanity trial. Four events were noteworthy.

A day before the change of venue hearing Ross called me like clockwork. I customarily briefed him ahead of time regarding any upcoming hearing because he hated surprises. This call, however, was not about tomorrow's proceedings.

"David, I don't have any eyebrows," he announced in obvious distress.

"What do you mean you don't have any eyebrows?" I asked.

"I don't have any eyebrows. I don't know what happened to them. I've been hearing rattlesnakes in my ears. I need to talk to Fisch."

"Ross, I'll call Fisch and have him contact you," I said, bewildered.

Chapter 13: Sans Eyebrows

"Can you tell me how you might have lost your eyebrows?" I asked matter-of-factly, trying not to make Ross feel worse than he sounded.

"I don't know. I'm losing it, David. If nothing gets resolved pretty soon, there may not be anything left for you to defend."

"Just hold on, Ross. Walter and I will see you tomorrow and I'll have Ralph call you as soon as possible." I called Dr. Fisch and asked him how bizarre this illness could get. His reply was essentially *"You ain't seen nothin' yet!"*

The next afternoon before court, Walter and I met with Ross in the jail. Sure enough, his eyebrows were missing, appearing to have been carefully removed — perhaps shaven. He didn't seem self-conscious or upset; an unusual placid response by someone normally obsessed with his appearance. He had no clue how the loss occurred. He even asked the guards; they were clueless as well and frankly most likely unmoved by their loss. As a result, we began the change of venue hearing sans one pair of eye coverings and their unresolved caper.

We lost the motion but, aware of our client's fragility, we alerted Hugh Thompson, the jail's warden, to Ross's potential for self-harm. Shortly after our alert, we became aware of three other strange episodes mentioned by Thompson; he referred us to deputies William Ruppart and Troy McCarty.

Ruppart related an incident that happened on April 19, 1984, after Ross finished a phone call. Ross used a phone in a very small, secured area called a visitor's pod. From an adjoining room, Ruppart observed Ross through a plexiglass window. When Ross finished the call, Ruppart walked in the pod to escort Ross back to his cell.

"He was sitting in his chair," Ruppart said, "had a blank stare on his face, and his head was down. He made no effort to notice that I was there." Startled by Ross's demeanor, Ruppart left and summoned his supervisor, Sergeant Craig Smith.

After less than a minute, Ruppart and Sergeant Smith returned to the pod. Ross's appearance had not changed.

"His head was down, and he was staring," Ruppart continued. "It was a catatonic stare, a stare into nothingness. His eyes were somewhat opened ... his facial muscles appeared to be completely relaxed. His head was down, and his shoulders slouched."

Ruppart went to use the intercom from the adjoining pod to talk to Ross. "I asked him if he was all right. I got a mumbled type response that he was okay." Ruppart's experience struck a chord with me because about a month later, I noticed similar behavior by Ross.

It was April 25; he and I were in a court hearing. As was our practice, he was seated to my left. I turned to him because he suddenly became very quiet. He was staring into space, again appearing almost catatonic. He looked forlorn. As I had done on previous occasions whenever he looked depressed, I began to rub his back. I asked him if he was okay and if he could tell me what had happened. He turned his head slightly to the left. His eyes began rolling back and forth. He flexed a bit, turned to me and said, "I'm sorry. What did you say?" He began talking like Steve or Justin.

Another deputy sheriff, the 6'2", powerfully built Troy McCarty, told me what then happened after that hearing ended when he escorted Ross from the courtroom to the jail. The courtroom door, which opened up to a landing and then stairs that led down to the jail, was located just to the left of the defense table. On this occasion, Ross had been initially acting normally. But that changed.

"As he stepped through the door," McCarty explained, "he paused for a minute, looked at the wall, put his left hand on his forehead, fell into the wall, and slid down the wall onto the floor of the landing."

"And tell me what you saw while he was on the floor?" I asked.

"His head was bent down and there was no movement at all. He was just looking down at the floor."

"Did that seem unusual to you?"

"Yeah, it's never happened to me before; it was the first time I ever experienced something like that."

"Did either of you then speak?"

"I bent down on the stairs and asked Carlson how he was. He said in a semi-angered tone of voice that he was okay."

I didn't know what to make of the incident: did Ross have a short fainting spell because he was ill or dehydrated, or was it something else? I didn't know.

McCarty then told me about a similar situation that occurred

Chapter 13: Sans Eyebrows

on May 8, 1984. Both he and Ruppart were clear on their dates because they had to document so-called unusual incident reports on a log for each prisoner. In any event, after court ended on that day, Ross had remained at the counsel table to talk to Walter and me. Once we finished, McCarty came to the table to escort Ross downstairs. Ross initially seemed fine, then something happened.

"After Ross stood up, he seemed to pause for a minute. Again, he grabbed his forehead, slumped down, hit the table, and fell onto the floor," McCarty said. "He was looking down at the floor. I asked him if he was okay. He again responded angrily that he was." McCarty looked perplexed. He had never before witnessed this kind of behavior from any prisoner.

After discussing these incidents with Dr. Fisch, he was convinced that these instances, combined with the pre-homicidal evidence we had amassed, were proof that we were representing an unusually sick young man. Now, our goal became: how to best present this illness to a jury.

CHAPTER 14

Justin, Steve & Norman

To succeed in our goal of persuasively presenting MPD to our future jury, Walter believed we had to strengthen our arsenal of expert witnesses. As a result, in March of 1984 he hired another psychiatrist, Dr. Robert Fairbairn. After several sessions with Ross, Dr. Fairbairn also diagnosed him as suffering from MPD and concluded he was insane when the murders were committed. Now, with the sanity trial scheduled to begin in June, we needed to figure out the best way to portray Ross's illness to a jury. Using our experts to merely explain MPD and why Ross fit the criteria wasn't enough. We believed the jurors had to see for themselves how Ross looked when he changed from one personality to another. To me, there was only one solution. We had to videotape Ross and try to capture his switching from one personality to the other. Walter agreed.

If nothing compelling resulted from the taping, we had no obligation to disclose any of it to the DA. On the other hand, if the tapes were powerful, we could use them to spur a plea deal, or failing that, use them at trial. There was little, if no, downside to the strategy. Since Dr. Fairbairn by now had developed a good rapport with Ross and fit Walter's strategy of needing a psychiatrist to sell the diagnosis because of their medical education and training, we asked the doctor to conduct the interview. Initially, Ross was not thrilled with the idea of videotaping, believing the unusual way he functioned was going to be broadcast to the public and subject him to criticism of being weird. However, after hearing the arguments in favor of taping, he eventually agreed to it.

Chapter 14: Justin, Steve & Norman

On May 10, 1984, Dr. Fairbairn, Walter, me, and our video operator met Ross at the jail. The interview room afforded us was large enough to accommodate our group. To avoid the possibility of a curious sheriff's deputy viewing our experiment, I covered the room's two-way mirror with a white sheet. Ross entered the room holding his omnipresent notebook and greeted us with a smiling, "Gentlemen, how are you all?"

Ross looked as though he was going out for a casual dinner, impeccably dressed in a yellow, buttoned-down shirt with sleeves twice folded up his forearm, dark blue slacks, and spit-shined black shoes. For an experiment that could determine whether he spent the rest of his life in jail, I thought he would appear nervous. The opposite was true; he seemed perfectly at ease.

Ross sat down and faced Fairbairn, whose back was just a few feet from the entrance to the room. The video technician set up to the right of the doctor. Since Walter and I wanted to be as unobtrusive as possible, we sat in the corner of the room to the right of everyone. The room's artificial illumination was bright enough to avoid the need for camera lights, another potential distraction to Ross.

Beforehand, Walter and I had agreed with Fairbairn that the doctor would do all the talking. If Ross became uncomfortable with our presence, Walter and I would leave the room.

The preparations in place, the 6'1", Canadian born and fiftyish looking Fairbairn began by asking Ross, "What's your understanding of what today is about?"

"Well," Ross said, looking quite relaxed, "I assume it would be of some possible benefit as far as understanding the way I am. Besides, it might be interesting for me to watch myself."

"Whom am I talking to now?" Fairbairn asked, leaning forward in his chair to hear the response.

"Justin," Ross revealed with a straight face.

Justin! I sure as heck didn't expect that reply. That was the first time I had ever heard Ross refer to himself as other than his birth name. A part of me said, "Oh, right, give me a break!" although I admittedly felt chilled upon hearing the response. This was much different than Ross supposedly telling someone he had a twin named Justin. Here, the client, whom I knew only as Ross, was saying with a casual, straight face that he was someone called Justin. Either Ross just pulled off an Academy Award performance, or he was a very sick kid. Before I became too mesmerized by the strangeness before me, Fairbairn noticed something that was not new to me. He asked, "What happened to your eyebrows?"

"I don't know," Justin replied, breaking out in a wide grin. "I woke up one morning, and they were gone. I'm a little self-conscious about them missing, but '**we**' make the best with what '**we**' have."

"We? Who's 'we'?" Fairbairn asked.

Justin was reluctant to answer and tried to avoid doing so, but Fairbairn gently pushed him. "Give it a try. Who is 'we'?"

"'We' are collectively a unit," Justin explained very matter-of-factly. "All of us. Myself, Justin, Steven, Gray, Blue, Michael, Stacey, Black, and Norman."

"Can they hear us now?"

"I don't know. I'm not sure," Justin admitted.

"Tell me about yourself."

"I enjoy nice surroundings, nice things. I like good food. Unfortunately, this is not the Savoy, the Ritz, or the Astoria. The amenities here are not fantastic." This Justin, I thought, had a cute sense of humor ... little glib, touch of sarcasm ... kind of reminded me of the younger of his two lawyers in the room.

Fairbairn pressed on, asking what role Justin played in the system's communications scheme.

"He's an integral part of communication ... Justin handles everything that requires tact or knowledge of things like fine dining, wines, that type of thing."

Although Fairbairn's role was that of an interrogator, he questioned in a pleasant but firm way. For the most part, the doctor's expressions remained neutral. Apparently confident that his patient was trying to cooperate, Fairbairn relaxed. He sat back in his chair, his left leg draped over his right knee. The doctor's slight wavy, short-gray hair and tan, handsome looks may have appealed to Justin's emphasis on socializing, but it was the doctor's probing skills that proved effective.

"How old are you, and where were you born?" Fairbairn asked.

"Sixteen. I believe I was born in Minneapolis."

Chapter 14: Justin, Steve & Norman

"You believe?"

"I'm not sure."

"How about 'we'?"

"Well, collectively as a unit, I suppose was born in Minneapolis."

"That's puzzling to you?" Fairbairn asked, seizing upon Justin's equivocal response.

"Well, it makes sense, and yet it doesn't ... that's not my area of expertise."

I watched the exchange between Ross and Fairbairn closely. I was scrutinizing Ross, looking for some inappropriate smirk, the slightest slip-up, or anything else to suggest he was a malingerer. If this MPD thing was contrived, I wanted to find that out before anyone else. So far, I saw nothing that looked suspicious.

Just then Fairbairn surprised me by asking Justin, "Could you bring out Steve? I need to talk to Steve."

I didn't realize you could just ask to speak to another personality, and they would appear. I thought for sure Fairbairn's request would catch Ross off-guard. I figured if Ross were a phony, he would burst out laughing and say "Okay, you caught me!" However, that didn't happen.

Justin didn't say anything. There was no smile. Instead, he turned his head slightly to the right. His eyes darted back and forth a few times, and then they stopped. He sat more erect and rested his hands on his lap. He looked back at Fairbairn, and the two fixed on one another for about a second.

Fairbairn extended a cordial "Hi."

"Hello. How are you?" came the soft reply. A more solemn look had replaced Justin's personable smile.

"Whom am I talking to now?" Fairbairn asked.

"Steve," was the faint response.

I was blown away. An entirely different persona overtook Ross's body. An impassive and serious face overcame this second personality. My cautious skepticism was placed on hold.

"I can't hear you," Fairbairn said softly.

Steve's face cringed. He looked perplexed. "I'm not, ah, real big on this. What's going on?"

"Very fair question," Fairbairn acknowledged. "Let me ask you,

Steve, what do you think is going on, and then I'll explain everything to you."

"I had an opportunity to discuss with Walter about some videotaping," Steve said. "I'm really not the one you should be talking to. I'm not real good at these things."

"You mean that someone else could do it better?" Fairbairn asked. Steve nodded his head, affirmatively.

As Fairbairn explained the purpose of the videotaping, Steve leaned forward so as not to miss anything Fairbairn said. The doctor then pushed on. "How old are you?"

Steve managed a wide grin and briefly looked down. "Do we really have to go into that?" he asked.

Fairbairn insisted upon an answer.

"42," Steve revealed, without flinching but returning to his flat demeanor.

"What's it like being 42?"

"There's some advantages to it. Knowledge is quite a handy thing. It's a trade-off for youth. We gain wisdom. However, there are some problems."

"How so?" Fairbairn asked.

"Well, I get a little more tired. I'm continually going to the bathroom."

"What do you mean it's a trade-off for youth?"

"The wrinkles ... loss of athletic ability ... loss of a number of things. I think it's a fair exchange for the wisdom that you gain throughout the years."

"Tell us about Steve's function," Fairbairn instructed.

"My function is basically to ... deal with facts and specific data and process them."

"This next question is a tough one," Fairbairn cautioned, "but, what do you think of your mental health?"

Steve was unfazed. "Well, from my own personal standards, I find it quite natural and understandable. From society's standpoint, it's not natural and it's not healthy. But we all have to survive — Walter, David, everyone. We adapt ways to survive, and I've adapted a way to survive that works for me."

Chapter 14: Justin, Steve & Norman

"Which is?" Fairbairn asked.

"Through divergent personalities. Division of labor."

"You're sounding boringly logical," Fairbairn said, half kiddingly.

Steve was not offended but instead agreed. "Well, basically, I am," he said, smiling.

I sensed that I was experiencing something very real. The change from Justin to Steve occurred as naturally as Walter and me taking turns at the courtroom podium. Gone was the outgoing and suave 16-year-old, and in his place emerged a serious and shy adult. In court, I had seen Ross change from one behavior to another preceded by the eye roll. At the time, I didn't know the significance. However, now each personality was identifying himself by a different name, displaying individualized characteristics and deadpan conviction.

"Could I talk to Blue?" Fairbairn asked.

"I don't think so," Steve replied. Again, the doctor was undaunted, mentioning that Blue had telephoned him yesterday.

Steve stopped talking and stared at Fairbairn. His large, dark eyes temporarily stood silent and then began to roll again. He sat back in his chair, lowered his head, and brought his left hand to his mouth. His right hand was resting on his lap. He looked at Fairbairn and seemed terrified. Tears began welling in his eyes. Fairbairn tried to console him by touching his right hand.

"Hi, this must be really scary for you," Fairbairn began. There was no reply. Blue looked around the room, first at the cameraman and then at Walter and me. He looked so scared. He returned to look at Fairbairn who asked, "Do you remember me, who I am?"

"The doctor," Blue whimpered with the look of a frightened infant who seemed to want no one but his mommy.

"Do you remember my name?"

"Doctor Fairbairn," Blue replied, continuing to weep.

I could feel my heart racing and beating against my shirt. Twenty-year-olds don't all of a sudden act like sobbing children in front of their doctor, lawyers, and a complete stranger, our videographer. This seemed too genuine to be faked.

I felt sorry for Ross and wondered, was this really how fragmented the human mind can become from repeated acts of abuse?

Just in the Nick of Time

I recalled my Dennis the Menace days and my parents' occasional physical response to my disobedience. However, after every attempt at behavioral modification, my mother and father hugged me and said how much they loved me. I did not believe that Ross Carlson ever experienced this essential post-affection to his parents' discipline.

"Can I help you in some way?" Fairbairn asked. Blue paused. He raised his head and removed his hand from his mouth. His eyes darted back and forth. He sat up in his chair and looked at Fairbairn. Gone was the weeping child.

"Hi," Fairbairn said, greeting the current entry.

"Hello doctor, how are you?" came the flat reply. Steve was back. "There's salt," he added, as he sat up and linked his hands onto his lap.

"Explain that," Fairbairn said.

"Wetness in the eyes ... the residual effects of a lump in the throat ... tightness in my joints ... seems like time has been lost. That's why it's good to have a watch with me."

Fairbairn asked about the difference between time lost and time stolen. Steve explained that whenever he had a salty taste in his mouth and felt he had lost some time, it meant that Blue or Gray had probably been "out." When he was left with a metallic taste and a feeling that time had been stolen, he assumed that Norman or Black had been around. Justin didn't leave him with any particular taste or absence of time; therefore, Steve preferred that Fairbairn continue his discussion with Justin. The doctor, however, had a different agenda.

"What are our chances of getting Norman out?" Fairbairn asked.

"Well, I'm not terribly thrilled with his behavior as of late," Steve revealed. "If you were to threaten me with a crowbar, I think you'd get Black," he said. Fairbairn wasn't quite yet ready for Black and preferred to meet Norman first. Before doing so, however, the doctor stood up and moved his chair a few feet further away from Steve, anticipating I assumed the entrance of a more hostile personality once the doctor heard the mention of Black.

Steve asked for a cup of water, and Walter took it to him. After taking a sip, Steve set the cup on a table behind him where he had previously placed his notebook. Fairbairn pushed again for Norman.

"That's going to be tough," Steve said.

Chapter 14: Justin, Steve & Norman

"This is a tough business," Fairbairn countered.

Steve became quiet. His eyes darted back and forth. Suddenly, our client glared at the camera and straightened up in his chair.

"What the hell is that thing doin' here?" a gangster-like dude barked while looking directly at the camera. Again, the transformation was unbelievable, but also very real. This character sat straight up and looked like he was ready to rumble. This was an action guy, not a word guy.

"What do you think?" Fairbairn replied.

"Now, what the hell are you guys up to?" this fourth personality demanded, looking over and staring directly at Walter and me, and sounding like every street punk you never wanted to meet. Are people really going to believe all of this, I kept on asking myself? This is just too bizarre, I thought!

"We're videotaping you because you're a sick man who needs to be ..."

"Fuck you!" the voice bellowed, cutting Fairbairn off. "You're nuts buddy. I'm fine. There ain't nothin' wrong with me." Hello, Norman, I said to myself. Sounds like you're a bit of a hoodlum. Fairbairn must have gotten a similar impression.

"You're kind of a rude guy," Fairbairn said.

"Hey, look, buddy," Norman said with a touch of a Stallone-type Rocky inflection. "I'm not here to make you happy ... you know. I'm here doin' my time. I leave people alone. I want them to leave me alone. I don't like finding myself in weird situations."

"What's weird about it?"

"Yeah, you try wakin' up in the middle of some fucker sittin' there videotapin' you!"

MPD concepts that I had been studying were now coming to life. Doctors talked in terms of "amnesia" between personalities, but those who suffered the illness, like Ross, used words like "blacking out" and "waking up" to express the same notion. Some of the hazy pictures that had formed in my mind from reading the literature were now becoming clearer. Imagine who was teaching me: a 16-year-old bon vivant, a bland 42-year-old intellect, a weeping child, and a street punk!

"You got a smoke?" Norman asked.

Besides Norman's less than angelic language, this last request of his was also a first. Never had I seen Ross, or whoever else had been in my presence, smoke or even ask for a cigarette.

As the two continued talking, Norman looked at the water cup that Steve had placed on the table. "What are you looking at?" Fairbairn asked.

"Glass of water!" Norman replied, as if he had no idea how the cup got on the table. "Amnesia between Norman and Steve," I thought to myself.

Believing that we had witnessed a good sense of Norman, Fairbairn attempted to move on. "Could I talk to Steve again?" Fairbairn asked.

"Who the fuck's Steve?" Norman replied.

"The fella I usually deal with," Fairbairn explained.

"Hey, that's not my problem. You wanna' talk to Steve, go get Steve. By the way, these are cheap fuckin' cigarettes." Norman dropped the cigarette on the floor and stamped it out. He then sat back and lowered his head. His eyes began to dart back and forth for a few seconds.

Steve reappeared. "Hi, I'm losing time," he announced with a slight grin.

"How do you know that?" Fairbairn asked.

"Metallic. It means some time's been stolen."

"Any idea how much?" Fairbairn asked.

"No," Steve replied as he casually picked up the cup of water that he had earlier used and began drinking. "This gentleman's been filming for a while," he continued. "Like I say, without a watch..."

Fairbairn's conversations with these personalities were removing most of my doubts about whether Ross suffered from MPD. Ross's methods of deducing which personalities had been "out" were original and unique to him. Nowhere had I read anything in the literature about a salty or metallic taste, or lost or stolen time. These were not concepts that Ross could have studied in any book or seen in any movie in order to learn how to fake this disorder.

It was now time to try to meet Black. Fairbairn's announcement

Chapter 14: Justin, Steve & Norman

seemed to raise the anxiety level in the room, especially since he had brought restraints with him. All agreed that the attempt to meet Black would be made after lunch. Because Steve thought Black might emerge more easily with fewer people around, Walter and I agreed not to return to the room after lunch.

After grabbing a quick bite with Fairbairn, Walter and I waited in the jail lobby until it was time to leave. More than an hour passed. It shouldn't have taken that long. Finally, Fairbairn emerged. He looked pale, a dramatic change from his tanned, energetic appearance of the morning. We couldn't wait to discover what had happened. First, we'd return to the jail, say goodbye to Ross, and then drive back to Denver.

CHAPTER 15

Black & Blue
& Finally Ross, Too

Entering the highway, Walter activated the "fuzz buster" on his dash and shifted into his Indy 500 mode. He was eager to return to Denver. At the start of our drive, Dr. Fairbairn looked ashen. That seemed odd because when Walter and I said goodbye to Ross, he acted as if he had just enjoyed a friendly chat with the doctor. However, once Fairbairn leaned forward in the back seat of Walter's car and recounted in detail the events of the afternoon session, we well understood the doctor's pallid look. Fairbairn spoke nonstop for the 40 minutes it took to drive to the outskirts of Denver. Walter and I couldn't wait to get to his office to play the video of the afternoon's session. However, our dash to the VCR was thwarted once we arrived closer to downtown Denver and I-25's five o'clock traffic.

"Walter, would you please drive over these cars?" I asked. He returned a smile.

Our first stop was the doctor's apartment and before we dropped him off, I left him with one question to ponder, "Is Ross competent to stand trial?" Walter and I had previously discussed this legal concept with Fairbairn before this videotaping, but, at the time, he didn't have enough information to say one way or the other.

Now, he answered, "Let me think about it." We asked him to think about it soon, especially based on what he described had taken place during his afternoon session with Ross.

Upon finally arriving at Walter's office, we beelined it downstairs

Chapter 15: Black & Blue & Finally Ross, Too

to his small library where we cleared the conference table of law books, loaded the VCR, and watched what had so shaken Fairbairn.

There was Ross — Mr. Casual GQ — sitting in his chair politely fielding Fairbairn's questions once again. After a few questions, Fairbairn reached for and held Ross's left wrist.

"What can you tell me about your wrist?" Fairbairn asked, holding Ross's wrist, which we had all previously noticed was completely enveloped by a grossly disfiguring three-inch wide scar, but none of us had ever asked him about it. Ross dutifully responded.

"Well, if you're asking us collectively, I think I can answer that. When we were very young, ah ... nineteen months old, a kettle of boiling water tipped over and scalded my left arm. The cuff of the wool sweater burned onto my wrist."

"Do you have any memory of that?"

"I don't. Someone else might, maybe Gray."

"You think Gray might have memory of that?"

"I don't know if it's memory or what we've been told. It's like when I was at Pueblo for evaluation, I essentially parroted back to the doctors what the police had told me happened the night my parents were killed." Just then my eyes wandered away from watching the two people talking on the screen.

There was a stark contrast between my sitting in the same room with Fairbairn and Ross versus watching them on the TV screen. In my view, the difference was significant and could pose a problem for us at trial.

In the morning, when we were all sitting together, I felt I had been in the actual company of Justin and the others. However, now it seemed as if I were looking at actors, and bad ones at that. What a difference the monitor made! It crystallized the caution expressed by both Wilets and in the literature that MPD can tend to look phony, kind of like bad acting. It was evident we needed to figure out a way to get the jurors in the same room where Walter and I had been earlier that morning. I didn't know yet how to do that and left the issue for later. I returned my attention to the monitor.

"I'm willing to give it a try," Steve said, responding to Fairbairn's request to meet Black and for permission to use leather restraints in the process. Steve then provided Fairbairn with a helpful clue in the event problems were encountered with Black. "To get me back, throw a mathematical problem or something at me. It'll engage me," he instructed.

Fairbairn said, "thank you for the tip." He began painstakingly binding Steve's arms to the respective arm rests of the chair, and then stooped to one knee while securing Steve's feet to the legs of the chair. Steve sat still, occasionally tugging at the chair to ensure that Fairbairn was tying the restraints tightly enough.

"Are you all right?" Fairbairn asked.

"I think I've got enough movement to at least let blood flow," Steve replied.

Fairbairn now figured it was time for the moment of truth. "Tell me about Black."

"Black steals time from me," Steve began. "When there is a dangerous situation, he pretty much protects Gray. If there's a life-threatening situation, Black'll disengage that situation."

"Disengage?"

"Shut it down ... whatever is threatening us. He's skilled in martial arts. He's the kind of person that'll do whatever's necessary to rectify a situation."

"How?"

"Usually very physically. If you were to say, come after me with a hammer, Blue would kick in. Then maybe Gray, and then probably in rapid succession the closer you drew, probably Black. You would be disarmed immediately."

"O.K., let's bring Blue back."

Steve paused. His eyes began darting. He sat back in his chair, lowered his head, and brought his left hand to his mouth. His eyes started to tear.

"Hi, how are you?" Fairbairn asked gently. "Do you want a Kleenex?"

"No," Blue responded, weeping.

"You look awfully scared. Can you tell me what you're thinking?"

"No."

Suddenly, Blue stopped sobbing. Another personality

Chapter 15: Black & Blue & Finally Ross, Too

emerged; his jaw tightened. He clenched his fists. His body seemed to be bursting with the energy of a fully stoked locomotive. He jerked his right forearm upward. The chair rocked to the left. He did the same thing with his left forearm. The chair rocked to the right. He repeated the movements twice more, appearing stronger and more determined each time. He squirmed, twisted, and managed to loosen his arms from the restraints. The fiery character finally freed his right arm from the chair. The leather straps dangled to the floor like an unraveled spool of thread. The individual angrily pointed at the camera.

"Don't ever ... ever lock me up," he ordered sternly. He menacingly turned to Fairbairn, who had remained still since Blue disappeared and was as compliant as possible, clearly taken aback, believing Gray was going to emerge once Blue disappeared. That didn't happen, reaffirming what I had learned in the literature that the personalities usually emerge spontaneously not because some therapist wanted to see them. The unpredictability and bizarreness of this disorder were clearly on display.

"Sorry," Fairbairn replied apologetically probably wondering if he was about to suffer a similar fate as that of Rod and Marilyn Carlson.

Black, the obvious newcomer, extended his draped, right arm with straps toward Fairbairn. "Take this off me. Now!" he demanded.

Fairbairn did not move. His face had become expressionless. He appeared resigned to do nothing else to further provoke Black.

"Three times seven!" Fairbairn said firmly, but not loudly. The doctor paused briefly, obviously awaiting a rescuer. Black did not respond. He continually glared at Fairbairn.

"Three times seven!" Fairbairn repeated — this time much louder.

Suddenly, Black dropped his right hand to his side, paused, and replied, "Twenty-one." Poof! Someone else had emerged.

"Steve?" Fairbairn asked, his eyes widening and a smile about to form as if he had just been reunited with a boyhood friend.

"Lost time, huh?" Steve asked calmly.

Relieved, Fairbairn broke out in a full smile. "So much for my puny restraints," he sighed as color gradually returned to his face and his body relaxed.

"There's nothing you can do to restrain him," Steve explained.

"I'm embarrassed that I put these on so ineptly ... Steve? Am I talking to Steve?"

"Um-hum. Well, this is strange because I lost time. It wasn't stolen from me. Last thing I remember, it wasn't stolen from me."

"What do you remember now?"

"Well, I have a metallic taste in my mouth now, but I remembered having a salty taste. That doesn't make sense." He looked away, appearing preoccupied. The camera continued to focus on him. I wondered what was happening.

Fairbairn figured this was a good time to end the session. "I guess Walter and David can join us now," he said, leaning forward in his chair and about to stand up.

Steve wasn't yet ready. "Is it necessary right now?" he asked, rubbing his arms.

"What do you think happened?" Fairbairn asked as he sat back in his chair.

"I presume you threatened me and Black intervened. That's all I can presume."

"How do you think that happened? What clues do you have?"

"I don't remember if I let Justin talk to you or what, but ... did we talk about striking me?"

"You suggested that. You talked hypothetically. You said if I were to come at you with a hammer. You don't remember saying that?"

"Well, I remember ... oh, a long time ago, we discussed ah ... you know that ... probably a couple of sessions back."

"Whom am I talking to now?" Fairbairn asked intuitively.

"I don't know. It's strange."

"You don't know who? It's not Steve?"

"No. Not really. Feels like they're pushed together."

"Is Ross available?" Fairbairn asked.

"That's ... who I think it is."

"So I'm talking to Ross now?"

"Yeah, I think so. This is really unusual." Ross was smiling and looking around the room.

I smiled back at the monitor. I had never seen such a happy

Chapter 15: Black & Blue & Finally Ross, Too

face on our client. I, therefore, couldn't imagine what had so upset Fairbairn when he emerged ashen from the afternoon taping.

"Ross hasn't been available for weeks," Fairbairn recalled.

"No, but I know who you are," Ross revealed.

"Who am I?"

"Doctor Fairbairn. And we've talked quite a bit. We've spent a lot of time discussing things. I can remember things, kind of ... it's nice ... it's really nice." Ross was beaming like an infatuated teenager.

"You're a little emotional," Fairbairn observed with an approving smile. "That's together, too?"

"Yeah," Ross paused. "It seems in right proportion."

"How do you explain it?"

"I don't have any explanation for it."

"I wonder," Fairbairn said. "For a moment ... only five or ten seconds ... you shared Black with me. You told me how to bring you out of that ... and it worked very well. It was after that ... that I think maybe Ross came together. Do you believe sharing the whole package with me helped?"

"I don't know. The last time I remember being out was when I was lifting weights. It was a long time ago. Long time..." Ross paused for a while. He looked around the barren room again seemingly searching his mind for some answers.

"Makes you sad to remember how long it was?" Fairbairn asked.

"Yeah. Seems a lot has happened since then."

"Let me check and see how your memory is. How old are you?"

"What year is this?"

"I will tell you," Fairbairn said, "but tell me first what year you think it is. What does it feel like?"

"It feels like two things. It feels like the year I graduated, and it feels much later ... much later."

"You graduated in what year?"

"'82."

"And it feels much later. What does that feel like?"

"I know I've been locked up for a long time, haven't I? It's '83?"

"'84. This is April ... '84. So, how old does that make you?"

"20. No, 19 ... 19. 'Cause I was born in May, and if this is April."

"What's your full name?"

"Ross Michael Carlson."

"Do you know where you are?"

"I'm in Douglas County Jail."

"Do you know why?"

Ross thought for a moment. "Kind ... kind of. I don't..."

"Tell me the kind of."

Ross's face blanched as if he had just discovered the worst news of his life. "I don't think I should."

"You don't think you should?"

"No. It seems like it's awful serious if it's what I think it is."

"It's awfully serious," Fairbairn replied grimly.

"Answer me this," Ross pleaded, looking as if he already knew the answer to his next question. "Where are my parents?"

"Your parents are dead," Fairbairn responded softly.

Ross began sobbing. Tears streamed down his cheeks. He dropped his head downward, turned it to the side, and rubbed his eyes with the back of his hand. He looked like the most helpless human being on the planet. I wanted to jump through the screen and comfort him. Fairbairn reached out.

"Do you want me to hold your hand?" Fairbairn asked, touching Ross's hand gently. Ross continued crying.

"I don't want to leave you alone like this. Stay here, Ross. I want to help you."

Ross paused. He stopped crying. His eyes darted back and forth for a couple of seconds. He sat up in his chair, crossed his right foot over his left knee, looked at Fairbairn and said apologetically but confidently and affably, "You'll have to excuse me for a moment. Would you by chance have a ... Kleenex or something available?"

Fairbairn offered his handkerchief and asked, "Whom am I talking to?"

"Justin," was the reply as he dabbed his eyes with the doctor's handkerchief.

"Do you remember who I am?"

Justin said, yes, while returning the handkerchief and acting carefree and as if nothing unusual had happened during this day. After

Chapter 15: Black & Blue & Finally Ross, Too

some small talk, the two agreed it was time for Walter and me to return to the room. The tape ended.

During the past hour, Walter and I had said nothing to one another. We just watched. When the tape was over, Walter looked at me and said, "Wow!" I didn't feel like saying much except to reply that I thought it was pretty incredible and that I wanted to take some time and think. I left Walter's office and said I would talk to him later. While driving home, I felt terribly sad. Vivid memories about other people in my recent past had been triggered while watching the tape.

A couple of years earlier, a dear friend's son, named Brett, long-diagnosed as an incurable paranoid schizophrenic, had been hospitalized in a Denver treatment facility. Then, Brett was Ross's age and possessed the tanned, physical features of a country-club tennis player.

When I occasionally visited Brett at the hospital, he would tell me how badly his head hurt. "If I could only stop the voices, Dave," he would agonize, "my head wouldn't hurt anymore." I couldn't fix his pain. I could only listen and be his friend.

His parents tried every possible treatment, but nothing worked. Brett eventually found the solution. He committed suicide.

A few hundred yards away from Brett, living in another wing of the hospital, was my son Curt, then 16 years old. Curt was housed with other youths whose histories cried out for intervention.

When Curt first came into my life in the fall of 1968, he was the cutest three-and-one-half-year-old I had ever seen. He had golden-blond hair, bangs to mid-forehead, big blue eyes, and a gleaming smile. After his mother and I became engaged, Curt called me "Daddy David." Within a millisecond, I became putty in Curt's hands.

After returning from my honeymoon, I obtained a formal decree of adoption legally changing Curt's last name to Savitz. When we walked out of the courtroom holding hands, he asked me "Are you my real daddy now?" I looked down at him and proudly said "Curtis J. Savitz, you bet I am!" That was the summer of 1969.

In 1974, Curt's mother and I divorced. I knew the split broke Curt's heart and I promised him our relationship would never change. Although I kept my vow, Curt was nevertheless overcome by so many confusing and complex issues.

Just in the Nick of Time

His teenage years were turbulent ones requiring individual and family psychotherapy. When he was 15 years old, an inpatient program was recommended as providing the best opportunity for long-term success. Otherwise, he was facing a potentially destructive future. I didn't hesitate to make the decision. Treatment was long and painful but a resounding triumph.

Curt was a child who was loved and who deserved every chance to live a healthy and happy life. Ross Carlson, the biological child of Rod and Marilyn Carlson, was denied the same opportunity. I couldn't imagine why a parent, biological or otherwise, would ever create a harmful environment for their child.

What happened during Ross's childhood that was so horrific, causing his mind to split into different parts? Who did unspeakable things to Ross and why? Why did Ross kill both of his parents, and why didn't I feel anything for them? Had I been sucked into feeling sympathy for Ross by some romantic feature of this case, or was I distraught because I honestly believed that cruel people did bad things to innocent children? I wanted some answers but wasn't sure how to find them or from whom. I would try and figure out a way while preparing for the sanity trial; it was scheduled to start in about a month.

CHAPTER 16

Birthday Cake, Matzo Balls, & a Fig Newton

On Wednesday, May 16, Dr. Fairbairn called my office just before noon and answered the question I had posed to him less than a week ago. "David, I just spent the weekend in Los Angeles at a conference on MPD. Ross is very sick and definitely incompetent. There is an 80% chance he can be cured and restored to competency. The diagnosis will be solidified because of the treatment."

Based upon our knowledge of MPD and Fairbairn's opinion, Walter and I had no choice. We were obliged under Colorado law to file a Motion to Determine Competency. We did so on May 18.

Ross was not happy about the motion of incompetency because "he" didn't want any more delays in the case. The problem was we didn't know who **"he"** was at any given moment during our interactions with him. In order to lift his spirits about this new development regarding the issue of his competency, ten days after we filed the motion, we decided to make May 28 special for him.

May 28, 1984, was not only Memorial Day but also Ross's twentieth birthday. For a surprise, Walter, Dr. Fairbairn, and I brought cake and presents to the jail. After first inspecting the cake to ensure it did not contain a hacksaw or derringer, the sheriffs brought Ross into the visitor's room. He was not expecting us.

"Gentlemen, what are you doing here?" Ross asked. "You should be relaxing and enjoying the holiday."

Ross noticed three wrapped packages on the bunk bed and

cake and ice cream on the table. "Happy birthday!" the three of us said nearly in unison.

Ross managed a weak smile. "I wish you gentlemen hadn't gone to the trouble."

"It's your birthday, Ross!" I said.

"Open your presents," Walter added. "Bob and I each brought you a book. David got you a shirt."

I made Ross cut the first piece of cake. You would have thought I had asked him to divvy up a casserole of spam and Brussels sprouts. He sighed but complied begrudgingly. Bob dished out the cake and ice cream as Walter handed Ross his presents. Something was wrong. Ross was uncharacteristically quiet while opening his gifts. Then, he spoke.

"I don't want to celebrate my birthday," he said testily. "I don't want any of this. You should have just stayed in Denver."

"Now, what's this all about?" I thought to myself. We had given up part of our holiday to spend with this ungrateful SOB, and this was our thanks. Suddenly, I lost my desire for cake and ice cream. I was tempted to take back my blue oxford shirt and say, "Up yours!" but then Fairbairn chimed in.

"Your lawyers could have spent the day with family and friends, but instead they planned something very special for you. I can't believe how rude and ungrateful you are. I think we're entitled to some explanation." Fairbairn's tone was surprisingly confrontational compared to his usual solicitous approach.

Unshaken, Ross looked impassively at Fairbairn and replied bluntly, "I don't like birthdays. I never celebrate them. I was always told I didn't deserve any presents. I appreciate your coming down here ... thanks very much."

That was it — short and sweet. Just like Justin — right to the point. No more details and no emotion. An abrupt silence filled the room. Bob, Walter, and I looked at one another. The ice cream on our plates began to melt in sync with Ross's ingratitude. The three gift-bearers had been spurned. There didn't seem to be anything more to say. We got up, said our goodbyes, and left.

I felt as gloomy as the stark, narrow corridor that led from the

Chapter 16: Birthday Cake, Matzo Balls, & a Fig Newton

jail's visiting room to the sheriff's receptionist's desk. I became upset not only because my benevolence had been slapped in the face, but also because Ross evidently had never been made to feel special on his birthday.

That's the way we Savitz kids were made to feel. That's the way my friends' parents made my folks feel. And that's how my friends and I made each other feel. After my divorce, I had always circled August 11 in my calendar. I wanted to make sure my son, Curt, knew I was glad he was born. After being with Ross, I realized that not all children were made to feel as special. Upon driving back to Denver, Walter, Bob, and I vowed to work even harder to get Ross his much-needed treatment.

Two days later, the defense team of lawyers, doctors, and investigators congregated around my office conference room table at 8:30 in the morning. With legal pads in hand, files lined up the width of the table, and monitor and VCR ready to go, we were camped in for the day.

To win the competency hearing, we had to prove that Ross suffered from MPD, and, as a result, could not assist or cooperate with us in his defense. Our zeal ran high, but so did our naiveté. We underestimated the importance of the competency issue and felt we had little chance of winning that hearing. Because of our pessimism, we were actually looking ahead to the sanity trial, which was scheduled to begin a few days after the conclusion of the competency hearing. Since Dr. Fisch was our only doctor with any kind of clinical and forensic experience regarding MPD, the consensus was that we needed a nationally known expert to win the sanity case. At 10:00 that night, we called it a day after agreeing upon the expert I should contact. I made the call the next day.

"What city, please?"

"Lexington, Kentucky, Dr. Cornelia Wilbur. It's on Regency Road."

"Thank you. Here's the number."

Dr. Cornelia Wilbur was the famed psychiatrist whose fascinating treatment of a female multiple, Sybil, was recounted in a best-selling book of that name published a decade ago. I wondered if someone so well-known would even give me the time of day.

What was I going to say, "Dr. Wilbur, since you treated Sybil, can you come to Denver and help us with a double homicide?" I didn't even know if she was still practicing. The MPD literature described her as professor emeritus of psychiatry. Our doctors felt that most jurors would be familiar with the story of Sybil and would give instant credibility to our case if Sybil's doctor was testifying on our behalf.

"Hello. This is Dr. Wilbur."

"Good morning, Dr. Wilbur, my name is David Savitz..." I told her why I was calling and of the upcoming sanity trial schedule. She immediately eased my anxieties.

"You know, Mr. Savitz, I have a niece who also is a lawyer, and she happens to live right outside of Denver — Aurora, I believe."

"I know the city well, doctor. My son lives there with his mother."

"I don't know if I can be of immediate help to you, Mr. Savitz, because I just got over a killer of a virus — in fact, I just got out of the hospital. But anyway, tell me a little bit more about Ross's family history."

After listening to an overview of the case that included Marilyn Carlson's conception out of wedlock, Linnea Hill's unforgivable response to her daughter Marilyn's pregnancy, and Ross's early childhood, Dr. Wilbur's next comment floored me.

"Sounds to me like the grandmother," the doctor said without hesitating. "Fits the classic history of grandmothers who sexually abuse their grandchildren between the ages of two to seven."

After picking myself up from the floor, I wondered if the doctor had experienced a delusional reaction from the medication she was taking. Before I could say anything, Dr. Wilbur continued.

"I haven't seen a multiple who was not sexually abused before the age of eight," she said. "Rigid people with sexual underpinnings, like Baptists, commit sexual abuse. You tell Justin that it is terribly important for the afterlife of all of the personalities to give up the one secret regarding who sexually abused him. Tell him that Sybil's psychiatrist said it was OK."

I acted attentively and uncritical as Dr. Wilbur spoke, but I couldn't help thinking, "Who in the world is going to believe this — the grandmother!"

Chapter 16: Birthday Cake, Matzo Balls, & a Fig Newton

When I was a youngster and our maternal grandmother Emma lived with us, I would occasionally sit with her in our kitchen while we listened to her favorite radio shows, including the comedy of Jack Benny and Rochester. Believing she deserved an equally good turn, I introduced her to reruns of one of my favorite programs, the spellbinding mystery drama, The Shadow. The opening lines of *Who knows what evil lurks in the hearts of men? The Shadow knows!* followed by an eerie cackle, were great entertainment to a young Butchie. Grandma Emma agreed. My paternal grandmother Sarah also brought me equally fond memories.

Her great gifts to me consisted of countless kisses, matzo balls as hard as hockey pucks, those special letters at college, and summer days of nostalgia. When we would sit on our front porch enjoying a nice summer breeze, she loved to recall in her distinctive Yiddish accent how a matchmaker introduced her to my grandfather Julius in 1910, that he took the train from Wilkes-Barre to Brooklyn to meet her and brought her two fresh challahs as a gift. When I went to college, she wrote me letters addressed to "Mr. Butchie-David Savitz." Her letters were easily readable because she wrote in a clear cursive style with huge letters that I swear could have been used as the top line for an eyesight test. Each sentence of her letters contained only about a half dozen words. The envelope always contained her trademark treat: a stick of gum.

I had such a rich history with my two grandmothers! I also knew that not all families enjoyed such treasures. I had to stop and think. I needed to understand that I grew up in La La land and was showered with love and nurturing by everyone in my family. My folks and we kids did things together: we biked along the Atlantic City boardwalk in the summer, drove to Miami Beach for vacations during spring break, and never missed a relative's Bar Mitzvah. We were Ozzie and Harriet and the Walton families all rolled up in one. However, never in my wildest imagination did I believe that children would have been maltreated in the manner described by Dr. Wilbur.

Dr. Wilbur was giving me the benefit of her years of working with this illness. She was the guru. I was the novice. For me, one of the most difficult aspects of the case was my ability to separate my life's experiences from the realization that some families do not love their children. I could not dismiss the doctor's wisdom in spite of how extreme it sounded.

"Dr. Wilbur, will you be able to examine Ross for the sanity case?"

"I'm taking my boards in June. I can't be available until July."

That was too late for us. The sanity trial was set to begin in June.

"Can you recommend anyone else?"

"Yes," she said, "call Dr. Richard Kluft in Philadelphia. He's the best there is — probably has diagnosed and treated more multiples than anyone else in the country." I was familiar with Dr. Kluft's name from the literature. I called him immediately. He was eager to help, but swamped with patients.

"You know, Mr. Savitz, the best forensic presentation I've ever seen was done by Fig Newton." My mind, of course, immediately flashed to cookies, but I resisted saying something stupid.

"I'm sure there's a story behind that."

"His first name is actually Bernauer, but everyone calls him Fig. There are others who are good but not as good as Newton. Stay away from anyone involved in the Bianchi case, especially Orne." I immediately jotted down "Orne-Bianchi" on my legal pad and placed a large asterisk to its left.

Dr. Kluft gave me Newton's contact information and invited me to get back to him whenever I wanted. I assured him I would. Within minutes I reached Dr. Newton in Santa Monica. "Call me Fig, Mr. Savitz."

"I will if you call me David."

"Fair enough."

By this time, I was proficient in summarizing the case. Dr. Newton listened patiently, but as I underscored the problems with the sanity case, he took me by complete surprise.

"Well, don't you want me for the competency hearing? That's the most critical part of your case. The way he's switching from one ego state to another — how do you know which one's in court and following what's going on? If you don't win the competency issue, you're going to have an even tougher fight with insanity. If he's found incompetent because of MPD, he'll have to be treated to be restored

Chapter 16: Birthday Cake, Matzo Balls, & a Fig Newton

to competency. The MPD will become fully revealed during his treatment, allowing you to use the state's doctors during the sanity trial that he suffers from the illness. This will make your task at the sanity trial that much easier." I made a double star on my notes by the reasons why Newton believed a multiple was incompetent.

"Well, doctor, I didn't think there was any way you could come here on such short notice. We'd love to have you, but today's Friday, and the competency hearing starts on Monday."

"That's no problem. I can fly out tonight, examine Ross tomorrow and work with everyone on Sunday, providing I'm able to help. Our son works outside of Colorado Springs; my wife can visit him while I'm working with you. I'll stay in Denver until I have to testify."

"I can't ask for a better deal than that, doctor. After we hang up, I'll make arrangements for a video technician to meet you at the jail."

"That's not necessary. I travel with my own equipment."

"That's great!" I replied, obviously surprised that this expert traveled with his tools of the trade. "Well, call me back with your flight information and I'll pick you up at the airport."

When I hung up the phone, I was ecstatic and couldn't wait to call Walter. We both agreed we might actually have a chance to win the competency issue.

Friday night, June 1, at Stapleton International Airport was not the best place to meet a stranger. This was one of the busiest graduation weekends of the entire spring, and the vehicles were stacked two deep waiting for arriving passengers. After about a half-hour of scouring the hordes of people outside Continental's baggage area, bingo! The doctor and I caught one another's roving eyes. After all, he was the only arriving male passenger with short gray hair, a woman by his side, and carrying what looked like video equipment.

Fig had arrived with his wife Brownie (again I resisted commenting), whose lean frame, gray-streaked hair combed flush back, and prominent cheek bones revealed a woman appearing much younger than her 63 years of age. The lovely Brownie quickly announced she knew her husband and I had much to talk about, therefore, she was perfectly content to sightsee as we drove to their hotel.

During our trip amidst nonstop conversation, I became more and more enthralled with Newton. Soon I began to believe — "Louie, I think this is the beginning of a beautiful friendship."

With Newton, I thought, our chances had just increased significantly of providing Ross with a new beginning. After all, his life that began 20 years ago did not start off very well.

CHAPTER 17

Born into Sin

During mid-October 1963, a terrified, 17-year-old Marilyn Hill informed her devoutly, religious parents that she was pregnant. The expectant child's father was Marilyn's sweetheart since the eighth grade, the nearly 18-year-old Rod Carlson. Marilyn's parents, Reverend Harvey and Linnea Hill, reacted as if a pitchfork had been plunged into their hearts. They were furious with their daughter's reprehensible immorality. Since the Reverend was the spiritual leader of the Minnehaha Baptist Church of Minneapolis, how could he, a disciple of Christ, continue to decry fornication and bless the covenant of marriage when his own daughter engaged in such blasphemy The Hills felt they had no choice; they had to resign from the church. The congregation, however, would not hear of it, referring instead to God's process of reconciliation described in Matthew 18:15.

> "[15] Moreover, if thy brother shall trespass against thee,
> go and tell him his fault between thee and him alone; if
> he shall hear thee, thou hast gained thy brother."

On October 30, 1963, Marilyn Hill and Rod Carlson nervously stood before their church's deacons cloaked with shame. They publicly confessed their sins, repented, and asked forgiveness for having dishonored themselves, their parents, church, and heavenly Father. The church elders unanimously granted absolution. Rod Carlson's parents, Henry and Mildred, who were also members of the same church, quickly forgave their son and Marilyn and never expressed the kind of disdain for them as the Hills had done. One of the Hills, moreover, remained particularly bitter.

Linnea Hill reportedly told her daughter that the public humiliation had been unbearable and that she wished Marilyn were dead. With her reaction, Mrs. Hill allowed her pride to override God's mercy in defiance of James 4:6 ("God opposes the proud but gives grace to the humble") and at the risk of the repercussions wrought by Matthew 6:15 ("But if you do not forgive men their sins, your Father will not forgive your sins").

Despite her mother's apocalyptic wishes, Marilyn married Rod in a small, private ceremony and gave birth on May 28, 1964, to their son, Ross. Despite their blemished start, the newlyweds were determined to overcome the blight on their lives. The brunt of snide jokes by her classmates, Marilyn shunned her friends and focused her energies exclusively on her husband and child. Rod worked at odd jobs after school to help support his wife and baby. After finishing high school, the teenagers entered the University of Minnesota and devoted themselves to academia, both finishing in the top five of their graduating class.

While attending the university, Marilyn and Rod staggered their schedules. Marilyn stayed home with Ross when Rod went to school. When it was time for Marilyn to attend class, Rod either worked or took care of Ross. When both teenagers had to be away from the house, Rod's parents, usually Mildred Carlson, babysat and often kept Ross overnight.

Mildred and Henry Carlson were hard-working people who lived a simple and frugal life. They were described by friends as compassionate and eager to see their son and his new family succeed. The Carlsons often dipped into their savings and lent the young couple money during rough times. Marilyn's parents, on the other hand, found it much more difficult to fully embrace their daughter's premature motherhood.

The Reverend and Mrs. Hill saw morality in black and white terms. To many, the spiritual couple appeared emotionally insensitive and standoffish. Those traits were thought to reflect their view of people as behaving either right or wrong. However, in an effort to

Chapter 17: Born into Sin

mollify their displeasure, the Reverend Hill took the lead in engaging his wife and himself in their daughter's new life.

The Reverend presided over his daughter's wedding, made his home available for her and Rod to live in until Ross was born, and arranged for Marilyn to work at the church's personage one day a week. Marilyn would always bring Ross with her when she worked at which time Linnea Hill would help care for her grandson. When Ross was around two years old, the Hills moved from Minneapolis in 1966 so the Reverend could join a congregation in Chicago.

In an effort to start a clean slate of their own, Rod and Marilyn moved to Colorado when Ross was five years old. There, they both began elementary school teaching careers in the town of Littleton, a suburb of Denver. They supplemented their income by selling Shakelee vitamin products, operating a neighborhood-lawn-mowing business when Ross became old enough to push a mower, and borrowing money occasionally from Rod's parents. At the time of their deaths in 1983, Rod and Marilyn owed the very generous Henry and Mildred Carlson $35,000. It was money they used to enhance Rod and Marilyn's lifestyle, such as down payments for a larger home in 1978 and a new Cadillac Seville in 1980.

Rod and Marilyn wanted to appear as if they had made it on their own. The young couple strove to present an image to the outside world of leading the perfect, successful life. They avoided letting anyone inside their circle of two. Theirs was a life shrouded in secrecy and marked often by extreme behavior.

Two months after Ross's arrest in the dynamite case, Henry and Mildred Carlson flew to Colorado during Christmas 1982 for a two-week stay at their son's and daughter-in-law's home. Henry and Mildred, however, abruptly cut their visit short by several days. It seemed that Marilyn refused to spend any time with her in-laws, making them feel like intruders. Marilyn would make dinner for everyone but then retire to her bedroom instead of sitting at the dinner table. In reality, Marilyn had become an emotional recluse since Ross's arrest in September. Neither she nor Rod ever shared the facts of Ross's aborted attempt to purchase dynamite with their parents, or anyone else.

I learned a more disturbing glimpse of Ross's early home life when I met with Dr. Fairbairn at his office to prepare him for the upcoming competency hearing. For the most part, Ross was the historian of what the doctor recounted. However, it was a history that Ross consistently related to other evaluators as well.

When I asked the doctor about Ross's earliest memory, Fairbairn flipped to a page in his notes and read the following passage: "The floor, 12-inch square tile, black and white swirling pattern in bathtub. Twenty-four months; the remains shoved in my face; felt smothered."

Fairbairn laid down his notes as he described to me this now familiar toilet-training episode. "He was trying to slough it off as really not a very important event," Fairbairn said. The lesson Ross learned was "to control my internal functions so that would never happen again."

Even when he turned older, Ross did not recognize the depths of his father's unreasonableness. Fairbairn provided an example of what had occurred when Ross was a teenager.

"Once he awoke during the middle of the night because he had to use the bathroom," Fairbairn reported. "After he flushed the toilet, Ross's father became livid for having had his sleep disturbed. Rod Carlson instructed his son never to use the toilet again while people were sleeping. The next time Ross had an untimely urge, he omitted the flush component. Instead, he would set his alarm a few minutes before he knew his father would arise that morning. Ross prayed Rod would not awaken sooner. When the alarm rang, Ross made a beeline for the bathroom and emptied the toilet." I couldn't help but shake my head in disbelief as Fairbairn related that and other incidents.

Fairbairn continued to recite from the notes of his April 11, 1984, interview. Ross reported "once I slammed my finger in the car door. My father said big boys don't cry. Ever since, I haven't."

Fairbairn explained that to please his parents, "Ross had to find a way to escape pain and to never cry or feel." Ross never found a solution. Instead, an insidious illness found him.

Fairbairn proceeded with his recitation. "Crayons in my pocket, age 5 or 6, melted in the dryer. Remember getting hit ... spoon, belt, fist."

The doctor read further. "Once coming out of the shower, age 5 or 6. My father lifted me up to the bathroom window. I remember fighting and screaming. I was trying to get down." This was Rod

Chapter 17: Born into Sin

Carlson, displaying his son nude for the neighborhood's consumption, Fairbairn explained. Rod's sadism, however, didn't end there.

Fairbairn reported that Ross had recounted how his father sometimes awakened him in the morning for school by taking Ross's pillow and placing it over his son's face. Soon Ross would start gagging for air and wake up screaming. Eventually, Rod Carlson would remove the pillow and say, "Time to wake up!"

When Justin spoke to Fairbairn, that personality revealed, "One time my dad tried to hit me over the head with a hammer because I forgot which day the garbage was picked up. My father became enraged because that meant the garbage sat around until the next collection day. I really thought he was going to kill me. Black kicked in and took the hammer away from him."

"But where are the acts of sexual abuse?" I asked Fairbairn." According to the literature and Dr. Wilbur, those acts typically are the etiology of MPD."

"David, my understanding is that they are Ross's secrets, which only skilled and intensive, long-term therapy can uncover." The importance of the competency hearing thus became more and more evident. To be sure, Fairbairn related behavior of a very abusive father; Walter and I would soon learn more.

We spoke with Dr. Fisch about his sessions with Ross. The doctor took out his note pad and quoted Ross.

"She felt God was punishing her for having me. Their love was conditional, depending upon what I did. They never touched me. I went with a girl. She touched my leg. I craved it."

According to Dr. Fisch, one quirk about Rod Carlson, which even his own neighbors verified according to the DA's own discovery, was the extremes with which Rod sought perfection. After a winter snowfall, Rod would instruct Ross to remove the snow from the front and back yards with their snowblower. Once the grass had dried, Ross then had to mow and fertilize it to prevent the lawn from losing its optimum height and color.

What Ross had revealed so far to our doctors about his abusive upbringing was universally believed to be just the tip of the iceberg. The defense team realized that the above events did not reflect the kind of extreme and/or continuous maltreatment that normally resulted in MPD. The literature and anecdotal histories provided by Drs. Wilbur and Newton usually involved repeated acts of sexual abuse or other horrific treatment. Fig had cautioned us that Ross would have to undergo extensive therapy before the full nature and extent of his secrets would ever become known. In order to accomplish this, we had to first convince Judge Turelli at the upcoming competency hearing that Ross was incompetent.

CHAPTER 18

Spark Plugs & Judge Day

On Monday afternoon, June 4, 1984, the dirt and gravel parking lot that abutted the one-story Castle Rock courthouse was filled with vehicles for the start of *People vs. Carlson*. As Judge Richard Turelli took the bench, several of our witnesses, a handful of curious spectators, and a throng of press occupied the modest courtroom. Characteristically, the press grabbed the front row seats so their sketch artists could have the best vantage point. Cindy Lebel, the reigning Miss Littleton, Colorado, and a reluctant defense witness, sat with her father in the middle of the courtroom and tried to be as inconspicuous as possible. She looked as though she were about to undergo her first root canal.

After taking a last glance at the opening statement he had penned on his notepad, Walter sat poised, awaiting the proper invitation from the judge.

"Are you ready to proceed, Mr. Gerash?" Judge Turelli asked.

Bob Chappell interrupted before Walter stood up. "If it pleases the court, the People wish to file a motion recusing your Honor from these proceedings."

"What is this BS?" I thought. Walter and I were handed a copy of the motion. Chappell and his co-counsel, Michael Watanabe, wanted no part of Judge Turelli. They cited the Colorado statute that allowed them to peremptorily remove the trial judge from this phase of the case. It was a deft move and caught us and the judge completely by surprise.

Just in the Nick of Time

During the last several months, Judge Turelli had witnessed much of Ross's strange behavior in the courtroom and had read about other similar type incidents in motions we had filed. The prosecutors wanted an untainted fact finder to determine the issue of competency. Judge Turelli looked disappointed as he read the motion. Walter and I read our copy. The law required that he withdraw from the case until Ross's competency was adjudicated by another judge. As I began to explain to Ross what was happening, Judge Turelli spoke.

"All right counsel, the court will have to make arrangements for a different judge. There will be a short recess while I call the judicial administrator."

The DAs, noticing we had several witnesses lined up to testify, were banking that no other judge would be available for at least several days, if not weeks. This way, they would have time to interview our witnesses and become better prepared for the hearing. Ross was unhappy with the expected delay.

"God, can we get this show on the road!" he lamented. "I can't take any more of this. Just put me in prison. I don't want to go to the loony bin."

Ross's oft-articulated preference for jail to the mental hospital wasn't new to me. Other of my clients, faced with the same choice, expressed similar sentiments; they'd rather be branded a criminal than thought of as someone who, in Ross's vernacular, was "nuts." However, there was no way Walter and I were going to expose our poster-boy, mentally fragmented, youthful client to the salacious horrors of prison life.

"Ross," I said, "you're not schizophrenic or psychotic; those are the illnesses usually associated with someone thought of as crazy. Let's see what Judge Turelli has found out."

Ross flashed me one of his thanks, David, but-I'm-not-convinced looks.

After about a half-hour, the judge returned, grinning slyly as if he had just swallowed the tweetie bird. "Gentlemen, the judicial administrator has just advised me that former Colorado Supreme Court Justice Edward Day will be available this Wednesday to take over this case."

Chapter 18: Spark Plugs & Judge Day

Judge Turelli finessed the DA's right out of their starched shorts. Chappell, of course, remained stoic. While he served in the Army, he was probably the platoon's prize soldier — obedient and never remonstrative, even at the most outlandish order. He displayed the emotions of an English butler and was not easily ruffled. However, neither he nor Watanabe could have expected that a new judge would be available on such short notice.

Judge Edward Day, like many retired judges, handled a limited number of trials every year whenever a judicial emergency occurred in the state. After hearing of Judge Day's appointment and as we drove back to Denver, Walter and I began to compare our experiences with his Honor. At first, we questioned whether, at 76 years of age, Judge Day might be a liability to our case. Would he be so entrenched in the psychiatry of the '60s and '70s and not open to the recently emerging, although controversial, diagnosis like MPD? Walter didn't expect there would be a problem.

"David, I've known Day for a long time. He used to be a reporter for the Rocky Mountain News before he practiced law. He knows how to dig for a story; he won't jump the gun. He's written some good opinions in criminal law while on the Supreme Court ... I've argued cases before him. He'll be great!"

I had my own reasons for believing we had lucked out with Judge Day. A few years ago, I tried an auto theft case before him in nearby Jefferson County. Even though my client was convicted of a lesser offense and later sentenced to a short prison term, I thought Judge Day's service was terrific. After the case, I wrote a letter to the Colorado Supreme Court extolling the virtues of the retired judges' system and Judge Day in particular. I wasn't sure if his Honor would remember me, but he couldn't possibly forget my client.

One night during the trial, as my client and I were walking outside the courthouse, we noticed Judge Day standing perplexed by his big, old Cadillac. His car wouldn't start, and he didn't have a clue why.

Unabashedly, my client offered his assistance, indicating that neither a simple wrench nor sophisticated machinery was needed to correct the problem. The implications of such naive benevolence and brazen confidence caused me great consternation, given the nature of the theft accusations against my client. His Honor didn't think twice about the offer and gladly accepted. He wanted to go home and obviously considered it foolish to look a gift horse in the mouth.

With my approval, my client opened the automobile's hood, jiggled a few wires, ignited a couple of spark plugs, and triggered the roar of the engine; the judge was on his way. Fast forward about three years, and Judge Day was apparently not experiencing any chronic vehicular problems because in just two days, he was about to drive from his home and preside over the competency hearing of an accused double murderer.

Wednesday, June 6, 1984 — what a way to celebrate my 41st birthday! It was beginning to seem like trying a case on my birthday was an annual rite of spring. At least, it had appeared that way during the past three years.

Last year, I had represented an NBA player in a paternity suit. Two years ago, it was a Denver firefighter on trial for smoking a joint during a lunch break. You'd think I would pamper myself on this particular day — take the day off, or better yet enjoy a week's vacation in some exotic spot. In reality, I was about to start what I liked doing best.

As the trial's first day was about to begin, Ross and I conferred at the defendant's table while Walter was schmoozing with the press, who had been given permission by the judge to sit in the jury box. The media was hoping to see Ross switch personalities. The judge's clerk and court reporter walked into the courtroom, signaling that Judge Day was soon to follow. Walter quickly sat down. The issue of Ross Carlson's competency was about to begin.

CHAPTER 19

Before the Homicides

Because we had filed the motion asserting that Ross was incompetent, the burden was on us to prove our claim. After each side gave their opening statements, we led our evidence with one of Ross's former classmates. Judge Day then took a mid-morning recess. At the defense table, I was speaking with Ross, while Walter was reviewing his notes for the next witness. Two members of the local network press approached us, having had their curiosity spurred by Walter's morning revelation during his opening statement that Drs. Fisch, Fairbairn, and Newton had conducted dramatic videotape sessions with Ross. The reporters asked Walter for copies of the tapes. Naturally, Walter declined the request. The two walked away discouraged, but, I sensed, undaunted.

Ross, keenly aware of the media's interest, looked at me with Darth Vader eyes and said, "David, there's no way those tapes are going to be shown on the 5 o'clock news. Unless you want a very ugly scene, you make sure no one gets them. Do you understand?"

There was something about getting orders from a 20-year-old who looked like he had just popped out of a Stephen King novel that did not set well with me. Just a few minutes ago, Ross's demeanor had been non-combative. Conversation with him had been pleasant. I resisted the temptation to comment on his surly attitude. Instead, I paused, counted silently, and reminded myself of his illness's unpredictability. I turned to him and calmly reiterated my earlier promise.

"Ross, as I told you before. We will never give up those tapes without a fight."

Just in the Nick of Time

After additional testimony from another of Ross's friends, it was time for the noon recess. The sheriffs would now return Ross to the jail which was situated directly next door to this courthouse in Littleton (the transfer from the Castle Rock courthouse was necessitated because once Judge Turelli was forced to withdraw, a courtroom for Judge Day had to be located in the same judicial district; a courtroom at the Littleton courthouse was available). Access to the Littleton jail, however, required walking down one flight of stairs, out a back door, and through an alley. The route was not without its obstacles — the vulturous press was still circling the hallways, hoping to snare the tapes. I decided to accompany Ross back to the jail. As we walked outside the courtroom, television beat reporters carrying microphones and accompanied by camera personnel converged upon us like a swarm of bees. I was in front of Ross, and the sheriffs were behind and on both sides of us. "Who are you now Carlson ... Black, Justin, who?" someone asked loudly in a mocking tone.

I quickly turned around and saw a reporter for Channel 4, Paul Day, no relation to the judge, reaching into our cocoon with a microphone and shoving it toward Ross. Day had a smirk on his face and was goading Ross. "Who are you now, Carlson? Show us how you change," Day continued. Ross ignored the intrusion, but I was enraged at Day's crass insensitivity.

I shoved the microphone away and screamed inches from his face, "Get the hell out of here! Don't you ever do that again!" I could feel my facing turning a stunning shade of bright red. My heart was racing. My blood pressure had obviously spiked into the next stratosphere. I refused to tolerate anyone ridiculing Ross in my presence.

Day froze. He looked startled. His eyes bulged. He shouted something back. My replied rage muffled his retort.

The sheriffs and I spirited Ross down the stairs and outside the courthouse. Day didn't follow. Ross was taken next door to the jail. I stood alone outside the courthouse and wiped the perspiration from my forehead with my handkerchief.

After a few minutes, I walked back inside and slowly returned to the courtroom. It was empty because of the recess. I sat down at counsel's table. "That son-of-a-bitch, grunt-sucking, motherfucker!"

Chapter 19: Before the Homicides

I muttered to myself. I sat back, closed my eyes, and took a few deep breaths. If Day wanted a fair fight, he would have to deal with me, not a fragmented soul like Ross. After a few minutes and having calmed down, I opened my eyes. It was time to return to the important business of the day: our testimony.

We had begun the hearing by establishing that Ross's different personalities and attendant amnesia existed long before the night of the killings, August 17, 1983. Susan Rhoads and Cindy Lebel were our first two witnesses; Michelle O'Hagen was on deck to lead off the afternoon. Each young woman had known Ross during different times from 1981 through August 1983.

Susan Rhoads was a classmate of Ross's at Heritage High School. She recounted that one day during their senior year of 1981/1982, Ross walked into Courtesy Ford, a car dealership where Susan had worked part-time. Ross was talking to a salesman and portraying himself as a very successful businessman with lots of money to spend. He was dressed "casually rich," wearing a leather or suede jacket. Seeing Ross, Susan walked over to him and said in front of the salesman, "Hi, how are you?"

Ross replied with a blank stare, saying "I'm sorry, you have me confused with someone else." Rhoads couldn't believe Ross's rudeness. She persisted in trying to get him to recognize her, but to no avail. Ross looked at her again with "a completely closed look on his face" and insisted he didn't know her. Rhoads was blown away. "I have never had anybody I know look me straight in the eye and say, 'I don't know who you are,'" Rhoads testified.

A few days later at school, Susan confronted Ross, wanting an explanation. Ross, however, clearly "had no idea what I was talking about," Rhoads recalled. She tried to persuade him otherwise. However, Ross was equally convincing that he had not run into her at the dealership. Susan felt the incident was so strange that she mentioned it to her father, who was at a loss to explain Ross's behavior.

Cindy Lebel was Miss Littleton of 1984 and had aspirations of a national title. When the competency hearing was supposed to begin with Judge Turelli presiding, Cindy and her father had insisted on meeting with Walter and me.

The Lebels implored us not to call Cindy to the stand. They believed the publicity of Cindy's having dated Ross and then testifying for him in a murder trial would harm her chances of advancement to Atlantic City. Cindy was a very attractive young lady, but I believed she should have been content to having achieved the title of Miss Littleton. However, after that meeting, Walter sensed that Cindy might not be the most forthright of our witnesses.

When it came time for Cindy to testify, she recounted that she and Ross first met in 1980 while sophomores at Heritage High. They began dating in 1982 during their senior year and occasionally saw each other last summer. In fact, she and Ross had a date scheduled for Saturday, August 19, the night after Ross's parents were found dead.

When she and Ross did go out, Lebel said, she was not interested in an exclusive relationship. Cindy's testimony was consistent with what she had told our investigator, Gene Tardy, except for one crucial piece. She had emphasized to Tardy that after informing Ross she wanted to date older guys, Ross suddenly began acting very mature. In fact, Ross told her on a number of occasions he was actually 42 years old! When it came time in court for Lebel to recall Ross's exponential jump in age from 19 to 42, she expressed a hazy memory. After receiving permission from the judge, Walter approached Lebel in order to show her a document. I thought to myself: watch out Lebel; you asked for it!

Lebel looked at Walter as he drew closer. She cleared her throat and fidgeted a bit in the witness chair. Walter held a piece of paper, which he had removed from his trial notebook. Lebel must have seen some courtroom dramas on television because she preempted Walter's next question. "Maybe I'm not understanding your question. Maybe that's it," she said, looking up at Walter as he placed the document in front of her that had been written by our investigator Gene Tardy.

"Mr. Tardy asked you if this statement was accurate ... 'he had the mannerisms of a late 30-year-old or early 40-year-old American male,'" Walter said, pointing to a particular passage in Tardy's investigative report.

"That's true," Lebel agreed.

"Didn't he tell you that he was 42?"

" ... Sometimes when he called, he would say 'I feel older

Chapter 19: Before the Homicides

today,'" Lebel responded. "That's when I asked, 'How old do you think you are?' And sometimes his answer was, '42.'"

Before Lebel sat down, Ross wrote me a note on a yellow, post-it regarding their supposed date of August 19. It read, "I have no recollection of having made that date." I stored Ross's revelation in my incompetency bag since later in the hearing I would be called to testify why I thought Ross was incompetent.

Did Ross's lack of recall mean the personality hearing Lebel's testimony was not the same one who actually made the August 19 date? Or, was this mere human forgetfulness? The latter explanation was a common, human frailty. The first possibility, however, was the most worrisome since that dynamic bore directly on whether Ross could assist in his defense. How could Walter or I effectively cross-examine witnesses if our client's diseased mind rendered him unable to remember past events? Without such recall, our client couldn't inform us of the details of an encounter to enable us to question a witness about them.

The last of our female, pre-homicide witnesses was Michelle O'Hagen. Michelle testified she was first introduced to Ross in November or December of 1982 by 14-year-old Kelli Olson[1], who had been dating Ross then. At the time, Michelle was attending Cherry Creek High School. Ross, who Michelle understood was 18 years old, had entered his first year at Metro State College.

Michelle had maintained a friendship with Ross until the Carlsons were killed. During most of that eight-month period, Ross acted like the 16- and 17-year-old high school kids who hung out at the ice-skating rink. However, around Kelli, Ross would act much older, like around 40. It was the "words" he used. Michelle noticed this switch in ages from 16 to 40 "about five or six times." Just then, Ross passed me another note. "I don't remember this girl at all," it said.

Every so often, Michelle continued, Ross would talk about his twin, Justin Time, who "was sent away at the age of three to Arizona ... because he was mean to Ross." At one point during the spring of 1983, Michelle said, Ross told her and Kelli that Justin was back in

---

1. The true name of Ross's girlfriend has been fictionalized as Kelli Olson in order to protect the individual's privacy.

Colorado and would be going to Cherry Creek High.

"I was absolutely convinced by talking to Ross that Justin was another person," Michelle admitted. One day, Kelli met Michelle at Cherry Creek High to see if they could meet Justin. Much to their disappointment, they discovered he had not yet enrolled there. Hagan's testimony concluded a good day of evidence for the defense.

When the first day's testimony ended, Walter and I still had work to do. We were scheduled to testify the next day about how our client's disorder rendered him incompetent. Therefore, we had to meet with a local lawyer, Marty Miller, whom we had hired for the sole purpose of examining us. After that meeting, I went home to relax; my birthday present to myself.

CHAPTER 20

The Lawyers Take the Stand

I had already mapped out the next couple of hours in my mind as I arrived home and hit the play button on my answering machine.

"Hi, Butchie-David! This is your beautiful, younger sister Carol. (I was too gallant to ever tell her that throughout our lives she would always be two years older.) Happy birthday from Jimmy, me, and the boys. Hope you're having a good day. Daddy told me you're in trial. Is it the boy who killed his parents? God, how can you represent someone like that? Does he really have all of those ... ?" Saved by the beep — the machine's limit was 20-second messages.

"Hi, David. This is your mother (as if I had forgotten her voice after 41 years). Daddy and I send our love ... just wanted to call to wish you happy birthday." I could just picture my dad sitting on his leather recliner with the television remote nearby and ready to be handed the phone if I had been home. As always, I had received their birthday card with an enclosed check for $50 and a note to have a nice dinner on them. I had set their card next to the one from my Uncle Joe, which contained a check for $41 and Happy 41st written on the subject line, and then his customary note on the card: "One year old on D-Day!"

I listened to the rest of the well-wishes from family and friends, including one from Robin, who had left town with her daughters to visit her sister in northern California. After having lived together for nearly two months, Robin knew I would be totally absorbed in Carlson and would treat everyone else at home as invisible. I next took a respite from the day's events by taking a six-mile run.

Just in the Nick of Time

The Highline Canal bike path, lined on each side by huge cottonwoods and with a picturesque orange sunset in the horizon, provided the perfect place for a soothing escape from the tumult of a trial. Within a span of 50 peaceful minutes, I was able to rehash in my mind the day's testimony, map out tomorrow's, and rid myself of any ill will that I may have harbored toward the insensitive Paul Day. I picked up the pace with a mile to go and then sprinted as fast as I could the last 200 yards before ending at my house. I walked a couple of minutes to cool down and then stretched a bit. I was ready for trial day number two.

The next morning, Ross was escorted into court, appearing fresh, eager to go, and dressed smartly in a pink shirt, gray slacks, and gray tie. He sat down next to me, arranged his legal pad and pen in front of him, and greeted Walter and me with a smile and a "Good morning, gentlemen." Then looking at me, he said, "I hope you got a chance to enjoy your birthday, David. I'm sorry if this trial spoiled it for you."

"Ross, I had a great evening ... thanks. This didn't spoil anything for me. Are you ready for another good day?"

"I like your optimism, David, but I'm not sure I enjoy people talking about how strange I am." With that, Judge Day entered the courtroom and assumed the bench.

To lead off the day, I called Dr. Philip Young to testify regarding Ross's fainting spells. Dr. Young was a Castle Rock general practitioner who had a contract with the sheriff's office to provide emergency and acute medical care for their prisoners.

The doctor saw Ross on May 8 after the second of his fainting spells, which occurred as he was about to be escorted from the courtroom by deputy sheriff Troy McCarty. Ross told Dr. Young he didn't recall having fainted earlier that day. Ross also mentioned not having remembered other "oddities of behavior" that friends, like Susan Rhoads, Michelle O'Hagen, and Cindy Lebel, had described him doing.

The doctor performed a battery of neurological tests and checked Ross's blood pressure, all of which were normal. Young diagnosed Ross as either suffering from a physical illness, like "psychomotor seizure," or a mental illness, such as "split personality."

Chapter 20: The Lawyers Take the Stand

When I asked the doctor to consider that Ross recently had a normal EEG, Young concluded that the mental illness diagnosis was the more likely cause for the fainting spells.

Young's testimony was a bonus for us. During his examination, the doctor had no idea what charges Ross was facing. Indeed, that was not his focus. Dr. Young evaluated Ross just like he would any other patient who had walked into his office. Yet, the doctor made a diagnosis of "split personality" that sounded as close to MPD as we could have hoped. Young's testimony had now set the stage for Walter and me to take the stand.

After Walter took the oath, Ross began to fidget a little. I rubbed his back and whispered to him that everything would be okay. I then had to leave the courtroom because the prosecution insisted that I be sequestered while Walter testified.

While in the hallway, I felt like a preschooler who had been placed in a time-out while everyone else in class got to play. After I reviewed the notes of my anticipated testimony for the umpteenth time, I began staring at my new surroundings, which now were outside Judge Day's courtroom. I proceeded to draft a letter in my mind to the county commissioners. "Dear Sirs: Please brighten up the drab hallways in your courthouse. Paint the walls, hang some pictures, replace the hard wooden benches, buy some magazines ... ."

Meanwhile inside the courtroom, Walter had taken center stage. Shyness or equivocation were as foreign to Walter as stage fright and stammering were to Sir Laurence Olivier. From all accounts, Walter sounded equally as comfortable as a witness as he did an advocate. Being aware of the outline of his testimony, I knew exactly what he was prepared to tell Judge Day. Walter first talked about his background: in 1943, he left high school at age 17 to join the Army; after the war, he went to UCLA and graduated from there in 1949; he next pursued his love of history and obtained a Masters in that subject from the University of Chicago in 1951; he then returned to LA where he worked as a union organizer for three years. After finally deciding upon a law career, he attended UCLA's law school for two years, married and had a child. For his third and last year of his law studies, he moved his family to Denver and finished at Denver University's law school in 1956. During his 28 years practicing criminal law, he had handled scores of murder cases.

Walter admitted he wasn't easily convinced of MPD's legitimacy because "sometimes the histrionic manifestations are incredulous. You think it's suspect." According to accounts of the cross examination I had later received, Chappell challenged the diagnosis and its attendant amnesia, believing our doctors' suggestive techniques had planted the MPD concept in Ross's mind and that our client had absolutely no memory problems.

Walter disagreed, saying that the issue of amnesia had become a critical concern for us when we tried to reconstruct what happened the night Ross's parents were killed. Judge Day seemed to side with Chappell. He interrupted Walter, saying there was pretty good evidence that Ross had a perfectly clear memory of that fateful night when he provided "one of the most detailed accounts of a person's actions from supper time to bedtime I've ever seen" Chappell evidently sensing he had forged an alliance with the most important man in the courtroom, remained quiet as the judge pressed Walter further.

The judge referred Walter to the February 8, 1984, report by the state's psychiatrist, Dr. Alan Fine. Ross was quoted in Fine's report as having lured his parents to the remote area in Douglas County where they were killed under the pretense of showing them a mailbox he had built for some friends. The judge read specific passages from the report. "He pulled out a gun. The mother said 'I don't want to live. This is hell. Go ahead and shoot me.' I shot my father first, then mother. Bang! Bang!" The judge put down the report and said, "Seems like pretty good memory to me." Court was then recessed for the day.

That was not the kind of explosive boom with which Walter had hoped to end his day's testimony. Walter and I huddled after court with Marty Miller to review what points Chappell may have scored and to formulate our strategy for the next morning.

The following day, Walter's testimony continued. I brought the daily paper to keep me occupied until it became my turn to testify. Occasionally, I was distracted by the comings and goings of other courthouse visitors.

Chapter 20: The Lawyers Take the Stand

Down the hallway to my left, a woman in a pale blue, ill-fitting dress left a courtroom in tears. She was comforted by a friend who wrapped her arm around the distressed soul. "How am I going to make it on so little child support?" the woman wondered as she and her friend walked toward me. I turned my head away so as not to be intrusive.

A teenage boy in jeans and a T-shirt was led by his mother down the stairs that serviced the courthouse's four floors. The boy's head was tilted to the left because his left ear was in his mother's grasp. She obviously felt this act of maternal bonding was necessary so her son would understand the consequences of repeated shoplifting charges.

Finally, a very sensuous-looking, young female with blond hair, wearing a white skirt and red sweater, which in tandem revealed the best of her natural qualities or enhancements thereof, exited the elevator that was on the opposite side of the hallway and a little left to where I was seated. The young lady was accompanied by a nattily-attired man whom I knew to be a lawyer. As they walked past me, they were discussing an undercover officer's apparent misunderstanding of the client's social invitation. They entered another courtroom down the hall.

This trilogy of sorrowful characters was merely reflective of the courthouse's daily business. I returned to my paper and read about London's 40th anniversary celebration of D-Day. I saved the sports section for last.

Meanwhile, back in the courtroom, Walter dealt squarely with Ross's purported rendition of the murder scene. Walter directed the judge to look at Dr. Fine's handwritten notes that he made while talking to Ross and compared those notes to the doctor's final written report.

"Dr. Fine's seemingly literal notes are quite different from his report," Walter said, pausing slightly and then reading Fine's contemporaneous notes of Ross's narrative of that awful night.

"I pulled out a gun. Things were speeding up like I had been shot out of a cannon. My mind was doing 200 miles an hour. I seemed to be watching it. I'm big on movies. It seemed like a movie. I was watching it from another place. I saw my shoulder. The camera concentrated on my shoulders. My mother said, 'I don't want to live.

This is hell. Go ahead and shoot me.' Shot father first, then mother. Bang! Bang! Father said nothing. Why would he give up like that? It doesn't make any sense. I think I wanted them to stop me from killing myself. I gave them ample opportunity and they didn't stop me. All they had to do is reach out and take it, but he didn't. Then again, he never took it. Then I ended up shooting myself."

Walter explained that Ross's out-of-body description of the murder scene was indicative of "a dissociative reaction, or break from reality" about which Dr. Fisch would later testify. According to Walter, Judge Day closely studied Fine's notes as Walter read them out loud. When Chappell then finished his examination of Walter, I was finally summoned from my temporary banishment.

Testifying was not a completely foreign experience to me. My first time was in 1974 — to obtain my divorce. Although it was not contested, one of the parties had to say the magic words, "the marriage is irretrievably broken." There was no need to force my soon-to-be-former wife to endure the public embarrassment of uttering those words so I was elected to do so by default. Discussing my own human frailties as a husband in front of a courtroom of strangers was not my idea of a good time.

A few years later, I had been hired as an expert witness in two cases to discuss the reasonableness of a lawyer's fees. Those were easier experiences, in part, because I was evaluating someone else's positive work. Now, however, I was being asked to speak about something much more delicate — a client's mental deficiencies.

I had been taught since law school that, except in rare circumstances, lawyers are forbidden from revealing communications between them and a client. Therefore, this setting presented one of those exceptions and a very fine line to tread. Walter and I had explained to Ross that what we were prepared to say in court would be for his best interests. The problem was we didn't know which personalities understood that explanation and which ones did not.

After describing last December's meeting with Dr. Wilets, my subsequent study of MPD, Ross's diagram for me of his personalities and his unusual behaviors in court, I was asked about the moving events of the Fairbairn videotaping. As I began to recall that day to Judge Day,

Chapter 20: The Lawyers Take the Stand

I could also see members of the press from the corner of my eye writing feverishly on their note pads.

Recollections of my client switching and, in particular, the sight of the personality Ross sobbing and changing to a dry-eyed Justin like the end of an automatic-sprinkler's cycle, still affected me. However, I kept my emotions in check to avoid being accused of pulling at the judge's sympathies.

Not once did Judge Day interrupt as I spoke about that day. When he wasn't taking notes or studying an exhibit I had prepared, he was peering at me. Walter was sitting with his feet propped on top of his briefcase in order to alleviate his recent back pain. He too was writing nonstop. Other than an occasional cough from the spectator section or the sound of a note page flipping, the courtroom was quiet.

I glanced at Ross whose head was bowed. He was staring down at the defense table. His hands were cupped, resting on the temples of each side of his head. I couldn't tell where or who he was. A part of me wanted to step down from the witness box and see if he was okay.

"When different personalities emerged during Dr. Fairbairn's interview, did they appear to be contrived?" Marty asked.

"During that morning session, I vividly remember my heart pumping so fast," I stated. "I was so keyed up. When we broke for lunch, I was off the ground because I had experienced something very emotional and very real." Within my peripheral vision, I again noticed the fervent activity at press row. Soon thereafter, court adjourned for the day.

The next morning, the resumption of my testimony was temporarily shelved. Three media lawyers sat patiently in the front row of the courtroom. Counsel had just filed a motion for copies of our tapes and were anticipating the opportunity to present their argument to his Honor. Little did these barristers know their pleas had as much of a chance of succeeding as Curly, Larry, and Moe headlining legitimate theater.

The only way the press could possibly get their hands on the tapes was if we decided to show them in court. If we elected to do so, the judge would then have to balance Ross's rights to privacy and a fair trial in the upcoming sanity phase against the right of the public to know. If the judge weighed that question in the media's favor, we would refuse to introduce the tapes and devise other ways to bring that evidence before the court.

After studying the lawyers' briefs, Judge Day invited the DAs and us into chambers. That homey ambience of family photos and leather couch belonging to the resident judge, however, failed to disarm Walter. The fire in his belly was stoked with coals of disdain for the media. He was about to explode out of his dark velvet suit and excoriate the press for its intention to display our client on the ten o'clock news as some freak of nature.

Judge Day, however, preempted Walter's imminent outburst. With the disarming calmness of an exalted town patriarch, the judge looked at Walter and said firmly, "You know, Mr. Gerash, I don't have to see the tapes. I'm sure your doctors can do a very good job of describing their sessions with the defendant. I wouldn't require any more than that. If you don't introduce the tapes, I don't have to rule on these motions." Walter's natural color returned — his outrage doused with judicial perspicacity.

The three media lawyers picked up their briefcases and walked disappointedly from the courtroom. The press's ghoulish appetite would have to be satisfied another day. It was now time for Bob Chappell to cross-examine me.

Dressed in a well-pressed, conservative suit, probably a 40 regular, and with his brown hair trimmed to military preciseness, the deputy district attorney could easily have moonlighted as an FBI agent with one exception — his mustache. However, there was no mistaking Chappell's prosecutorial skills.

In court, he was cool and deliberate. As an experienced trial attorney, Chappell first checked to see that he had the judge's attention. Upon receiving eye contact from Judge Day, Chappell began.

His initial questioning focused upon my inexperience with the disorder and lack of objectivity. I obviously could only speak about MPD as a lay person and admitted that I had studied the illness for less than a year. I acknowledged that balancing effective representation of a client with the need to maintain objectivity about the client's defense was sometimes a struggle.

Chapter 20: The Lawyers Take the Stand

Chappell asked if I still had any doubts that Ross suffered from MPD upon discovering that he studied psychology in college. Of course, that didn't matter. It's a well-known psychological phenomenon that individuals who feel they're stranger than the general population often try to learn why.

The prosecutor also inquired whether, during my representation of Ross in the probate court, he had told me he had enrolled in a trusts and estates course at Denver's Metro College? Again, I replied in the negative, knowing we would argue to the judge during closing statements that such a question was like implying that someone who took a basic chemistry class was probably guilty of manufacturing illicit drugs.

When Chappell ended his cross, he gathered his notes and walked back to his seat. The boyish-looking Michael Watanabe greeted him with a nod of approval.

As I left the witness stand, I couldn't help but wonder what impact, if any, my testimony was going to have on Ross's future. As I settled down next to Walter, he flashed me a smile. Marty gave me a wink. Ross, however, remained sitting with his face downward, focusing intently upon his tablet. He was drawing. His left hand firmly gripped the left top margin of his paper, preventing it from moving. I looked down to see what was so preoccupying him. He had been painstakingly designing perfectly straight geometric figures without the aid of a ruler. Who knew what journey he had been traveling? It certainly didn't appear to be the one I had just finished.

CHAPTER 21

The Defense Experts Take Center Stage

After the first week of testimony, I devoted Saturday, June 9, to escape from the case's intensity. Up at the crack of dawn, I took off for a seven-mile run in sunny, 55-degree weather. After an obligatory pause at Mister Donut for coffee and an apple fritter, I went to my office to catch up on a few hours of work. The remainder of the afternoon was spent putting the finishing touches on a 25th anniversary party happening that night for my friends, Carl and Marsha Scheer.

The Scheers had played a pivotal role in my meeting Robin last December — Carl for his having to travel out of town on business during the Carik Christmas party and Marsha for inviting me as her escort that evening and my fortuitous meeting of and falling head over heels for Robin Childs. The least I could do in return was to organize a surprise black tie dinner celebration at the Normandy French restaurant attended by the Scheer's two children, special friends, an abundance of hugs and kisses, and a bunch of fun toasts. The break, however, was brief.

Sunday was another day of preparation. Monday, we would begin the expert phase of our case and paint the sorrowful portrait of someone who never enjoyed a celebration of fun and frivolity with his parents and their friends.

Drs. Fisch, Fairbairn, and Newton would testify to their evaluations of Ross and corroborate Walter's and my views regarding incompetency.

Chapter 21: The Defense Experts Take Center Stage

A key theme of our experts was: MPD is a "disease of secrecy and hiddenness." Since Dr. Fisch had previously treated a few patients with the disorder, his "clinical experience had taught him that none of the alter personalities would reveal incidences of abuse without involvement in a trustworthy therapeutic relationship. Such an alliance could take several months. Then, complete fusion of the various personalities into one integrated individual could take anywhere between 18 months and three years," he stated. As an expert in hypnosis, Fisch further related that "it was only through the integration process with hypnotherapy as part of the treatment that the full nature and extent of the abuse would be revealed."

Both Fisch and Fairbairn emphasized the conundrum facing multiples, who have raised a mental impairment defense in a criminal case such as this one. Since child abuse, usually sexual, was the *sine qua non* of MPD, during the eventual sanity trial, Ross's lawyers would want to show the commission of this kind of abuse against their client in order to convince the jury that Ross suffered from the disorder. Because the abusive incidents can only be uncovered during treatment, which Ross has not undergone, he has been unable to inform his attorneys about the episodes, thus preventing him from assisting in his insanity defense. That "failure to assist his attorneys," according to the doctors, therefore, rendered Ross incompetent under Colorado law.

After Drs. Fisch and Fairbairn discussed their interviews with Ross and their opinions of his incompetency, the groundwork for Dr. Newton was laid. I had met with Dr. Newton on Sunday to prepare him for his testimony, or, more accurately, he prepared me for his testimony! I had learned long ago from Walter that attorneys should never believe they possess even a smidgen of the knowledge accumulated by top notch forensic experts and that a trial lawyer can be most effective in such situations by merely pointing the baton and becoming nearly invisible as the expert explains the various movements of the particular symphony to a judge or jury. When we met, Newton told me exactly what he intended to say during his testimony and the questions I should ask to elicit his responses. I was prepared and called him to the stand with my baton in hand.

As he eased into the witness chair, the doctor lowered the

microphone to adapt to his 5'9" frame. The much taller Fairbairn had just preceded him. I took Newton through his qualifications.

In 1960, he treated his first MPD patient; since then, the doctor had seen a total of 37 people with that disorder. In 1967, he produced a training film regarding all facets of MPD. His numerous publications about the illness included a chapter in an upcoming psychology book. Courts in California, Oregon, and Hawaii have admitted him as an expert in MPD and hypnosis, and two of those cases dealt specifically with the mental capacity of a multiple.

After having been trained in hypnosis by a world authority, Dr. Roy Dorcus, Dr. Newton earned the designation "Fellow" from four prestigious national organizations dealing with that methodology. Those qualifications led to his appointment as an examiner for the American Board of Psychological Hypnosis. His term as president of the Society for Clinical and Experimental Hypnosis had ended just this year. Throughout his career, he had been the recipient of his profession's highest awards in psychology and hypnosis.

Dr. Newton spoke in a mildly raspy voice, which I surmised, had resulted from countless hours of psychotherapy trying to heal the pain and suffering of so many distressed souls. I stood quietly at the podium as the doctor answered, looking most often directly to Judge Day, who usually returned his characteristic neutral gaze.

"Without any exception in my experience, hypnotizability is always a characteristic of the multiple," Newton stated. Newton explained that hypnosis lowers the patient's resistance and anxiety to therapy and the therapist, making it easier for the patient to establish rapport and discuss his background with his therapist. In addition, alter personalities are more willing to emerge under hypnosis.

Dressed in a light gray, striped suit and charcoal gray tie, Newton communicated in relaxed and confident tones, just like he had while educating me for the first time two weeks earlier in his motel room. There, he had been clad in slacks and a short sleeve shirt, sipping coffee into the wee hours of the night and, during breaks, talking about his dream of retiring in a couple of years to Bozeman, Montana, and fly fishing in that state's crystalline waterways. I told him he could retire when the Carlson case was over.

Chapter 21: The Defense Experts Take Center Stage

In describing how an individual became afflicted with MPD, Newton provided this narrative. I stood at the podium, laid my pen down next to my notes, and just listened until I knew he had finished.

"Typically, there is a family where spouses have opposite parental attitudes and behavior," he began. "One parent may be harsh, unforgiving, exacting, critical, and extremely punitive toward the child. The other parent will be docile, subservient, and generally jaded about the child's rearing. The second parent usually sees no problems with the manner in which the child is raised. Finally, the child is abused both physically and psychologically and told the family's behavior must be kept **secret**."

"The child longs for security, approval, and love from both of his parents. However, what he receives are rejection, criticism, and punishment. The child then stuffs into his subconscious the anger, hurt, and fear he feels from his parents. This is called repression, which the child does on an **unconscious** level."

"This is a child who is very bright and imaginative. Since he is unable to receive happiness and joy from his parents, he creates imaginary playmates who provide him with these niceties. Now, there is just so much pain a child can stuff into his subconscious before his head will burst. At some point, his repressive mechanism reaches the point of overload and failure. His psyche then affords him two choices — become psychotic or split. Some children become the former. Others develop MPD. The result is strictly an unconscious process."

When Newton had revealed this process to me during our pre-trial preparation, I was riveted by his explanation. Now, while Newton testified, I could see that Judge Day was as captivated as I had been. I spoke next only when it became apparent that he had answered my question and was ready for the next one on my list. I peered quickly over at Walter and saw his look of approval. Ross was drawing again, and Dr. Fairbairn sat at his side as his comforter, if needed. I asked the next question, and Newton continued.

"For those children whose ego splits, a wall of denial, repression, and amnesia is built between the parts. On one side of the wall is the happy and compliant child. On the other side is the depressed and fearful child. If that wall were not present, the happy child could never pull off his existence because he would always remember the unhappy events which led to his original split.

With this splitting or dissociative mechanism in place, the child's ego can later separate again as the situation warrants. The child uses his imaginary playmates as the identities of the different parts. In Ross's case, he had named his playmates Justin, Steve, Gray, and so on.

"One split, however, brings its own problems. After the initial split, we now have a happy and a sad side. However, we are missing an intellectual side. Accordingly, a need arises for other splits in order for the entire individual to function. The subsequent splits solve some problems for the individual but create others. We now have many parts with walls of amnesia constructed throughout the system.

"What do we do when it becomes necessary for parts with different features to respond simultaneously to a life's situation?" the doctor rhetorically asked as part of his prepared remarks. "It is not so easy," he explained and then continued with additional questions and answers. "Furthermore, how do we avoid being detected when we subconsciously need to split from one part to the other? Often that can be accomplished by switching quickly and subtly. Other times it cannot be helped that the switches are obvious and dramatic. Most of the time, people do not even associate the dramatic switches with anything being wrong. They merely observe that sometimes so and so does strange things or acts differently."

Newton's message was as clear as a Montana stream. Confident that I had captured the judge's attention and understanding, I had Newton list the evidence and features of MPD which existed with Ross. The doctor included everything from the circumstances of Marilyn Carlson's pregnancy, to the voice differences among the personalities, to the configuration of personalities, or "ego states" as Newton referred to them. He emphasized that the configuration, which Ross had drawn for me in jail, could not have been copied from any text or publication because they were so unique to Ross.

Newton was our final witness. Both Bob Chappell and Michael Watanabe were ill-prepared to challenge the bases of any of our doctors' findings and opinions. Their cross examinations of our experts were feeble. Instead, the prosecutors were banking on their own experts to convince Judge Day that Ross was a faker and manipulator.

CHAPTER 22

The Prosecution's Experts Follow

After accompanying Fig outside the courthouse and flagging down a cab to take him to the airport, I hustled back to the courtroom. As I walked to the defense table, I heard speech which sounded so affected that I actually thought someone was playing a joke. As I looked around and regained my bearings, I quickly realized my intuition was off the mark. I had to bite my lip.

Chappell was standing at the podium asking questions of a witness. Walter was busily taking notes with his feet propped upon his briefcase. Ross and Dr. Fairbairn, whom we had asked to continue remaining at our table to comfort Ross because he was splitting so much during our experts' testimony, appeared engrossed in conversation unrelated to what was occurring from the witness chair. As I sat down, both Ross and Fairbairn greeted me. "I heard you did a great job with Newton," Ross said.

"Thanks, I thought it went well," wondering which of Ross's alter personalities had been present during Newton's testimony. "Is this really Norma Livingston?" I asked him.

"Yes, David."

Testifying was a dark-haired woman in her early 50s who sat in the witness chair erect and as stiff as a starched shirt. She was a staff psychologist at the State Hospital where Ross was sent early in the case for evaluation after we announced he was pleading not guilty by reason of insanity. Livingston was one of the hospital doctors who evaluated him for sanity and competency. Her hands were folded on her lap, and her attention was focused upon Chappell as if she were frozen in place. As a fifth grader, I had an English teacher, Mrs. Ruggels, who doubled as our school principal. She was a stickler for proper enunciation as was Livingston. At the time of fifth grade, Mrs. Ruggels appeared to be around the same age as that of my grandmothers, probably because Mrs. Ruggels had gray hair and wore her stockings bunched around her ankles, although I doubted she could sing like Grandma Emma or make matzoh ball soup like Grandma Sarah. Anyway, what do ten-year-old kids know about the age of adults, other than believing they're really old? One day, Mrs. Ruggels, in her role as principal, summoned me to her office because I was seen throwing snowballs at passing cars during the noon hour; she wanted to know why a 10-year-old would do such a mischievous deed. Granted, she was unaware of my chocolate milk caper, but such a question seemed so ingenuous. Ten-year-old kids do stupid things because they want to.

Livingston sometimes answered a question from Chappell with the same kind of incredulity and deliberate and precise language as Mrs. Ruggels had expressed to me years before. Livingston seemed perturbed with Chappell for asking her questions to which he obviously knew the answers and with her curt responses was seemingly scolding him for doing so. Livingston clearly was not versed in the ways of the courtroom. Upon listening to Dr. Livingston, I wondered if she were the reincarnate of Mrs. Ruggels.

I remember reading Dr. Livingston's report several months ago when she had diagnosed Ross as a mixed personality disorder, a garbage pail designation, and concluded that he was malingering a thought disorder, i.e., faking a psychosis. The latter opinion was based primarily upon reports from the hospital's recreational therapist who observed Ross playing basketball on two separate occasions.

During the first basketball outing, Ross performed as if he had never played the game, dribbling the ball like a "sledgehammer," and shooting as if he were shot-putting. On that day, Ross, according to the therapist, clearly knew that staff was present. The next time, however, unaware that staff was watching, Ross organized the other patients into two teams and played like an all-star hoopster. Although

Chapter 22: The Prosecution's Experts Follow

Dr. Livingston probably did not know the difference between a basketball and a bowling ball, she concluded that Ross had obviously exaggerated inept athletic prowess while being observed by staff. Since Ross scored normal on the standardized psychological tests and exhibited no bizarre behavior on the ward, he, according to Livingston, was obviously faking his dismal basketball skills on that first day. During his cross-examination, Walter exposed the doctor's modest academic credentials, her utter lack of any understanding about MPD, its features, and diagnostic criteria, and the paucity of evidence upon which she based her diagnostic conclusions and opinions of malingering. I couldn't help but believe the prosecutors were relieved when Dr. Livingston eventually ended her testimony and the first of their two psychiatrists, Dr. Scott Reichlin, took the stand.

Only two years post-residency, one of which had been in private practice, Dr. Reichlin sported a full beard, which, to cynical criminal lawyers like me, suggested the doctor was trying to cosmetically hide his youth and inexperience. In reality, a 32-year-old shrink does not become imbued with the intelligence of Freud two years into the world of forensics.

Although Reichlin had never diagnosed, treated, or observed any patient with MPD, he, nevertheless, believed Ross was faking the disorder. The doctor emphasized two points:

(1) The personalities were not complete or complex enough to be considered separate, full-blown personalities. The various "characters" whom he saw on our doctors' videotapes seemed like nothing more than mere "cardboard cutouts" or two-dimensional figures; and

(2) The behavior of some of the personalities observed on the tapes was too dramatic and inconsistent. Reichlin mentioned Norman whom he described as sometimes exhibiting an Italian, Stallone-type accent and on other occasions, displaying a less pronounced inflection.

Reichlin admitted his knowledge about MPD came primarily from reading the literature. He acknowledged an unawareness of Ross's child-abuse history. He admitted unfamiliarity with the incident at Courtesy Ford where Ross was seen by his high school friend, Susan Rhoads, but only to deny he had been there when confronted by Rhoads at school a day or so later. Reichlin agreed the event was arguable evidence of true amnesia. Finally, he conceded he had misinterpreted Ross's MMPI test results conducted a year before the homicides and which Dr. Fisch believed were so significant to the reliability of the diagnosis. Reichlin agreed the MMPI results showed no malingering.

The weak slate of state experts changed, however, with the testimony of Dr. Alan Fine. Dr. Fine epitomized the unassuming kid next store, who went off to college and returned a success. A single, good-looking professional with a thick head of dark, wavy hair, Fine was someone who mothers would want to stop at a Safeway and invite to dinner to meet their daughters. He owned three traditional suits: a blue, a dark brown and, his favorite, a gray. We saw the blue and brown ones during earlier interviews of him. He wore the gray when he took the stand at 3:30 on Tuesday afternoon, June 19.

It was almost a year ago to the day that Fine had completed his residency in psychiatry at the University of Colorado. One month later, he began his duties as staff psychiatrist of the forensic unit at the Colorado State Hospital. Just six months after he started, Dr. Fine examined Ross.

Fine willingly met with Walter and me on more than one occasion to discuss his findings. He did not consider Ross a malingerer. Rather, Fine diagnosed Ross as having a mixed personality disorder with many antisocial features — essentially a young scoundrel with no incapacitating mental problems.

The doctor had viewed the Fisch-Fairbairn-Newton videotapes and also listened to an audiotape interview conducted of Ross by Dr. Fisch in early December 1983 when Fisch first examined Ross. Although Fine admitted that Ross exhibited behavioral changes on the videotapes, the doctor believed, however, that the interview methods used by Drs. Fairbairn and Fisch were too suggestive.

Fine argued that Dr. Fairbairn's asking Ross, "Who am I talking to?" might be good technique for treating a patient with multiple personality disorder, but was not very helpful forensically. That question frequently asked by Fairbairn, in Fine's view, planted and reinforced the notion in Ross's mind that he consisted of more than one part. The doctor also believed that Ross's so-called description of

Chapter 22: The Prosecution's Experts Follow

shooting himself was suggested. Fine flipped to the appropriate page of Fisch's audio taped interview with Ross and commented.

"This is Dr. Fisch speaking: 'As your double was shooting your parents, did your double notice anything unusual or different about them?'"

"And Mr. Carlson responds: 'No, not terribly. Well not true. My mother had said, I do not wish to live any longer. Just go ahead and shoot me.'"

"Fisch: 'Okay, if you can imagine that scene again. The thing I'd like to know ... does either or both of your parents seem to look like you, or do you seem to look like them?'"

"Carlson: 'Ah, they seem to look like me, and I look like them.'"

Fine had just struck one of our Achilles heels. Newton warned us that we did not have an absolutely pristine record in the form of the interviews conducted by Fisch and Fairbairn. However, Newton, nevertheless, had long viewed these exchanges highlighted by Fine as minor peccadillos — inadvertent, well-meaning, and certainly acceptable in a therapeutic milieu. Most importantly, these forensic missteps did not change Newton's view, and the view shared by nearly all of the eminent practitioners in the field, that one cannot develop MPD artificially, including by suggestive interview techniques.

During our private interviews with Fine, the doctor conceded that Ross's killing-fields account of the homicides fit the classical definition of a dissociated experience. He also spoke of his enormous respect for Dr. Newton's expertise and skills. Fine acknowledged that he neither studied nor had any previous experience with MPD, and he was refreshingly truthful in admitting to a prosecutorial bias.

The doctor was as honest as Mother Teresa. During cross-examination by Walter, Fine did not deny what he had told us during our pre-hearing interviews. In spite of these concessions, it was the sincerity of the doctor's pro-prosecution opinions that rendered him a credible witness. We were hoping, however, that the doctor's genuineness would be overshadowed by our extensive evidence of pre-homicidal events, the MMPI test results, and Dr. Newton's expertise. In addition, we still had one more explosive incident waiting in the wings, in the event it was needed.

CHAPTER 23

Our Ace in the Hole

Although the three pre-homicidal instances of forgetfulness testified to by Ross's classmates were symptomatic of MPD, the one incident we had hoped Judge Day would find the most compelling had yet to be heard.

Randy Staton was a gift from the gods, but, more important, a direct result of our media strategy designed to find a diamond in the rough. While watching television coverage of the competency trial, Staton saw a media interview of Dr. Fairbairn after the doctor had testified. The interview was precipitated by a strategy session Walter and I had with the doctor regarding how hampered our investigators had been in finding witnesses like Ross's three female friends: Susan Rhoads (the Courtesy Ford incident), Cindy Lebel (Ross said he was 42 years old), and Michelle O'Hagen (Ross had a twin brother, Justin).

We believed there probably were other people who could recall unusual episodes concerning Ross. However, because the Steve personality was the one with whom we were primarily dealing in preparation for the hearing, that personality had no recall of anyone who, for example, may have dealt with Justin. In addition, any incident that did involve Steve would not have appeared out of the ordinary to him so it wouldn't have dawned on him to tell us about it. As a result, during his on-camera press interview, Dr. Fairbairn issued a plea for people to come forward if they recalled an unusual past experience regarding Ross's forgetfulness. Staton responded and left word at Walter's office. Walter called him back as soon as he returned from

Chapter 23: Our Ace in the Hole

court. Walter called me soon after he finished talking to Staton and excitedly reported their conversation.

"Mr. Gerash, about five or six years ago Ross used to cut lawns in our neighborhood. He must have been around 14 or 15 at the time. That particular summer he mowed our lawn for a couple of weeks while my parents vacationed in California. I was around 19 years old and had knee problems so I couldn't do the mowing."

"During one of those weeks, I was inside the house and saw Ross cutting our lawn. A couple of hours later the doorbell rang. It was Ross, and he was very angry. He wanted to know who cut the lawn. He accused me of mowing it in order to beat him out of his $5.00. I thought he was kidding. I said, you cut the lawn earlier. He said, no, he didn't. When I told him that he did and that no one was trying to beat him out of his money, he suddenly had this blank look on his face. I gave him his five bucks, but he was convinced that I had cut the lawn."

"The incident was so bizarre that I mentioned it to my folks when they returned home. They just shook their heads. They didn't have any explanation. That day never made sense to me until this case. I've never forgotten it. Does this help you guys at all?" That was an understatement!

After Walter hung up, he became very depressed, feeling guilty about not having been as committed to the diagnosis as I had been. Doubts had always lingered in the back of Walter's mind about whether Ross suffered from the disorder until Station's story. That event, however, was compelling evidence of Ross's amnesia five years prior to the homicides and was the kind of blockbuster testimony we needed to substantiate that symptom and hence, the diagnosis. Walter and I had agreed to save Staton for the sanity trial, unless we actually had a shot at winning on the competency issue. After Dr. Reichlin finished his first day of testimony wherein he accused Ross of being a malingerer, I called Walter that night.

"Walter, I think we should call Staton in our rebuttal case. Reichlin said that Ross doesn't have MPD — that he's a malingerer. Fine will say if he has features of the disorder, it is artificial and was created only after Ross began working with our doctors. The time is now."

Walter agreed. He'd call Staton that night and arrange for him to testify after the People rested their case.

During the next day, as the prosecution was winding up its case, one of our staff waited outside the courtroom in the hallway for Staton to appear at a prearranged time. Around 1:30 in the afternoon of June 20, Staton walked into the courthouse. No one from the prosecution knew anything about him. Our lookout summoned me to leave the courtroom to meet our prize witness.

"Mr. Staton, Hi! I'm David Savitz, co-counsel with Mr. Gerash for Ross Carlson."

Staton had just come from his job. Dressed in jeans and a work shirt, he appeared to be in his mid-20s; he was of ample girth. A large silver ring holding numerous keys hung from a belt loop on the right side of his jeans. He was soft spoken and polite. After Staton repeated to me the story he had told Walter a few days earlier, I asked him a few questions that I thought the prosecution might pose. Staton was stone solid in his recollection of what had happened that summer day some five years ago. When it became time, I escorted Staton into the courtroom. Walter announced Staton as the defense's rebuttal witness. The judge swore in Staton. The courtroom observers inched forward in their seats obviously curious about what he had to add since he wasn't called in our case-in-chief.

Chappell was caught off guard with the simplicity and genuineness of Staton's story. The prosecutor's cross examination was shorter than the 3:00 p.m. chimes that could be heard ringing from the nearby train station. Staton was excused by the judge. We rested our case. After tomorrow morning's closing arguments, the case would be in the hands of Judge Day. Walter and I left the courthouse, believing we had ended our case on a high note.

Chapter 23: Pictures

Pictures

Ross's Heritage High School 1982 senior yearbook photo

Modeling photo of Ross in 1983

Just in the Nick of Time

Ross with parents in 1982/'83

Ross with Muffin in 1982/'83

Chapter 23: Pictures

Hammer used by father to strike Ross when he was a youngster

```
Mr. J.N.T.:

We have been advised by our contact at "Soldier of Fortune"
that you are interested in items we have access to.

We are located close to Denver. If you are still looking for
the items you mentioned, contact us through:

              Pat C. Clark
              P. O. Box 2648
              Littleton CO 80161

If you want to meet with us, name a date and time and location,
and we will have a representative available.

Our only stipulation would be that the meeting take place in a
shopping center parking lot. Also needed would be a way to
identify the person we are meeting (for instance, clothing and
vehicle  of person to be contacted).

Looking forward to doing business with you,



                                 Jack
                                 American Countrymen, Services Division
```

Letter in August 1982 from undercover cop to
J.N.T. (Justin Nicholas Time), who sought to buy dynamite
through *Solider of Fortune* Magazine; letter resulted in
the undercover arrest of Ross soon thereafter

Just in the Nick of Time

Mug Shot of Ross on 9/15/'82 in his dynamite case; he is 18-years-old

Page 1 of Marilyn Carlson's 4-page letter to probation department re Ross's dynamite case of September 1982

Chapter 23: Pictures

healing for about two days for the graft. At three he had many bouts with bronchitis and had many colds from which he could not seem to recover, so the doctor advised us to have allergy testing done. No specific allergies emerged so the doctor prescribed weekly shots to help him fight viruses.

From birth until Ross was two and one half, Rod and I attended night school at the University of Minnesota two nights a week. I was home with Ross all day and fed him and put him to bed before the babysitter arrived. When he was two and one half we started attending day school and I left him at a sitters (where there were no more than 2 other children) from about 8:00 a.m. until noon. I spent the afternoons playing with and reading to him and did not study until he was sleeping.

Ross started talking at about 20 months and was speaking in sentences at two. He was very verbal and everyone remarked about how bright they thought he was. When he was four he was campaigning for Hubert Humphrey. He loved books and would sit still for a long story. He had few playmates until we moved to Colorado.

When he was five we graduated from the University of Minnesota and obtained teaching positions in the Littleton Public School System. We moved to Littleton in August, 1969, and Ross started kindergarten at Centennial Elementary School.

Ross was eager to go off to school, but soon encountered difficulties. He had trouble learning the names of the letters of the alphabet out of sequence. We helped him some at home, but he was so frustrated that he backed off. The kindergarten teacher did not feel he should repeat kindergarten.

First grade was disasterous. He did not really learn to read, worked slowly and did not color neatly so he missed opportunities to do other activities that he found more motivating. After about two months he came home and said, "I either need to learn how to read smarter or talk dumber." His first grade teacher did not feel he should repeat, but did recommend summer school. He tried every trick in the book to keep from attending those six weeks. They used the same materials that he had been unsuccessful with. That same summer we bought him a miniature schnauzer. He wanted a dog so much. We still have Rag-A-Muffin who is a part of our family.

Ross was enrolled in Special Reading in second grade at Lewis Ames Elementary. He said that the kids teased him and tried to beat him up. School was not a pleasant place for him and whenever a math time test was given he would plead that he was sick and go to the office. We never

Page 2 of Marilyn Carlson's 4-page letter to probation department Re Ross's dynamite case of September 1982

heard that he was a discipline problem either until fifth grade when the teacher commented on his superior verbal ability. During this year he joined the Littleton Wrestling Club and did quite well. He was in Special Reading during fifth grade.

For his eleventh birthday at the end of fifth grade he received a set of World Book encyclopedias from us. By this time he could read and he read all summer. At the beginning of 6th grade he tested high enough in reading to get into one of the high reading groups. He was so thrilled that he called me at school and got me out of class to tell me. During the summer of sixth grade he played baseball. He was not one of the best players, but rode never concerned us. We were happy that he was participating.

During elementary school he had several friends, but not a "best" friend. We have no relatives here and most of our friends did not have children his age so I imagine it was often lonely for him.

When Ross entered junior high things seemed to be brighter for him. He liked the new bigger school and got about a 3.7 average for the first year. He was very good in P.E. We began working on our Master's Degrees, driving to Boulder daily to attend summer school at this time.

Ross had always behaved so well at home and treated us with much respect that we were troubled with the resistance he displayed in 8th grade. He maintained his grades, but was very hard to get along with. Ninth grade was better and we thought that things had evened out.

In 10th grade he began to lift weights and developed a great physic, now the girls began to call. He was only interested in the most popular and so was often disappointed. He played football in 9th and 10th grades. He was really an extra player and practiced hard, but got little playing time during a game. He decided not to play during his junior year because of this.

We were having many conflicts with him during his junior year over the car, curfew, and chores. In the spring of his junior year we had him see Dr. Foster Cline, a child psychiatrist from Evergreen. He had about five sessions with Dr. Cline and he suggested we back off and that Ross was just experiencing ordinary adolescent problems and then he discussed him.

We thought things were going well during his senior year and I was quite blue about the prospect of his leaving home. He talked of going to college, but never took the ACT TEST, or filled out applications. He maintained about a 3.75 grade point average at Heritage High School. After graduation he decided that he would attend Metropolitan State College because they did not require the test score and he could live at home where we could proofread his papers for

Page 3 of Marilyn Carlson's 4-page letter to probation department Re Ross's dynamite case of September 1982

147

Just in the Nick of Time

Page 4 of Marilyn Carlson's 4-page letter to probation department Re Ross's dynamite case of September 1982

Investigation of murder scene of the Carlson bodies on August 18, 1983

Chapter 23: Pictures

Carlson Cadillac parked in lot of Tamara Square Shopping Center allegedly by Ross after the killing of his parents on August 17, 1983

Incriminating contents of suitcase found in Carlson neighbor's bushes in September 1983

Just in the Nick of Time

KCNC-TV's six-part series, *One Man or Ten*, the murder weapon
(courtesy of KCNC TV)

Dr. Fairbairn explains purpose of videotaping to Justin
on May 10, 1984

Chapter 23: Pictures

Partial Dynamics of Ross's Switching during Dr. Fairbairn taping on May 10, 1984

The personality Steve is out after Justin switches during Dr. Fairbairn taping on May 10, 1984

Just in the Nick of Time

The personality Norman emerges after Justin switches during the Dr. Fairbairn taping on May 10, 1984

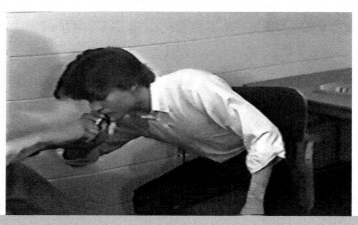

The personality Norman has borrowed a cigarette from Dr. Fairbairn during the taping on May 10, 1984

Chapter 23: Pictures

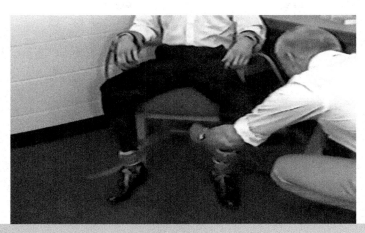

Restraints are being applied by Dr. Fairbairn to the personality Steve in anticipation of the emergence of the personality Black during Dr. Fairbairn's taping on May 10, 1984

The Sobbing Blue personality is "out" before the personality Black emerges during the Dr. Fairbairn taping on May 10, 1984

Just in the Nick of Time

The personality Black emerges and begins to free himself from the restraints applied by Dr. Fairbain on May 10, 1984

The personality Black has freed himself from restraints applied by Dr. Fairbairn on May 10, 1984

Chapter 23: Pictures

Dr. Fisch Hypnotizes the personality Justin during the doctor's videotaped interview on May 19, 1984

Just in the Nick of Time

While hypnotized, the personality Justin recounts murder scene during Dr. Fisch's taped interview on May 19, 1984

The personality Justin is Hypnotized by Dr. Newton during the doctor's taped interview on June 2, 1984

Chapter 23: Pictures

While hypnotized, the personality Justin switches to another personality, presumably Black, during Dr. Newton's taping on June 4, 1984

Dr. Martin Orne begins taped interview on April 17, 1988 with Ross, who has slipped into a sleep-like state

Just in the Nick of Time

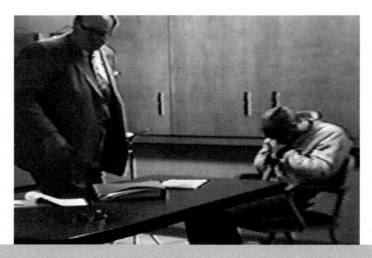

Dr. Martin Orne concludes AM session with Ross on April 17, 1988 because he remained in a sleep-like trance state the entire time

Dr. Michael Weissberg notes the time on April 17, 1988 when the morning session of the taped interview conducted by him and Dr. Orne of Ross has concluded

Chapter 23: Pictures

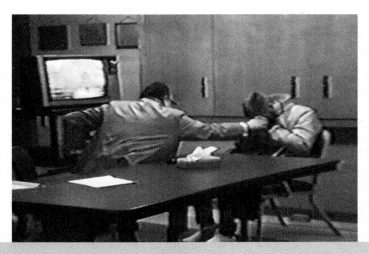

Dr. Martin Orne, during the PM Session of April 17, 1988, seeks to remove Ross's hands from his eyes

Fearing the personality Black had emerged after awakening the sleeping personality by trying to remove Ross's hands from his eyes, Dr. Martin Orne pulls back instinctively during the PM session on April 17, 1988

Just in the Nick of Time

KCNC-TV's six-part series, *One Man or Ten*, the ten different personalities of Ross Carlson (courtesy of KCNC TV)

Chapter 23: Pictures

Courtroom artist's sketch of David Savitz examining Dr. Fairbairn during competency hearing in June 1984 before Judge Day

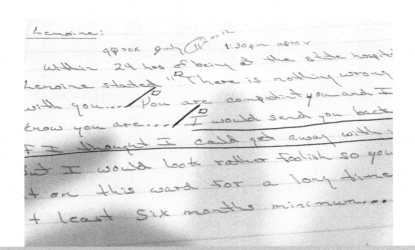

Top page of Ross's notes of his interview by Dr. Edward Lemoine 24 hours after Ross's arrival at Colorado State Hospital for treatment in July 1984, after having been found incompetent to proceed the previous month by Judge Day

Just in the Nick of Time

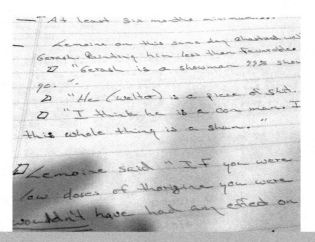

Bottom page of Ross's notes of his interview by Dr. Edward Lemoine, 24 hours after Ross's arrival at Colorado State Hospital for treatment in July 1984, after having been found incompetent to proceed the previous month by Judge Day

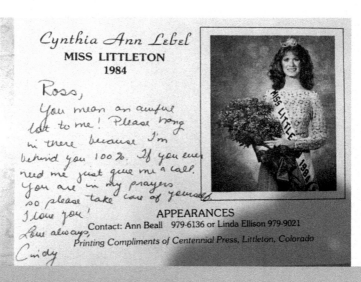

A photo and inscription by Cindy Lebel sent by her to Ross in 1984

Chapter 23: Pictures

Outside of one of the Christmas cards sent by one of Ross's personalities to David Savitz in 1985

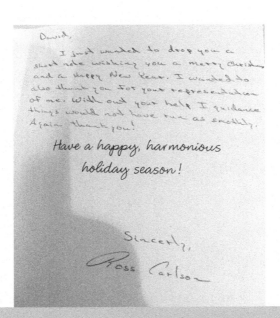

Written contents within the inside of the Christmas card that one personality sent to David Savitz in 1985

Just in the Nick of Time

Outside of the second of the two Christmas cards sent in 1985 to David Savitz by another of Ross's personalities

With warmest wishes for the holidays and the coming year!

Ross Carlson

Written message of the inside of the Christmas card sent in 1985 to David Savitz by another of Ross's personalities

Chapter 23: Pictures

Gift of Brian Davis Poster of White Iris sent by Ross to David Savitz shortly after David's wedding on December 13, 1987

The full Colorado Supreme Court (1975). Justice Edward C. Day is seated at the front left. Photo Credit: Paul Abdoo

Just in the Nick of Time

Honorable Robert Kingsley (courtesy of KCNC-TV)

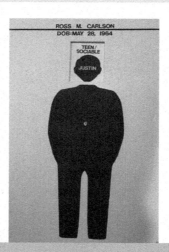

Demonstrative exhibit used by Ross's lawyers during September 1987 competency hearing before Judge Kingsley

Chapter 23: Pictures

ROSS M. CARLSON

ROSS	→ ORIGINAL PERSONALITY
JUSTIN	→ TEEN - SOCIABLE
STEVE	→ 42 YEARS - ORGANIZER
MICHAEL	→ TEEN - BOISTEROUS
STACEY	→ THE ATHLETE
BLUE	→ WEEPY CHILD
GRAY	→ TEEN - DEPRESSED
NORMAN	→ STREET PUNK
BLACK	THE PROTECTOR
HOLDIN	> THE PATIENT

Demonstrative exhibit used by Ross's lawyers during September 1987 competency hearing before Judge Kingsley

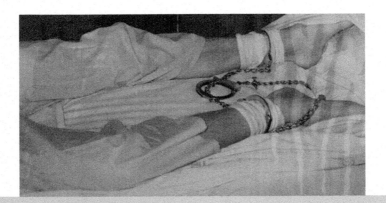

Ross's legs shackled to his bed at University Hospital after his attempted suicide there in late November 1989

Just in the Nick of Time

Dr. Michael Weissberg interviewed in February 1990 (courtesy of KCNC-TV)

Walter Gerash, Ross's senior counsel, interviewed in February 1990 (courtesy of KCNC-TV)

Chapter 23: Pictures

Deputy District Attorney Robert Chappell, state's lead prosecutor, interviewed in February 1990 (courtesy of KCNC-TV)

Dollygirl-sister raises her younger brother Butchie in 1946 before he pulls off the chocolate milk caper a year later

Just in the Nick of Time

David Savitz, his wife Robin, and their children Curtis, Rachel, and Kristin taken at Rachel's Bat Mitzvah on December 12, 1987

David's parents, Sam and Isabelle Savitz, taken at David and Robin's wedding on December 13, 1987

Chapter 23: Pictures

David and Robin with Carl and Marsha Scheer taken on wedding day December 13, 1987

Guests from Ross's case, who attended Kristin's Bat Mitzvah in July 1989, included Walter Gerash (top far left), Fig Newton (top middle with glasses) and Ralph Fisch (bottom left) (the couple between Walter Gerash and Fig Newton is David Savitz's principal editor for this manuscript, Vivian Epstein, and her husband Ted)

Just in the Nick of Time

Dr. Marvin Schwarz and his wife Kathy in 1986/'87

David and his three siblings: Carol, Edward, and Jack, at a family event in 2015

David Savitz, age 76, Walter Gerash, age 92, and former Carlson investigator Tony DiVirgilio on June 19, 2019

PART 3

CHAPTER 24

Judge Day's Decision

After closing arguments, Judge Day wanted the balance of the day to consider his decision, so he recessed court until the next morning. As usual, Ross asked that Walter and I stay after everyone else left so we could talk. The sheriffs afforded us our customary privacy in the jury room adjacent to the courtroom. One deputy sheriff sat outside our private domain with the door slightly ajar for security purposes.

"Gentlemen, thank you both for your effort," Ross said matter-of-factly. "Walter, that was an excellent closing argument. The judge seemed to listen very carefully. David, yours was a little dry, but you laid out the facts accurately and logically."

"Thanks, I guess," rationalizing that it was probably my client's Siskel personality that gave Walter an enthusiastic thumbs up and his Ebert part, a horizontal thumb to me. In my view, if one personality had sat through both closings, I surely would have received a much better grade. After receiving our scores, Walter and I then left, wishing Ross good luck in tomorrow's ruling.

When I returned to court the next morning, the courtroom clerk directed me to the hallway outside the judge's chambers. Walter greeted me warmly by the arm and whispered in my ear. "David, the judge found him incompetent. He just told me and Chappell." I muffled my excitement so as not embarrass my adversary who was standing a few feet away. The door was open to the judge's chambers; Judge Day was seated at his desk and writing on his legal pad. After a few moments, he signaled for us to go into court.

The press remained seated in the jury box, poised with their spiral notebooks and sketch pads. The television reporters had their camera cohorts assembled in the hallway waiting to capture some pearls of wisdom from the victors and a likely curt "no comment" from the losers. After Ross was escorted into the courtroom and sat at the defense table, Walter shared the good news with him. Ross responded with an insipid, "Thank you."

Initially, I was taken aback by Ross's unemotional response but then realized that the response was likely reflective of the particular alter personality to whom Walter was speaking. In this case, it was probably the 42-year-old, serious, intellectual, Steve, who would have been in charge of listening to and trying to make sense out of the court proceedings.

Ross then turned his attention to the back of the courtroom and caught the eyes of Mary and Jo Guess, a couple who had befriended him several months ago and remained steadfast in their support ever since. Everyone rose as the judge, carrying a yellow legal pad in his right hand, entered the courtroom.

Judge Day's decision was an overwhelming endorsement of our evidence and strategies. He talked about the vast experience of our experts and their convincing testimony versus the incredulous suggestions of malingering and manipulation raised by the prosecution's witnesses. He mentioned Dr. Wilets's utterance, after being advised of the murders, that Ross must be a multiple. He found that the testimony from Ross's lawyers was "essential and as reliable as the psychiatric evaluations" and persuaded him that Ross would ". . . not be able to participate fully or assist his counsel in his defense." Finally, the numerous pre-homicidal instances of "memory and time loss" testified to by classmates and neighbors, especially the

Chapter 24: Judge Day's Decision

Randy Staton incident, reflected classical textbook amnesia, establishing convincingly that Ross's illness existed before the murders.

While the judge read his decision, I felt enormous satisfaction. Walter and I had accomplished something good for a very ill, young man. I was hopeful that with treatment, Ross could live the remainder of his life without the psychological manacles of MPD. Ross, however, did not share those same dreams.

When we met with him afterwards in the jury room, there was no smile on his face, just a look of resignation. I thought he would be jumping through the roof, but again reminded myself: that's not what Steve is all about.

By prevailing in this hearing, we had delayed a sanity trial indefinitely where the result may have been disastrous. Ross now was afforded an opportunity for treatment where he could become an integrated person, and we, in turn, could learn about the horrors of his childhood. Our chances in a future sanity trial would thus be immensely improved. "What's wrong, Ross?"

"David, the state hospital will never treat me."

"Ross, we'll make sure the people who examined you during your competency evaluation, such as Norma Livingston, are not involved in your treatment. Let's try and see how it goes."

An indelible look of doubt permeated Ross's face as he was led away by the sheriffs.

CHAPTER 25

The Nightmare Begins

On October 19, 1984, my reliable GE clock radio awakened me at 6:00 a.m. just in time for the news. "Well, KHOW listeners, get out your shovels and put on those snow tires. An early winter has again arrived in the Rockies." I parted my bedroom window curtains and saw that my neighborhood was a blanket of fresh snow. There were no tire tracks visible on my cul-de-sac, which meant the paper boy had not yet made his rounds. His delay and the steady fall of white flakes did not portend an easy drive to court. If the weather was worse south of the metro area and all the way to Castle Rock, then this morning's hearing might be canceled. An hour later the phone rang. I had just finished adjusting the knot on my dark-blue tie and, knowing what suit jacket and silk pocket square were about to complete the finished ensemble, anticipated the overall feeling of a very tasteful GQ look.

"Dave, this is Judge Day."

"Good morning, your Honor," I replied, hiding my surprise at the 7:00 a.m. phone call.

"Dave, it looks like the weatherman was right. We're having one of those early fall snow storms. We have the hearing this morning, and, at my age, I don't think I can drive the thirty or so miles to Castle Rock in these conditions. You've subpoenaed Dr. Traylor and all of those people from the state hospital; they're probably already on their way from Pueblo. There's no way I can reach Pat Robb and everyone else now to stop their travels. I'd like to ride with you so we don't have to cancel the hearing."

Chapter 25: The Nightmare Begins

"That's fine, judge," I stated, while loosening my tie to facilitate the downward path of the lump in my throat. I felt uncomfortable about riding alone with Judge Day since a sacrosanct rule of ethics is for lawyers to avoid one-sided communications with the judge involved in their case. Even the appearance of impropriety is frowned upon. So, even though there would be no conversation with Judge Day about the case, his mere presence in my car would be viewed with suspicion. Since he was a former Colorado Supreme Court judge, I was confident he knew these rules, but I still felt uneasy, notwithstanding the significance of the hearing.

At 10:00 that morning his Honor was scheduled to hear the defense's request for contempt citations against a slew of hospital big wigs, including its superintendent, Dr. Haydee Kort. I had also subpoenaed Kort's boss, Dr. Frank Traylor, the executive director of the Colorado Department of Institutions. However, since the judge saw no problem with us carpooling, I arranged to pick him up since he was the one who initiated the contact. After I hung up, I immediately called Walter.

"Walter, I'm obviously not going to tell Day, 'No, your Honor, you need to take a cab to Castle Rock even though I live just a few blocks from you and have a car with front wheel drive'!"

"Well, I understand you'll be uptight, but the judge knows he can't discuss the case with you. At his age, he can't drive in these conditions. Plus, he's right; there is no way of contacting all of the witnesses now."

I was only slightly relieved by Walter's approval, and felt I was in store for the longest 30-mile drive of my career. To my relief, however, Judge Day made the hour-long trip whiz by. We discussed a variety of topics as far removed from the case and the law as Castle Rock was from my home.

When we finally arrived at the courthouse, I parked directly in front to avoid being accused of some sleight of hand. It just so happened that the DA's investigator, Bryan Bevis, entered the courthouse as the judge and I exited my car.

On my way to the courtroom, I thought about the evidence we were about to present that morning.

More than three months had elapsed since Judge Day signed the four-page Order of Commitment on July 10. On that day, the hospital's in-house attorney, Pat Robb offered no additions or deletions to the Order and stated, "We have no objection to it."

The Order stated that Ross was to receive "care and psychiatric treatment" for MPD and set forth an established procedure for treatment of the illness. No one from the hospital, who had examined Ross before the competency hearing, was to play any subsequent role in his treatment.

In the three months since Pat Robb's comments to Judge Day, not one millisecond of treatment for MPD had been provided Ross. His primary therapist was a registered nurse whose treatment was limited to checking Ross's pulse and blood pressure. Ross also received abundant doses of ridicule and disdain from certain hospital personnel.

Dr. Edward Lemoine, the Clinical Administrator of the admissions ward, was one of the first people to greet Ross when he arrived at the hospital. I shook my head in disbelief when Ross called me and regurgitated Lemoine's opening comments at their first meeting.

"Carlson, unless you want to stay here for the rest of your life, forget about MPD," Ross reported as Lemoine's opening salvo, and then continued. "I've known that blowhard Gerash for a long time. He's one half show and the other half BS. I know he cooked up that MPD defense. If I had my way, I'd declare you competent right now, but the judge would think I was a fool. I'll wait six months and then certify you as competent."

"Wait, David, that's not the best part," Ross forewarned.

To make Ross's return to the hospital an even better homecoming, none other than double-dribbling Norma Livingston participated in his first intake session. I mollified my anger at her participation and instead chose patience while Ross and I talked further.

"Ross, I know the hospital broke its promise not to have Livingston involved. You've just been there a day. Let's be a little more patient."

Chapter 25: The Nightmare Begins

"Okay, David, but I know these people."

I obviously didn't. Instead of treating Ross for MPD, the hospital spent the next eight weeks diagnosing him. The irony is that if an uninitiated outsider read the various diagnoses made by the hospital personnel of Ross since his arrival, one would have thought that several different patients had been evaluated. On July 10, 1984, the admitting hospital doctor wrote that Ross suffered from an atypical psychosis. On August 30, 1984, the hospital's Chief of Psychiatry, Dr. Robert Huffaker, believed Ross suffered from a mixed personality disorder (the same finding made by Dr. Alan Fine nine months before). On September 12, 1984, a staff psychiatrist felt that paranoid personality disorder was the source of Ross's troubles. It took an outside consultant from Denver, the well-regarded psychiatrist Dr. Jeff Metzner, to finally enlighten the hospital of what they were seeing right in front of their eyes.

We knew Jeff and were quite familiar with his résumé. We had retained him when we attacked the sanity statute last spring before Judge Turelli. Jeff had not met Ross then, nor had we spoken to the doctor since. Independent of our prior utilization of Dr. Metzner on the legal issue of sanity, the hospital obviously felt Jeff could also be objective on the issue of Ross's psychiatric treatment. On September 17, 1984, after an extensive review of materials and several interviews with Ross, Jeff reported that he had no reason to disagree with Judge Day's conclusions and Order of July 10, 1984.

Jeff stated it was vitally important that a skilled clinician treat Ross and that the therapist "makes the assumption that Ross is indeed suffering from a multiple personality disorder" and "not take an adversarial position regarding the diagnosis." Metzner further emphasized that "the most important factor in establishing alliance with Mr. Carlson is listening to him and taking a very nonjudgmental approach."

Talking to a wall would have netted a better result. The hospital, taking its cue from Dr. Lemoine's animus toward Walter and the variegated diagnoses from its first wave of physicians, ignored Dr. Metzner's recommendations and appeared to have discarded them in the nearest trash can.

As Walter and I learned about each of these events from Ross and read the numerous hospital reports, which we received routinely during the first several weeks of Ross's hospitalization, we became more and more incensed. Walter's response to Lemoine's comments was unprintable.

Our patience exhausted, we had filed a motion to have the hospital hierarchy held in contempt for their disregard of the Court's July 10th Order. Judge Day was to hear the hospital's explanation today, October 19, 1984.

Appearing mildly contrite during the hearing, the hospital hierarchy assured the judge that positive strides were just around the corner. The hospital staff was doing all they could in this very complex case, the judge was told. Neither Dr. Lemoine nor Norma Livingston, the hospital now assured Judge Day, would be involved in Ross's treatment. In addition, Dr. Lemoine would be cautioned about his intemperate remarks. Despite our pleas for some kind of punitive sanction, such as a brief contemplative period in jail, the judge refused to hold anyone in contempt.

During that afternoon's drive home with the judge, I was half relieved that Walter and I had come in second that day. At least no one could say that my ferrying his Honor to court had influenced the hearing's outcome.

Ross's outlook for positive care soon improved. As a result of his completion of a battery of psychological tests, the hospital's neuropsychologist, Dr. Gregory Trautt, found definite evidence of MPD and no hint of malingering. As far as treatment, Dr. Trautt wrote "the primary therapist should pay special attention to behavioral changes" and "should respond to him (Ross) in a supportive and reflective fashion." The hospital then assigned Dr. Trautt as Ross's primary therapist and its chief psychiatrist, Dr. Huffaker, as responsible for his overall treatment.

Walter and I finally became optimistic. Successful treatment would result in an abreaction of memories and uncovering of the incidents of abuse, all of which could be shared with a jury during the next stage of the case — the sanity trial. Moreover, the integration of Ross's mind would enable him to assist and cooperate with us in that trial. If he were declared insane, the yeoman's work of treatment

Chapter 25: The Nightmare Begins

would have already occurred and the remaining treatment necessary to restore him to sanity would hopefully be short.

On October 22, 1984, Ross began treatment. During the next few weeks, the treatment team observed at least three episodes of Ross dissociating and the emergence of different personalities. On October 31, 1984, Dr. Huffaker made it official — he formally diagnosed Ross Carlson as suffering from multiple personality disorder. It was the first time in its long history as evaluator and treatment provider for the Colorado court system that the Colorado State Hospital had ever made that diagnosis in a forensic setting. Dr. Huffaker believed it would take about two years to restore Ross to competency.

During November, Dr. Trautt observed incidents of Ross's forgetfulness similar to those that Walter and I had confronted. The doctor's notes of November 2, 1984, revealed one such example:

In the morning, he presented himself as a cool and very rational mature adult. His language, for the most part, was grammatically correct, and he used a high level of vocabulary. In the afternoon, the patient presented himself in a more adolescent fashion. His language was frequently grammatically incorrect, and he used a number of cuss words. Further, he appeared not to have any recollection concerning the morning session.

Toward the end of November 1984, Ross allowed Dr. Huffaker to hypnotize him on two occasions. By submitting to hypnosis, Ross added another solid layer to the essential foundation of therapeutic trust. Suddenly, however, that foundation turned to sand and toppled at the feet of Drs. Huffaker and Trautt. The prosecutors were strongly to blame for this collapse.

The DAs, still feeling the pangs of their competency defeat and the resultant barrage of press criticism, deployed their intrepid investigator, Bryan Bevis, to pursue another round of investigation. Bevis's mission was to interview members of the Carlson family in Minnesota and their friends and neighbors in Colorado to dispel the black cloud of abuse which now draped the Carlsons' tombstones. The Bevis interviews produced a mixed bag of information, but they did contain one recurring theme to which the prosecutors attached great significance.

Several individuals described the Carlsons as "too perfect" and Rod Carlson as a "stern taskmaster." Most friends noticed that neither parent seemed to interact much with Ross. A few neighbors had seen Ross practice karate in his back yard, but others never did. Some people said Ross always appeared to act his age, while others thought he acted older. Rod and Marilyn's best friends portrayed them as hard-working, church-going, and loving parents. Ross, on the other hand, was often pictured by these same people as spoiled and lazy. Despite these differences, one common thread permeated the statements: no one had ever seen the Carlsons abuse Ross emotionally or physically.

Why did that theme of no public display of abuse not surprise us? After all, wasn't it *de rigueur* for middle class people to beat their kids publicly so social services could be called and cart the young ones off to a foster home? Even a high schooler knows that abuse occurs predominantly within the hidden confines of one's home. And why was there no mention of sexual abuse in Bevis's reports? Did he not ask about it? Did he even know what to ask, and, if so, did he think a perpetrator would have excitedly come forward and told a family member, friend, or neighbor, "Say, let me tell you about the times I sexually molested Ross when he was a youngster." Did Bevis not know that in the 1960s and 1970s, the period of Ross's youth, that people committed unspeakable things against little boys? Or, again, was that not the kind of conduct that perpetrators admitted to their loved ones or best buddies?

In any event, Chappell packaged these statements and shipped them off to Dr. Huffaker in mid-December 1984, ostensibly to "assist in the evaluation and treatment of Ross Carlson." Then, in an act of therapeutic suicide and gross naiveté, and on the sole basis of the DA's discovery, Huffaker and Trautt challenged Ross at a treatment session, insisting that he recite chapter and verse of incidents of abuse. When Ross refused such an outrageous request since he was merely in the early stages of establishing a bond with each of these physicians, the doctors raised "major doubts" about his suffering from MPD. Confronted yet with new skepticism, this time by his own therapy team and their obvious lack of psychiatric sophistication, Ross had enough.

Chapter 25: The Nightmare Begins

In January 1985, he withdrew from treatment, and vowed never again to have anything to do with the hospital.

With its selfish act of egoism, the prosecution had presented Ross's caregivers with a dagger which they used to carve the heart out of the trust and rapport essential to the therapist-patient relationship. Three months of progress had been flushed down the toilet. Judge Day's Order was now a limp piece of parchment because of the hospital's ignorance and arrogance.

Meanwhile, Ross was content to wait out the hospital until a solution could be found. His dreary existence brightened, however, when a special person from the past unexpectedly re-entered his life.

CHAPTER 26

A Gentle and Perfect Beginning

For nearly a year and a half since the Carlsons' deaths on August 17, 1983, Kelli Olson and Ross did not know how to contact one another. That changed, however, when Kelli spent her Christmas break in 1984 visiting friends in Colorado and ran into Suzanne Keller. After receiving Ross's phone number from Suzanne's dad, Jack, who by then had been serving as Ross's conservator for more than a year, the 16-year-old Kelli quit staring at the number and finally mustered enough nerve to dial the state hospital.

"Hi, I was expecting your call," Ross said upon learning who it was. "It's nice to hear from you. How are you?"

Kelli loved hearing Ross's voice. She had to see him and asked if he could list her as an approved hospital guest. Of course he would; he'd let her know in a couple of days when she could visit. Kelli broke out into a huge smile as she hung up the receiver. She leaned back in her chair and thought back to October 1982.

As a high-school freshman, Kelli Olson's crush on 18-year-old Ross Carlson had become an obsession even though the two had never met. For the last month, Kelli couldn't take her eyes off Ross whenever he would show up at the local skating rink. Kelli's girlfriends consoled her, "Don't worry if he pays no attention to you — he has an identical twin brother named Justin." Kelli knew nothing about Justin, had never met him, and, as far as she was concerned, her friends could chase Justin. She wanted to meet Ross. Her lucky day arrived on October 8, 1982.

Chapter 26: A Gentle and Perfect Beginning

That morning, Kelli sat at her school desk, waiting for typing class to begin.

"Hi Kelli," her girlfriend Suzanne Keller said with a smile as wide as Kelli's IBM Selectric keyboard. "Guess who I talked to last night about you?" Zan said, teasingly.

"Ross!" Kelli responded, excited at the mere mention of his name. "What did he say? Tell me everything," she insisted.

"Well, the most important thing is he wants to meet you tonight at the skating rink."

"Oh my God!" Kelli exclaimed. Dreams do come true, she thought to herself. She gave Zan a big hug.

The next several hours of school took forever. The 2:05 p.m. bell finally rang. Kelli bolted out of her homeroom and hightailed it to the school bus. By the time she arrived home, she would have less than three hours to get ready. Life was not kind to a 14-year-old!

It was a beeline to the shower and then the most important decision of the evening. What should she wear? What was his favorite color? "Oh, why didn't Zan ask him what color he liked?" Kelli cried out loud. "Stay cool! Pick out something plain and simple," she told herself. The winning combination — jeans and a pale-blue sweater. Boy, it was hot in her room, she thought, as she fanned herself with her right hand. The five-minute drive to the roller rink would cool her down, she hoped. It was time to go.

"Mom, hurry! Let's go! I can't be late." Kelli's dutiful parent, Mary Croce, obeyed, transporting her daughter to the rink with nary a word from the normally loquacious teenager. Kelli had decided that even the most bland parent-child conversation would undoubtedly result in a delay to her rendezvous. She could not take the risk. "Thanks mom. See you later."

Kelli scurried from the car and headed toward the rink's entrance at 5:45 p.m. She knew Ross would no longer just be a fantasy by the time her mom returned at 11:30 to take her home.

The local roller rink was a teenage hang out. Even kids who had already graduated from high school found themselves lacing up their skates on Friday night. First-year high schooler Kelli felt mature beyond her years, and a college freshman like Ross would certainly agree.

Just in the Nick of Time

Kelli had been hanging out with her friends for about an hour when Tim, the DJ, announced it was time for a "couples skate." After the announcement, Tim skated to Kelli and said, "A tall, blond-haired and blue-eyed stranger is going to come over real soon."

"Oh, my God! You're kidding," Kelli screeched, her cries muffled by the rink's blaring music. Within seconds, a short guy with dark hair and brown eyes tapped Kelli on the shoulder. "Would you like to dance?" he asked. "Of course not, you dork; I'm expecting someone else," she was tempted to blurt out. However, she resisted the urge; she was raised better than that.

Unexpectedly, the second worst thing in the world then happened. Kelli and her dance partner skated right past Ross. "Oh, no," she said to herself. "He's going to think I'm with this guy." Kelli's life had just gone to hell. Within a few minutes, the dance with the interloper ended.

Two more excruciatingly long hours passed, and still there had been no appearance by a golden-haired prince with piercing-blue eyes. It was now after 9:00 p.m.; Kelli was talking to her friend Michelle O'Hagan. The 11:30 curfew was just two plus hours away.

Suddenly, Kelli's pulse quickened. Her palms began to perspire. The rink quickly felt awfully warm. Kelli noticed Ross skating toward her. She was standing with some girlfriends. She acted nonchalant as if she had not seen the approaching knight. Her peripheral vision, however, locked onto him. Ross drew closer and closer.

The ballad "Love Rules" filled the rink — that was no accident. Kelli had asked Tim to play it; she knew the song was one of Ross's favorites. Just two more roller glides, and he would be there. "Excuse me young ladies," Ross said politely. Looking directly at Kelli, he asked, "Would you like to skate?" Kelli's heart launched into a spirited palpation.

What are you kidding? Why do you think I sprinted home from the bus stop, arrived at the rink 15 minutes before it opened, wore my favorite sweater, arranged for your favorite song, and made sure no other male was within 100 yards of me? Who do you think I've been waiting for all night? Of course, I want to skate! However, now was not the time for brutal honesty, Kelli decided. Instead, she took a deep breath and casually replied, "Sure."

Chapter 26: A Gentle and Perfect Beginning

The rest of the evening was a blur — Ross and Kelli talked effortlessly as they skated, smiled, and laughed until 11:30. When they said good night, Ross asked for Kelli's phone number. In return, he handed her a business card. Centered in bold green letters were the words: **ROSS ENTERPRISES**. An address and phone number were printed in the corner. Such class, she thought.

Ross called Kelli every day the following week, but that was hardly enough. She wanted to be **with** Ross. Her wish came true on a Friday night when she and Ross had arranged to meet at the rink. After the two skated for a while, Ross said, "Kelli, I was wondering." He sounded so serious, Kelli thought. "Would you like to go somewhere and have a nice bottle of champagne?" Ross asked.

"Sure, that sounds like fun," the 14-year-old said in a gargantuan understatement. Kelli had never tasted champagne in her life, but who cared. She had seen enough movies and had heard enough adult conversations to know about the specialness of the drink with bubbles served in those cool-looking glasses. Ross could have asked if she wanted to go share a coke; the answer would have been the same.

The two drove from the rink in Ross's dark-blue Cutlass and parked on a ridge overlooking the city of Littleton. A full moon punctuated the sky while the city's lights flickered below. A mild breeze rustled the nearby trees. Ross made sure that soft music played from his car radio. He retrieved a bottle from the back seat, popped the cork, and toasted Kelli and their second Friday together. They began talking about one another's background. Kelli was dying to know more about Ross's twin brother, Justin, whom she understood lived out of town.

"Justin used to hit me a lot when we were kids," Ross explained somberly. "Because he was so mean, my parents sent him to Phoenix to live with our aunt. While living there, he changed his name to "Justin Nicholas Time." "He's a junior in high school now," Ross said. "Wait a minute," Kelli said, surprised. "How could he be in high school and you in college if you're twins?" Ross quickly answered, "I skipped kindergarten and first grade because, according to my parents, I was smarter than the rest of the kids. You see, they're teachers and were always teaching me things."

"Well, that would make you sixteen," Kelli said in disbelief since

Ross looked much older. Sixteen! This was fine with Kelli. Her parents couldn't object to her dating a boy only two years older, especially someone who was obviously an intellectual prodigy.

During the next few weeks, it seemed the only words Kelli spoke to her mom and stepdad were "Ross, Ross, Ross." As responsible parents, Rose Mary and Richard Croce imposed a curfew and insisted upon knowing Kelli's whereabouts at night. However, an 11:30 p.m. curfew was an unreasonable restriction on blooming love. As a result, Kelli utilized the classic staying-overnight-at-a-friend's-house ploy in order to generously expand her curfew and places of rendezvous with Ross.

On the Friday eve of Halloween weekend, Kelli was allowed to sleep at Jenny Barnett's house. Kelli, however, conveniently failed to inform her folks that Jenny's parents were away for the weekend. Coincidentally, Rod and Marilyn Carlson were also out of town. What a fortuitous set of circumstances! How would Ross and Kelli handle such serendipity?

Ross picked Kelli up at 8:00 p.m., and remarkably, another coincidence — Kelli was wearing the same color top as Ross. He had on a pink oxford shirt, and she, a pink polo sweater. By now, she had discovered his favorite colors; if only she had studied so hard in school!

Not wanting his parents' car to sit idly while they were away, Ross arrived in his folks' blue Cadillac Seville. "Yes, it's gorgeous," Kelli agreed, looking at the car but referring to someone else. "Italian sounds great," she said as Ross sought her approval for the evening's menu. He then drove to his house.

CHAPTER 27

Connecting as One

As Ross and Kelli entered the Carlson home, a small, gray Schnauzer eagerly rushed to Ross and was immediately grabbed and hugged by his master who, in turn, was licked feverishly. Muffin was Ross's companion and his pride and joy. Ross spoke about this furry, pointed-eared animal more than he did anyone else in his family. Indeed, it surprised Kelli that Ross rarely, if ever, mentioned his folks. However, she didn't press him.

"Sure, I'll have a glass of wine," Kelli said, having, before the date, quickly read about this beverage and learning that it too was made from grapes but that it came without bubbles. After filling Kelli's glass, Ross escorted her to the dining room.

Ross had outdone himself. The Carlson family china and gold silverware glistened against the dimmed lighting, regally awaiting the evening's fare. Always the gentleman, Ross steadied Kelli's chair as she sat. He then excused himself to the kitchen. Kelli couldn't imagine what array of delights was about to emerge.

Within minutes, Ross reappeared, carrying a large round tray. Kelli smelled one of her favorite aromas — melted cheese. Ross set down a piping-hot, pepperoni pizza an arm's reach away from Kelli. What 14-year-old would not consider this the perfect meal!

Just as dinner ended, a phone call interrupted the mood. It was Jenny, checking on her about-to-bust-curfew house guest. Kelli couldn't concentrate on the call because Ross was concentrating on the crease of her neck just below her ear. His kisses were soft. And she felt warm as a result.

"Jenny, I can't talk now. I'll call you later." Kelli hung up; she had little choice. Ross was leading her by the hand toward the stairs and up to the second floor. They entered his bedroom. It was surprisingly dull looking.

Kelli had expected something like mirrored walls and a chrome bed. Instead, a bed with a double mattress, covered by a simple, brown comforter, was bracketed by night stands at each side of the bed. There were no wall coverings, not even posters or pictures to serve as colorful accents to the room. The room's one highlight was a fancy stereo system situated within a vertically-tiered, front-opened cabinet. Scores of records were stacked diagonally under the turntable. Music from the expensive speakers filled the room. Overall, however, the space certainly didn't look like any teenager's bedroom Kelli had ever seen.

"Please make yourself at home," Ross said, motioning for Kelli to sit on his bed. He proceeded to select additional records. "Will you play *Take Me to The Top*?" Kelli asked.

"I think I can do that for you," he said, while lowering the volume. Having arranged the order of his music to be played, Ross sat down next to Kelli and continued what he had started downstairs. Like that first Friday evening in his car, his kisses were long and tender. Although she enjoyed the romance, she started to become nervous. She was in an environment conducive to more than just kissing. Ross reached toward the nightstand and turned off the lamp. The room went dark except for the small light of the stereo.

Ross took off his shirt, revealing a smooth, muscular upper body. Kelli began to tremble. Was she getting involved in something that might go too far? Ross took her in his arms and held her tightly. She felt so secure. He slowly raised her off the bed. They stood embracing.

Ross unbuttoned Kelli's blouse and removed her bra. She was determined not to allow this to go any further. Ross didn't even try. He merely guided them both back onto his bed.

The two lay down holding each other, ensuring that no one could pull them apart. Kelli prayed that the special feeling would never go away. "I was so happy. I could have stayed in his arms forever," she remembered. That evening, however, was merely the beginning.

Their relationship grew even stronger during the balance of

Chapter 27: Connecting as One

1982. Kelli had never experienced a better three months of adoration and kindness from anyone.

January 1983 then arrived. Later that month on a Friday when Kelli had no school, Ross picked her up around 9:00 a.m. and drove to his home. Ross's parents were teaching and wouldn't return until late afternoon. After spending a couple of hours in his living room, Ross turned to Kelli and said, "I'm tired of talking. Would you like to go upstairs?" Kelli agreed.

Ross sat on his bed, leaned up against the headboard and stretched out his legs. He scooted over to the center, making room for Kelli. She sat on her knees facing him. The two smiled at one another. He broke their brief silence.

"Well, you have a choice of what to do," he said. "Well, we can (a) eat lunch; (b) I can teach you how to drive; (c) We can make love; or (d) all of the above."

Kelli had known this day might arrive. Ross had not rushed their physical relationship. Kelli had insisted they take it slowly. Ross respected her wishes. He knew Kelli's ideal was to marry as a virgin. Kelli desired Ross and didn't know if she'd ever feel this way again. Some of her friends had gone all the way. She and Ross were in love. He made her feel like no one else did. She had made her decision.

"Well, all of the above."

"Really?"

"Yes."

"Would you mind pulling the shades down please?"

Kelli got up from the bed and closed the curtains. Ross pulled the brown comforter down to the midway point of the bed. "I'm embarrassed," Kelli said.

"Why?" Ross asked, while removing his shirt.

"Well, because I've never done this before, and ... I'm just embarrassed."

Ross held Kelli and began to remove her sweater, but it was fastened at the back by a pearl button. "Now, let me just turn you around so I don't tear anything," he said while turning her so her back was facing him.

He pushed away her long, brown hair until he undid the pearl

191

button of her sweater. After removing her sweater, he turned her again to face him. He plied her with soft kisses while navigating his hands freely and gently. She tensed as he touched her bare chest. She exhaled deeply and tried to relax.

Ross continued kissing her. He removed his pants and then knelt down and slowly removed Kelli's jeans while intermittently kissing her stomach and below her navel. She felt herself becoming more and more tense; she wrapped her arms around his head and pulled him upwards so they could kiss again. The two were wrapped within one another's arms. It was the first time Kelli had ever allowed herself in this situation. They got into bed and lay side by side. Ross pulled the comforter forward to cover their backs. He draped his left hand over Kelli's back. He began kissing her neck, then her shoulders, and next gave equal attention to the balance of her upper body. She closed her eyes and felt the warmth of his light touches. He turned his head to the right; she peeked and followed his right hand as it moved to the drawer of his nightstand where he retrieved some protection. She closed her eyes again. Her body began to tingle and shiver. Her goose bumps had goose bumps. She had dreamed about this moment; it was now real. She had found her love.

Ross pulled the comforter down to the foot of the bed and positioned himself on top of Kelli. Her mind and body throbbed with warmth and passion; it masked her brief pain. The two lovers connected as one. She did not want him to stop.

The next hour or so passed as though it were a fleeting moment. The two lay in bed tucked within one another's arms and covered by the comforter. The music had played in the background as Ross's record albums flipped onto the turntable from one to the next. His eyes were closed as Kelli rubbed her hand over his chest. Her finger touched his lips, and she leaned over to kiss him. He awakened and smiled. They kissed again. "Shall we get dressed and have some lunch?" he asked. That sounded good to her. What a wonderful way to start the new year!

The next few months were a roller coaster of events. At times, Ross was cheerful and happy, but during other times, he seemed so different. Kelli was confused.

Chapter 27: Connecting as One

One time, they were supposed to meet at the rink, and Ross didn't show. As soon as Kelli felt they were becoming closer, Ross would do something to avoid the next step. Sometimes he wouldn't call for a few weeks, although he never stayed away for more than a month. After such a lull, they would again resume being inseparable. Then, in August of 1983, Kelli's world came to an end.

For some months, her folks had their home for sale because her stepfather, Richard Croce's employer, was transferring him to Phoenix. When the house finally sold, all Kelli could scream was "No! No! No!"

A week or so before Kelli had to leave for Arizona, she and Ross sat in his car in front of her friend Jenny's house to say their final, "Goodbye." Kelli's eyes filled with tears. Ross placed his arm around Kelli's shoulder and said, "Why are the people I'm closest to always taken away from me? Please don't ever forget me." Kelli looked up at him and assured him she never would. His eyes also began to well with tears. Kelli had never before seen Ross so emotional. They hugged, kissed good night, and Ross drove away. Within a few days, Kelli heard the horrific news of August 17, 1983.

Now, nearly a year and a half later and certain that Ross could not have been involved in the murders of his parents, Kelli was effervescent with renewed infatuation.

CHAPTER 28

Their Love Has Endured

On January 1, 1985, Kelli drove into the 300-acre grounds of the Colorado State Hospital and was directed to the building which housed the forensic ward. There, she was met by a hospital worker and escorted down the center hallway which bisected the two medium-security wards. To the left of the hallway was ward F-10 and to the right was F-12 where Ross lived. A waiting room existed for each ward and was located before each entryway. The waiting rooms were enclosed, the exterior walls running about waist-high with glass then extending to the ceiling. For security reasons, the visiting areas were very basic — a couch, a few office-type chairs, one or two larger upholstered chairs, and a small desk which could seat two. No guards were present in the waiting rooms, allowing patients and their visitors as much privacy as possible.

A middle-aged woman and a young man, who appeared to be in his 20s, were sitting at the desk. Kelli stood, nervously awaiting Ross's arrival. She had no idea what to expect.

Suddenly, the door to the room opened and Ross entered. Considering his confinement, he looked as stylish as he could, wearing sunglasses and a blue-gray, V-neck sweater. It was the same sweater he was wearing in the photo of just him that sat on Kelli's nightstand at home.

Ross motioned for her to sit on the couch that was against a wall away from the other visitors. Ross wanted to know everything Kelli had been doing since they last saw one another. The conversation

Chapter 28: Their Love Has Endured

remained light and superficial — there was no discussion regarding the circumstances that had brought Ross to the hospital.

During the 90-mile drive from Denver to Pueblo that morning, Kelli had promised herself she would tell Ross so many things. She wanted to say how she had cried herself to sleep during the past sixteen months thinking about him. She wanted to say she'd wait for him no matter what happened in his case. The list she had created in her mind, however, could not reach her lips. Instead, she trembled from sorrow at the predicament of her first love.

Sensing Kelli's difficulties, Ross reached out and held her hand. "Relax, it's okay," he assured her. He leaned over and kissed her on the cheek. Kelli gave Ross a hug and began crying.

While holding her, Ross said, "They can take away anything they want from me, but they can't take my memories." Kelli's allotted visiting hour passed like a nanosecond. The two separated from one another and said goodbye, as tears continued running down Kelli's cheeks. She couldn't stop crying on her drive back to Denver.

Shortly after returning to Arizona, Kelli received a note. It read, "You are very precious to me." Ross drew a diamond at the end of the message. And just like that, the love between the two rekindled. Feverish letter writing and frequent phone calls quickly followed.

Since Ross was only allowed to dial collect, the brunt of the phone expense fell on Kelli. Fearing that her parents would notice the long-distance charges and put an end to the calling, Ross had a plan. Kelli would fill her pockets with quarters and find the nearest pay phone. From there, she would make prearranged, monthly calls without her parents' knowledge. Richard and Mary Croce's ignorance, however, lasted only a few months. Again, it was the nosey prosecutor's office that was the tattle tale.

In April, Kelli returned a second time to the state hospital. After that visit, an investigator for the district attorney informed the Croces that their daughter had seen Ross. The Croces were concerned about their daughter's choices and well-being, knowing that Ross was accused of a stone-cold double homicide of his parents.

They asked Kelli to see a psychiatrist. Begrudgingly, Kelli complied. However, after a few therapy sessions, the doctor agreed — there was no cure for unswerving love.

Ross and Kelli then decided there was no choice. They had to keep their ongoing romance a closely-guarded secret. Otherwise, their privacy would constantly be compromised. Kelli, of course, would be the big loser by virtue of a police informant or parental threat of a financial cut off. Ross was too protective of Kelli to have her suffer either consequence. He wasn't concerned about himself; no one could heap any more harm upon him.

Since January 1, 1985, Kelli Olson had become the bright light in Ross's otherwise dismal hospital room. The early love between the two had been reborn on that date. However, unbeknownst to Kelli, Ross psychiatrically was a very ill young man and wasn't getting any better.

CHAPTER 29

The Nightmare Becomes Worse

Toward the end of February 1985, Ross called. After exchanging our usual round of greetings, he provided me with a glimpse of his dismal life on his ward and one bit of good news. "David, I exist among lunatics who spend all day running up and down the hallway or urinating on the shower wall. I spend most of my day in my little room, reading, sleeping, or listening to music. Recently, the only decent interaction I've had with another patient is with a guy named Kashaun Dupree, who coincidentally also has MPD."

Ross explained that Dupree is currently being treated by a psychologist out of Colorado Springs, Dr. Barry Quinn. "According to Kashaun, Quinn fused his personalities before he ever got to this hell hole," Ross stated. "Since then, Quinn's been allowed to come to the hospital and treat Kashaun. I met Quinn, and he seems like an okay fellow." I immediately called Quinn and explored his doing the one-on-one therapy with Ross. Hoping to restore its credibility with Ross, the hospital agreed to the arrangement. A few weeks later after having spent a few sessions with Ross, Quinn reported that the two of them had established a good rapport, but also cautioned, "Ross's experience has not been very good at the hospital so treatment will take some time." Unfortunately, Quinn was never afforded that time.

The hospital pulled the plug on the arrangement during the spring of 1985, believing that Quinn was keeping the staff in the dark about his sessions with Ross and that this special privilege gave Ross too much control over his treatment. On April 19, 1985, we filed a motion to allow Quinn to continue as the therapist and outlined the salient events that occurred during the last year, including, the hospital's diagnosis of MPD, the opinion by Dr. Huffaker that successful treatment would take at least two years, the beginnings of treatment and establishment of rapport by Drs. Trautt and Huffaker, the obliteration of that rapport by the investigative packet that Chappell sent the hospital, the hospital's resultant skepticism about the diagnosis and their ludicrous demand that Ross recite chapter and verse of all the incidents of sexual abuse, Dr. Quinn's qualifications and success in treating Dupree, the doctor's establishment of rapport with Ross, and the hospital's junking that relationship because of their indifferent attitude toward Ross and his illness. The hospital responded, requesting that Ross be ordered to treat with them.

The three-day hearing began April 30, 1985, with Judge Day immediately taking Chappell to task for dooming Ross's therapy the preceding December. The judge told Chappell he was not pleased with the prosecution's conducting an investigation while the judge was staying at his winter retreat in California and then sending the results of the investigation to the hospital. Chappell, however, defended his actions.

"Since the issue of abuse was raised during the competency hearing," Chappell explained, "the People have the obligation to meet that defense at an eventual trial." Chappell was right about his duties as a prosecutor, but dead wrong to send his holiday package to the hospital. After the prosecutor and jurist concluded their exchange of point and counterpoint, the hearing took place with our presenting evidence in support of all of our points. We also called Kashaun to testify to highlight an incident regarding the hospital's careless attitude.

Kashaun, a bright, well-spoken African American man in his late twenties, talked about having confronted Ross in the ward a few months ago. Ross was acting like an "overbearing juvenile" whom Kashaun called Spike. Upon witnessing the behavior, Kashaun quickly ran to Dr. Trautt and told him to "come to the bathroom to check out Carlson." The doctor, however, ignored his own prior admonition "to pay special attention to Ross's behavioral changes" and declined

Chapter 29: The Nightmare Becomes Worse

Dupree's invitation and commended him for having "high standards." Trautt's response was a head scratcher.

After the hearing, Judge Day took the matter under advisement. Meanwhile, Ross returned to his 10 feet by 12 feet hospital room and his few possessions — a poster of a Lamborghini, his AM/FM stereo, several novels, and a few legal pads. For the time being, there would be no journal entries that he could record regarding treatment.

On Thursday, May 30, 1985, a phone message from the Colorado Attorney General's office required my immediate attention.

Need your help! Medical problem (brain related), want to do tests, he has refused, trying to work something out with another hospital, is serious.

The attorney general's office referred me to Dr. Dawn McNiece, the psychiatrist currently assigned to Ross's ward. The doctor relayed that two days ago, while Ross was at the cafeteria, he was observed sitting at a table and staring into space. Staff couldn't get him to respond to their questions. When he stood up to return his tray, his pants were soiled, having evidently experienced incontinence. McNiece explained that incontinence could suggest a brain tumor. She had asked Ross to undergo a neurological evaluation and provide a sample of his blood, but he refused to let the state hospital touch him. She therefore arranged to transport him to Denver General because that hospital was willing to do whatever was necessary. However, Ross would not agree to anything unless his lawyers approved.

I assured the doctor that if the situation were as grave as she had painted it, we would certainly cooperate. I spoke to Ross and asked him what had happened.

"I'm not sure, David, although I can surmise. You know how I hate birthdays and you know what date May 28 was."

"I know. You were 21 on Tuesday. Happy birthday."

"Thanks and thanks for not making a big deal out of it. As best I can piece together, one of the little ones probably got depressed, the 21st being pretty significant, and had an accident. It's no big thing. The hospital is just a little paranoid because you guys tear them up in court. They want to do all of these stupid tests, but there's no way I'll let them touch me."

Although Ross's explanation made sense, we still had to be cautious. Judge Day immediately signed an Order I prepared, authorizing the necessary tests at Denver General. As anticipated, the results were negative. Not surprisingly, the state hospital had never considered the May 28 incident as MPD related. Instances of the hospital's ineptness and recalcitrance continued.

On July 17, 1985, the judge ordered the hospital to allow Quinn to treat Ross. The judge's criticism of the hospital stated, in part,

> *If treatment of this disorder requires a one-to-one therapist-patient relationship; requires hypnosis by a treating therapist in whom the patient has confidence; requires trust on the part of the patient; requires conviction on the part of the physician concerning the disorder being treated; requires belief in the diagnosis of multiple personality disorder; then the hospital has no one on its staff who can adequately and appropriately treat the defendant.*

That shining moment lasted one whole day. On July 18, Dr. Quinn called to say the hospital would not pay him. On August 5, 1985, we filed a motion demanding that the hospital pay Quinn's fees. During the subsequent hearing, the hospital argued that its budget had no money for Quinn, therefore, if Ross wanted the doctor, he had to pay for the treatment.

During this hearing, we proved that every year the hospital's budget had allocated moneys for outside physicians in a variety of specialties. For the current fiscal year of 1985-1986, the hospital had contracted for $1,359,466 worth of such services. Of that amount, $20,000 had been set aside for podiatrists, including treatment for bunions. We also showed that the state's strategy of forcing Ross to bear the Quinn expense was another of its attempts to render Ross penniless. Unbeknownst to Judge Day, because disclosure of the state's overall strategy had not become relevant until now, their plan was tenacious but so was our resolve to defeat it.

A few months before this dispute regarding Dr. Quinn,

Chapter 29: The Nightmare Becomes Worse

Colorado's Attorney General had brought a separate lawsuit against Ross's conservator, Jack Keller, in the Arapahoe County probate court — a court distinct and separate from the one over which Judge Day presided. The Attorney General was the legal representative of the hospital in court matters and Carolyn Lievers was the AG's lawyer assigned to this case.

As Ross's conservator and the guardian of the trust moneys since October 1983, Jack Keller never refused any defense request for funds to defend Ross and consistently thwarted the state's efforts to tap into the trusts. Jack, thus, gave us a fighting chance to compete with the prosecution's enormous resources. On at least two occasions during 1984, the state had the temerity to send Jack bills for Ross's confinement at the state hospital — $9,794 for the period July 10, 1984, through August 31, 1984; and $10,394 additional through September 30, 1984. Jack refused the trust's payment of each bill.

The basis for the AG's lawsuit was a statute that allowed the state to sue for reimbursement of a patient's hospitalization. In the suit, the state sought a court order requiring Jack to approve the bills he had previously rejected and to pay other bills now due. The statute upon which the suit was predicated was designed to tap into a patient's existing insurance coverage or personal assets.

Ross had no insurance coverage. His assets totaled $1,600, which included the clothes on his back, a 1978 Oldsmobile in storage, an AM/FM stereo worth about $75, the few books that dressed his night table, and a few dollars to spend at the commissary. However, those assets were not what the attorney general had in mind; the state wanted to tap into the Carlsons' trust estates. The scheme was obvious — if the attorney general succeeded in depleting the estates, Ross wouldn't have the financial means to defend himself with private counsel and qualified doctors.

The hospital calculated Ross's daily patient rate at $138. He, therefore, owed $30,798 from July 10, 1984, through March 31, 1985. The total for a year would be approximately $50,370. If the state were successful in this current challenge, and if two years were still needed to treat Ross, the trust would be saddled with a hospital bill of at least $130,000 through March 1987. Jack Keller and his lawyer, Don

McCullough, challenged the hospital every step of the way. Although they lost the May 1985 suit in the lower court, they immediately appealed to the Colorado Court of Appeals. The appeal had not yet been resolved by the time of our current hearing before Judge Day regarding payment of Dr. Quinn. While the two court battles raged without resolution, Ross remained on the sidelines waiting to resume therapy.

Finally, on December 27, 1985, the judge ruled in favor of mental health over bunions. Judge Day found that Ross "continues to be the victim of multiple and protracted legal proceedings which are preventing him from receiving treatment." The judge said that the law required the state to provide Ross "with such care and treatment suited to meet his individual needs." Since the hospital had no one capable of providing that treatment, they had to fulfill their duty by paying Quinn.

The judge's Order was a bright day for the defense. Nearly a year had passed since the Chappell-Huffaker-Trautt treatment debacle. Ross was able to resume therapy with Barry Quinn. Walter and I again felt that Ross's treatment was back on the right track. Our optimism was short lived as a result of the Attorney General's appeal of Judge Day's orders.

On January 30, 1986, the Colorado Supreme Court issued an **ORDER TO SHOW CAUSE WITH STAY,** temporarily halting Judge Day's rulings. By a quirk in the law, the judge and Ross had to be joined as respondents in the appeal by the hospital.

In this unique situation, where defendant and judge were on the same side in a suit, the two could work together and strategize their response. Since Judge Day was in California for his annual winter respite, contacts between him and me were relegated to the phone. I didn't have to see the judge's face to understand his disappointment with the order from the Supreme Court of which he had been a member for 20 years.

"I don't know what they're thinking up there, Dave. If this young fella' doesn't get treated, this case will never end."

Walter was taking a well-deserved sabbatical and traveling so I prepared and filed our brief at the end of February. On July 16, 1986, I received a mailing from the Supreme Court.

Chapter 29: The Nightmare Becomes Worse

The court overturned Judge Day's rulings, concluding that only if the trial judge found "that in devising the treatment plan the state hospital staff failed to consider the relevant facts and exercise competent professional judgment" could the judge interfere with the internal functions of the hospital. Since no such findings were ever made by Judge Day, the right to treat Ross remained with the hospital.

There were feelings of gloom and doom in our camp while the hospital brimmed with elation and arrogance. Knowing that it was the only game in town, the hospital and prosecution would now pursue another strategy to remove the two thorns in their sides. Having Ross declared competent would take care of the second thorn, and it was the easier of the two since Ross wanted nothing more to do with the hospital and was prepared to do whatever it would take to accomplish that goal. The thornier and more sizeable problem, which had to be addressed first, was Judge Day. Soon, I would learn how the prosecution intended to rid itself of him.

CHAPTER 30

The Changing of the Guard

Ross assumed tunnel vision in his determination to convince the hospital that he was competent. He memorized all of the case materials we had sent him so he could impress the state doctors with his knowledge of the myriad court proceedings. He would talk to our doctors only about mundane matters and refused to discuss any topic relating to MPD. He wore dark-tinted glasses during his interviews so no one could see his eyes. He had developed a new personality, called Holdin, whose sole function was to appear competent and become free of the state hospital. In essence, Ross wanted to appear to the hospital as if he were holding it together; he wanted to "hold on" and avoid dissociating.

"As far as I'm concerned, he is getting sicker," Dr. Fairbairn told Walter and me in October of 1986. "He is worse off now than he was when I testified in 1984. I doubt he can be of any assistance to you. The development of a new personality is Ross's inherent and involuntary defense mechanism to the pain he's been suffering at the hands of the hospital," Fairbairn stated.

About a month later, Drs. Newton and Rewey examined Ross. They, too, were greeted by a torturous monologue of legal events and Ross's refusal to talk about MPD. "Ross was not going to say anything that suggested his incompetence," Dr. Newton explained. Newton and Rewey saw someone "very determined, very firm, and very angry about his situation. He was going to do whatever it took to persuade the hospital people that he was competent."

Chapter 30: The Changing of the Guard

Notwithstanding Ross's efforts to appear intact, the reality was that the only things he had together were those bundles of court papers he had memorized. His mind had become more fractured by this new personality created to adapt to yet another abusive figure in his life — the Colorado State Hospital. Walter and I were determined to free Ross from this pernicious perpetrator. We would take advantage of a Colorado law that permitted civil commitment of a criminal defendant who could not be restored to competency within the foreseeable future.

In early January 1987, we received the hospital's anticipated reports of Ross's competency. A restoration hearing was mandated to test those views. Because Judge Day was in Palm Springs for his annual winter getaway, he had to be informed about these latest developments.

On February 10, 1987, Walter and I wrote the judge and sent copies of the letter to Pat Robb, Bob Chappell, and Carolyn Lievers of the attorney general's office. Before sending the letter to Judge Day, I informed Pat Robb of its contents. She had no objection to any portion of it. Besides advising the judge of the hospital's findings that Ross had been restored to competency and the need for a hearing to address those opinions, Walter and I stated,

> *... we will be requesting, during the restoration hearing, the termination of the criminal proceedings ... pursuant to C.R.S., '16-8-114.5(2). We will then request that the defendant be civilly committed for treatment ...*

The statute we cited providing for civil commitment was enacted to reflect the decisions of several US courts that a state's indefinite confinement of a criminal defendant solely because of his incompetency was unconstitutional when it seemed unlikely the defendant could ever participate fully in a trial. We had no intention of asking for Ross's outright release from all hospitalization, but rather sought his civil commitment in a private facility. In our view, this remedy, albeit a longshot, was Ross's only hope in his current predicament. Our strategy was temporarily derailed less than two weeks later when we received a pleading from the DA's entitled *Motion for Substitution of Judge*. Its objective was to remove Judge Day from the case.

In their zeal to hit both Judge Day and me with Scud missiles, the prosecutors dredged up harmless events of two and one-half years ago, drummed up an allegation of misconduct, and showed a flawed understanding of the law. The motion's accusations of judicial impropriety and favoritism included my driving the judge to court for the contempt hearing against the hospital during the snowstorm in October 1984; Walter's and my recent letter of February 10, 1987, wherein we advised the judge of our intent to seek dismissal of the case; and a charge that must have been concocted in outer space, namely, that I drove the judge's wife in my car on a "shopping excursion." I seethed with prosecutorial disdain while reading the motion. It is one thing to be maligned by clients and the media. That comes with the territory of practicing as a criminal attorney. It can be disheartening to have to answer to well-intentioned but often misguided accusations of lay people. However, to be wrongfully accused by your brethren leaves one gasping for air.

The motion for substitution was heard by Judge Day on June 8, 1987. I had prepared Ross for the possibility that his Honor might step down because of his respect for the judiciary and his own sense of fair play. When the judge took the bench and began addressing the motion, only an occasional cough from court observers intermingled with his words.

Judge Day quickly got to the core of the matter. He stated, "I had made up my mind before this *Motion for Substitution of Judge* was ever filed that I was going to withdraw from this case." However, before giving the prosecutors the green light to celebrate his decision to step down, the judge chose to answer their charges.

"I'm not going to allow this motion to go unchallenged. In my 41 years as a judge, it is the most unprofessional act that I have ever seen attorneys display. The prosecution has challenged my impartiality, saying that I have been prejudiced in favor of Ross Carlson and against the People. That cannot stand up because the objective that I have sought from the beginning was to take the necessary steps as quickly as possible to bring this man to trial. Every motion that the defense has filed has been designed to accomplish that objective. However, there has never been one movement on behalf of the District Attorney to accomplish that result.

Chapter 30: The Changing of the Guard

"Indeed, the most flagrant *ex parte* action taken in this case was the one engaged in by the District Attorney and his investigator. Without seeking court approval or expert opinion, they sent the results of their investigation to the doctor who had started to treat this defendant, resulting in the doctor changing his mind about whether he believed Ross Carlson was suffering from multiple personality disorder. From that point on, Mr. Carlson withdrew from treatment because the confidence that is supposed to exist between patient and therapist had been destroyed."

The judge then dealt with the other very personal charges, his face reddening as he continued. "Listen to this allegation," he said, segueing into a discussion of the alleged "shopping" trip. "Now imagine this. During a conference call about a serious matter involving the defendant, I proceeded, while the Attorney General is on the line, to refer to Mr. Savitz having made himself of service to Judge Day's wife on a shopping excursion for which she was in need of transportation."

"Now, there are many statements that refute themselves, and this is certainly one of them. No judge or anyone else in his right mind would interrupt a telephone conference about a serious criminal case to engage in a conversation with Ms. Lievers listening in about Mr. Savitz having taken my wife on a shopping trip. The statement, of course, is not true because it never happened."

"First of all, for the last eight years, all of the shopping that Mrs. Day has done took place in Palm Springs. She has gone Christmas shopping at Joslins in Denver, but was accompanied by our daughter. I do all of our grocery shopping in Denver, and if I can't go, I'll have a neighbor friend pick up a few things for us. But we're not going to use an expensive attorney to do that kind of thing. That statement on its face is absolutely absurd. Absolutely absurd."

"Now, let's take paragraph number six where the astute investigator sees Judge Day exiting Mr. Savitz's car. That took place before the hearing on defendant's request for contempt citations. If there was anybody at the District Attorney's table who thought it was improper, all they had to do at the start of the hearing is say, 'Judge Day, as a result of having seen you ride to the courthouse with Mr. Savitz, I think this case ought to be continued because it is probably tainted.' If it was improper, why wasn't it brought to the court's attention immediately before the hearing? It so happens that all the citations were dismissed by me. Defense counsel didn't get anything out of it. So that shows bias and prejudice on the part of the judge with defense counsel?"

Judge Day picked apart the other allegations and saved for his closing foray the reason he had decided to withdraw before the motion was ever filed.

"Now we have the psychiatric miracle of the age. After leaving Mr. Carlson alone and doing nothing for about three years, I receive a report that he is perfectly competent to stand trial. When I got that report from the state hospital, which was way before this motion was filed, I said to myself, 'How can I believe those people down there when all of the medical evidence I had heard said it takes about eighteen months of treatment before most multiples are successfully fused?'"

"It would fly in the face of all competent psychiatric testimony if I listened to those people from Pueblo say that time cures all and everything will take care of itself. Well, some other judge is going to have to hear that kind of evidence because I certainly would not give it any credence. If this motion had not been filed, when I returned from Palm Springs, I would have had all the parties together and announced I was getting out of this case."

With that, Judge Day closed his involvement in the case and adjourned the hearing. The court personnel who had sat through the numerous proceedings during the last three years were both stunned and saddened. They knew the judge had no office, staff, or law clerks. He worked out of his home without the bare necessities of a sitting judge. Because of these limitations, he had to rely on common sense and the professionalism of the attorneys whenever he was assigned a case. He was hurt that his swan song after four decades as a judge was a stale and phony set of allegations.

As Chappell walked out of the courtroom, neither Walter nor I looked his way. Ross left the courtroom in his typical unemotional state.

Ten days after Judge Day withdrew, I received a phone call from the Honorable Robert T. Kingsley, saying he had been appointed to take over the Carlson case. I knew Judge Kingsley from his many years

Chapter 30: The Changing of the Guard

on the Denver district court where he had served a term as chief judge of the criminal division. While on the bench, the judge often presented a gruff exterior, could be impatient at times, and had a penchant for an occasional salty tongue, especially while conducting matters in his chambers. "Bring the son-of-a-bitch down," he once commented to a deputy sheriff in one of my cases after he ruled the miscreant had to be released from a lengthy prison sentence because of a prior judge's mistake. As Walter would say about Judge Kingsley, "he carried his emotions on his sleeve." Despite that, his Honor was as fair and honest as any judge before whom I had appeared.

Based upon our collective experiences, Walter and I concluded that Judge Kingsley was as solid a choice as any of the judges available in the semi-retired pool. After learning of this appointment, it was time for Walter and me to begin rounding up our witnesses for the second competency trial, Carlson II. Before plowing into that task, however, I had to first take care of some personal business.

CHAPTER 31

The Soul of an Angel

By the middle of June 1987, I had spent nearly three and a half years with Robin and her daughters, Rachel and Kristin. Since the end of Ross's case was nowhere in sight and Robin's 34th birthday, June 18, was fast approaching (the two events having no connection whatsoever), I had to make a decision regarding the latter.

When I left the house for work on the morning of Thursday, June 18, 1987, I had no birthday gift in my possession. Men fear the searing look from the 'love of their life' when they greet her on the morning of her birthday without a significant gift in hand. Having considered the ramifications of such an omission, I figured an invitation of marriage might make up for my gift-giving lapse.

Mindful of my sometimes-wry sense of humor, Robin reserved her decision until I called her mother in Los Angeles and asked permission. My future mother-in-law, Helen Kash, was elated, relieved that she could now substitute the letter "o" for her pet moniker for me, "my sin-in-law."

Having now irrevocably committed myself to the future Mrs. Savitz, I nevertheless wanted to obtain one more person's permission. Once I satisfied that obligation, which would then bind me to a relationship for at least the next several decades, I could get back to the Carlson case, which seemed to be taking nearly as long.

I would have to wait until Robin's and my upcoming July 10 trip to Toronto for her cousin's wedding to obtain the last approval. Toronto, Canada was the birthplace and last resting place of Robin's father, Ken Kash.

Chapter 31: The Soul of an Angel

As a single man in his mid-20s, Ken Kash had moved from Toronto, just across the Canadian-US border, to Buffalo, New York. There, he became a very successful jewelry merchant. At the age of 35, Ken was introduced to 19-year-old Helen Goodman of Toronto, a breathtaking Grace Kelly lookalike. After three months of weekend trips across the border, Ken and Helen married. They settled in Buffalo, where Robin and her two, older sisters were born.

At the age of 41, just five years after his marriage, Ken Kash suffered an unknown debilitating virus that eventually relegated him to a wheelchair until his death at the age of 61. Since Ken became ill when Robin was just two years old, her main impression of her dad was his incredible resolve to overcome his affliction.

Although Ken Kash became physically challenged as an adult, his mind continued to sparkle like the precious gems he sold. He was a voracious reader, who instilled that passion in his daughters by usually insisting that one of them walk with him during his weekly trips to the library and help him comb the stacks for a favorite book or two. He accomplished those joint outings with the aid of a tripod, often requiring the traffic light at the intersection of Buffalo's Main Street to completely sequence two to three times before he was able to cross it.

"As a little kid," Robin reflected to me one day when talking about her dad, "I was scared to death walking across that busy street, but obviously my father felt confident that city drivers in Buffalo would avoid hitting him and his young daughter." Having caught my smile when she told that story, she continued and said, "You and my father would have gotten along great because you both have that stupid sense of humor." I took that as a compliment, but I also knew I would have enjoyed knowing Ken Kash because of the indomitable spirit he had passed onto his daughter.

Ken and Helen Kash divorced when Robin was a teenager and Helen ventured to Los Angeles to start a new life for her and her three daughters. The daughters always traveled to Buffalo a couple times a year to see their dad, who remained an integral part of their lives. One of Robin's last memories of her dad was when she was twenty-two years old. Then, she flew from California to Buffalo in the summer of 1975 just so Ken Kash could meet his first granddaughter, the then nine-month-old Rachel. During that visit, Robin held Rachel while kneeling at the side of Ken's wheelchair. Ken Kash placed his hand on his granddaughter's head, prayed for her safety, and recited the children's blessing in Hebrew and then in English: "Y'si-mech El-o-him k'Sa-rah, Riv-ka, Ra-chel v'Le-ah," "May God inspire you to live in the tradition of Sarah, Rebekah, Rachel, and Leah." In November of that year, Ken Kash passed away. Twelve years later, I wanted to speak to my father-in-law and obtain his permission to marry his youngest daughter.

On Saturday afternoon, July 11, 1987, Robin and I visited Ken Kash's grave site. I told my father-in-law a little bit about myself, told him how much I loved his daughter, and said, "she has the face of a goddess and heart and soul of an angel." I said, "she has the right to live with me clothed by the sanctity of a marriage" and that "I will be good to her." He gave me his blessings. I placed a stone on his tombstone so that he would always be reminded of my presence. I left with both a twinkle and a tear in my eye.

After satisfying this last condition, I was able to return to Carlson with a clear mind and a blessed heart. I spent the next several weeks vigorously preparing for the September 21, 1987, competency hearing before Judge Kingsley.

CHAPTER 32

Hospital Friends

We had known that whenever Ross had another competency hearing, Kashaun Dupree would be one of our key witnesses. As a result, I kept in contact with Kashaun because I knew he would soon be discharged from the state hospital. When Kashaun earned his release from the state hospital in September 1986, he agreed to make himself available for any future hearing. He visited my office a few months after his release so I could tape record his recollection of four of his different experiences with Ross during the last two years. Relaxed and dressed in a light brown suit and tan sport shirt, Kashaun began.

"One morning during breakfast, I noticed Ross had stopped eating. His head was down with his chin nearly touching his chest. Little bits of food began dribbling out of the corner of his mouth. He sat still. I didn't know what was happening, so I bent over and asked, 'Ross, what's the matter?' He didn't say anything. He just looked at me. Usually, his eyes were dilated, but now they contracted something fierce. I realized he was probably dissociating so I sat with him for about 20 minutes."

"When chow was over, I took him by the hand and walked him to his room. I laid him on his bed and then left the room. I waited outside. A short time later, Ross came out and asked me what happened. When we returned to his room, I told him."

Hearing about incidents like this was important to me. Although I had been convinced since the 1984 competency trial that Ross suffered from MPD, and events since then reaffirmed my belief, sometimes tiny speckles of doubt would reemerge. I didn't want to be accused of wearing blinders, so I would sometimes ask myself: Was I being fooled by a master manipulator and extraordinary Shakespearean actor? Had I been so mesmerized by the press's fascination with this case that I had developed tunnel vision regarding Ross? Were the several doubting and novice shrinks at the state hospital right and our learned doctors wrong? Usually when I finished one of these reevaluations, I felt like scolding myself. My guilt sufficiently assuaged, I continued listening to my office guest while he described another experience, this time with someone he dubbed the "punk rocker."

"Yes, another time, I was sitting in the day room and noticed Ross coming down the hall. He was wearing rolled-up jeans and a muscle T-shirt, had a pack of cigarettes stuck under his left chest area, and his hair was spiked. What really blew me away was his gait — he had this kind of bounce to his walk like a punk rocker. He walked past me, sat down, lit up a cigarette and began puffing away like a chimney. I walked over to him, introduced myself and asked him for a cigarette. He didn't want anything to do with me, so he flipped a cigarette my way and essentially told me to 'Fuck off!' I nevertheless sat down and smoked a cigarette by him, but he essentially ignored me."

"It's Norman!" I said to myself. I then asked Kashaun if any hospital personnel had observed Ross at the time.

"A staff member, Laura Smith, came into the hall to deliver our mail," he replied. "She dropped everything on the table where Ross and I were sitting. I was interested to see if she would notice how different Ross looked. He normally dressed very preppie, combed his hair very neatly, spoke very pleasantly and, most of all, hated cigarettes — refusing even to be around anyone who smoked. Smith looked at Ross and, said, 'Well, Ross, I don't think I have anything for you.' She then left without any further comment."

I knew Kashaun had seen Ross when he turned 21. It was the day the Attorney General's office made that frantic call to me about Ross's episode of incontinence. Ross had been in the dining room with a staff member, Jim Quintana. Kashaun spoke to Quintana the next

Chapter 32: Hospital Friends

day and was so angered by the aid's comments about the day's earlier events that Kashaun went to his room afterwards and recorded them verbatim on a note pad.

Quintana's unsavory comments, Kashaun recalled, were, "It's time that 'Mr. Rich Kid' was knocked down some and shown who runs things here." "He said, 'Ross was lucky to find some stupid old, retired judge who fell in love with him and wants to protect him ... that the judge, however, is too stupid to realize he can't tell us state employees what the fuck to do ... and that we run the show, not him.'" "He went on to say, 'We can do what the fuck we want to with Ross and who in the fuck does Ross think he is? He has a better stereo and stuff than I do. He's just another nut just like the other patients. He'll have to look up to us. We ain't looking up to him.'"

I knew any judge would be profoundly interested in hearing Quintana's erudite analysis of Ross's situation. In Kashaun's report of a third incident, he described a character whom he had anointed with my long-forsaken nickname from my youth. I handled this part of Kashaun's recitation quite nonchalantly, avoiding any suspicion that he had mentioned a name which I had succeeded in burying when I moved to Colorado to attend law school.

"Around the summer of last year," Kashaun said, "the personality, which I had named "Butch," got into a rather heated argument with me. I feared Butch because his eyes would become dilated to the point where they were almost totally black. His veins would stand up on his neck, his muscles became tense, and his breath became extremely foul. To let him know I wasn't going to be confrontational, I acted very submissive. I tilted my head down and to the right, where it was practically resting on my right shoulder. Then, I closed my eyes for a few seconds. When I opened them, I noticed that the old Ross had returned."

Unbeknownst to Kashaun, he had described Black to a tee. Fearing that I might ruin Kashaun's train of thought, I avoided revealing that I had also known a Butchie, a chubby, freckle-faced kid from Pennsylvania, who, as a four-year-old, perpetrated the chocolate milk caper and later, when in grade school, threw snowballs at vehicles driven by unsuspecting motorists, prompting stern discipline from

Mrs. Ruggels. With that secret in tow, I listened as Kashaun proceeded to recount the last of the four unusual events.

"In September 1986, after I had moved to Ward F-10 in preparation for my discharge from the hospital, the staff allowed me to visit Ross one night. When it became time for me to leave, Ross walked me to the door. As we were about to say goodbye, his eyes started flooding with all kinds of activity. Ross turned into this little kid that I had seen for the first time in December of 1984. As he had done then, he grabbed me, started crying and said, 'Please don't go, please don't leave me, I need you.' It touched me because no one ever has said that to me."

Kashaun's description of Blue was right on the money. I checked the tape to ensure there was enough space on it for Kashaun to talk about another sympathetic figure at the hospital, Ben Ramos. If something ever happened to Kashaun, I wanted to make sure I had preserved his words about Ramos. "To your knowledge, did any hospital employee ever alert a fellow staff member about Ross's behavior?"

"The only staff person I have ever heard say anything about that was Ben Ramos. However, when Ben notified other staff about observing Ross dissociate, he was told not to acknowledge that behavior ever again. If he did, there would be consequences."

Both Ross and Kashaun had previously told us about the hospital's banishment of Ben Ramos to the Siberia of hospital wards. When we finally located Ramos at his home, he was eager to talk with us. Walter and I spoke with him over the phone also in anticipation of using Ramos as a witness in a future competency hearing. I took notes as Ramos spoke to us.

In 1979, Ramos started working as an aide at the state hospital. During 1982-1983, Ramos attended vocational school in Pueblo, where he obtained his psych tech license. In August 1983, he began working with Kashaun who had just arrived at the hospital following an insanity adjudication in Colorado Springs. According to Ramos, shortly after Kashaun's arrival, the staff diagnosed their new patient as a "sexual sadist." However, Ramos learned that before Kashaun had entered the hospital, he had been diagnosed with MPD and was in treatment with Dr. Barry Quinn.

Chapter 32: Hospital Friends

After learning more about Kashaun's history, Ramos realized the hospital may have mis-identified his true illness. Since Ramos's job was to implement the treatment program designed for Kashaun, he approached the ward psychiatrist regarding this inconsistency. The psychiatrist said he wouldn't recognize MPD and that "if Mr. Dupree and you want to go through the DSM III and choose a diagnosis that is closest to MPD, go for it!" Ramos recalled that he and Dupree accepted the invitation, combed through the diagnostic and statistical manual of mental illnesses, and chose the diagnosis of mixed personality disorder, a hospital garbage pail favorite.

In early 1984, when Barry Quinn came to the hospital to treat Kashaun, Ramos worked alongside the doctor and learned about MPD. This learning process occurred during a two-year period.

Shortly after Ross transferred to ward F-12, Ramos discovered that the hospital's newest celebrity arrival and adjudicated incompetent had also been diagnosed with MPD. "This prompted me to watch him much more closely," the 29-year-old Ramos recalled. "I was surprised to learn that members of Ross's treatment team did not believe in the diagnosis and knew nothing about its features or treatment," he told Walter and me while we interviewed him on the phone.

"I witnessed Ross's dissociative process frequently. He would often write his name on the blackboard using different handwriting. Sometimes he wrote with a left-hand slant; other times in childlike printing, and frequently in very legible cursive. Another time I saw him in the day hall, wearing a T-shirt, with a pack of cigarettes rolled up in his sleeve. He was smoking as if he were used to it. I knew that Ross hated to be around smoke," Ramos continued.

"Another time, I saw Ross in the ward, upset after having just met with Dr. Trautt. It appeared Ross was in the midst of a dissociative episode. I spoke to him, while carefully noting his mannerisms. After we finished speaking, I waited for about 45 minutes until approaching Ross again. When I pressed Ross, he could not remember that we had just talked."

"I mentioned each of these incidents to staff or documented them in the chart. After reading the chart, Mike Chittenden, the ward's Clinical Administrator, and Dr. Trautt became angry and ordered me to refrain from talking to Mr. Carlson. Shortly after that, I was suspended from my duties and transferred to another ward."

"In your opinion, can the hospital treat Ross Carlson?" Walter asked Ramos.

"Establishment of a trusting relationship and alliance are of paramount importance with MPD," Ramos answered like a sophisticated therapist. "That kind of attachment cannot occur at the hospital because new therapists are always introduced into a patient's treatment. As a result, there is never enough time for an MPD patient to build a solid foundation with any one therapist. The Colorado State Hospital is currently the worst environment for an MPD patient."

Listening to Ramos was like hearing the deafening echo of Gregory Wilets's words more than three years later. Now, instead of hearing a grandfather clock tick in the background of attorney Gerald Pratt's wood-finished conference room, I was watching an analog clock marking time on Walter's desk.

Wilets's admonitions of early December 1983 had been realized in spades. The realities of the matter were now being honestly recounted by a compassionate hospital worker who was merely doing his job — Ben Ramos. Sadly, none of the highly educated professionals or well-paid administrators, who ran the 300-acre state hospital, would admit they were incapable of treating such a challenging illness. Instead, they were resigned to warehousing people like Ross. So, by the fall of 1987 when his second competency hearing was about to begin, Ross Carlson at 23 years of age was no better off, and, by some accounts, was in worse condition than he was on the first day he set foot on the campus of the state hospital as incompetent to proceed more than three years ago. Sadly, the only people who best understood Ross psychiatrically and who could explain him to Judge Kingsley were his learned defense doctors, a crafty veteran defense lawyer and his younger protégé, a former state mental patient and his disenfranchised therapist, and a banished hospital lay employee. I had a good idea what I would say to the judge when I took the stand again.

CHAPTER 33

Understanding the Many Sides of Ross Carlson

As a result of my four years of experiences with Ross, I was usually able to tell when he had switched from one personality to another or had awakened from "escaping" from the world around him. To the casual observer, Ross's chronic escapism, which often took place in court, appeared as if he were sleeping or daydreaming. However, in reality, to avoid the pain of hearing testimony about his disorder or family history, Ross would "float or space everything out" and travel to another place. Most clients who take a catnap during sometimes less than scintillating judicial proceedings will easily awaken when they are lightly nudged or softly spoken to. This was not the case with Ross as typified by any number of examples from the many court hearings during which we sat next to one another.

During such instances, Ross would be dressed like a fashion plate, seated to my left, with his legal pad and pen lying in front of him on our defense table. However, his eyes would be shut, and his head bowed. His elbows would be perched on the arms of the chair, and his hands, slightly cupped and barely touching, rested on the lower part of his forehead. His breathing would be normal and relaxed. He could not be awakened either by a whispered admonition about polite courtroom protocol or by a light tug at his arm. He would only re-enter the proceedings spontaneously, or if he were shaken vigorously.

Another of his signature looks was more worrisome: dark, dilated pupils staring vacantly into space as if his experience of a horrific event had been frozen in time. That peculiar gaze seemed to epitomize more than anything that life was an unhappy ordeal for Ross. If you had just met Ross and observed that expression, you'd likely keep your distance. His sleep-like escape mechanism, however, was the more dominant presentation.

Throughout the course of this case, whenever Ross would emerge from one of his floating episodes, he would pause, look to the side with his eyes spasmodically fluttering back and forth for a few seconds, turn to me and usually say, "Where are we, David?" He actually meant — what had happened during the proceedings while he was "gone"? I would then bring him current. Sometimes when I would ask what he thought had taken place, particularly during one of our phone conversations or private meetings outside of court, he would confabulate and use his deductive reasoning to fill in the lost time as best he could. Often, however, the gaps in memory between personalities could not be recovered and without fusing the personalities the "lost" information could not be shared with us attorneys. One such example occurred when Ross called me on May 22, 1986.

"David, do you remember me mentioning Kelli Olson? I dated her before I got in this mess. She moved to Phoenix shortly after I got arrested; she wrote that diary I sent you."

"I remember reading it. It was called *Too Perfect*. You and she met, I believe, in the fall of 1982."

"That's right. Well, anyway, I've written her a few letters, and she calls me from time to time. She called yesterday and said two of her friends, Ashley Best and Mark Van Doren, claimed to have received letters from me within the last few weeks. The problem is, David, I don't recall writing either of these people."

Ross was concerned because whenever the prosecutor's investigator, Bryan Bevis, received a tip that Ross was writing to anyone, he would appear at the front door of Ross's pen pals, ready to seize the letters for future court use. Since Ross's current letters to friends were usually quite harmless, I wasn't too worried. The problem was we didn't know how many pieces of correspondence Ross was unable to account for and what the contents of those materials were.

By the summer of 1986, Ross had enough of the hospital, and the feeling was quite mutual. Although he had devised a plan to

Chapter 33: Understanding the Many Sides of Ross Carlson

appear competent whenever evaluated by the state's doctors, he knew Walter and I would always insist upon separate examinations by our experts whenever we received competency reports from the other side.

"That's fine, David," he would say upon learning that I had scheduled an examination by one of our doctors, "but I can't stay here any longer. There's no way these imbeciles will ever treat me. I have to be where someone like Dr. Newton can treat me. I need the judge to see what a hell hole it's been since the last time we were in court. He really hasn't seen me for about a year and a half."

In early October of 1986, I first learned from Dr. Fairbairn that Ross's new personality, Holdin, had been created to accomplish Ross's competency scheme. "David, when Ross walked into the room where I was seated to evaluate him, he was carrying multiple packets of papers approximately one and a half feet thick. He greeted me in a matter-of-fact way, shook my hand, sat down at the table, and waited for me to say something. I was shocked at how cold he acted toward me because we had spent all that time together two years earlier," Fairbairn painfully said. He continued.

"After he rambled on for a few minutes, I decided to zero in and ask him with whom I was talking. He avoided answering but eventually mumbled the name, Holdin." I listened as the doctor described this newly-created personality.

"After Ross Carlson arrived at the hospital as incompetent in July 1984, Holdin developed," Fairbairn said. "Since this personality had never met me, he treated me like a stranger. I asked repeatedly to speak with the person who had been phoning me during the past year, but Holdin refused, calmly explaining that he was unable to do that." What most upset Fairbairn was Ross's appearance.

"David, I was shocked. Ross appeared as a shrunken version of how he looked two years ago. In the past, he was so muscular presenting with his well-developed, weight-lifting body, his intense eye contact, and his virile, assertive manner. Now, his eyes are hidden behind dark tinted eyeglasses which he apparently wears indoors all the time. He wore a loose fitting, long-sleeve shirt, sported a wispy blondish-red beard and slouched forward with a stooped posture. Evidently, he has lost eleven pounds during the past few months since being taken off his food supplements. There is no sense of strength or danger about him now. His current demeanor was goofus; he looked like a crazy inmate on the back wards of a state hospital," Fairbairn described.

No one should have been surprised at Ross's mental deterioration. He was not going to improve without treatment. To my knowledge, Holdin never called me, but I honestly didn't know one way or the other. However, around the beginning of December 1986, Ross phoned me, speaking in his old familiar analytical Steve-like tone. By this time, we had an idea that the state hospital was preparing reports to Judge Day that Ross was now competent, although we had not seen them yet.

"David, at the next hearing, you should examine Trautt, Greene, Ramos and Kashaun since those are the most important witnesses. I'm not really sure we should call Fairbairn. He annoys me. He's always challenging me. Plus, the money in the trust is running low. I'm wondering if I still need Walter."

I listened to this all too familiar rant. One day he loved Fairbairn; the next day he couldn't stand him. At times, he didn't even remember him. One day Ross would leave case strategies to Walter and me; the next day he was the conductor. Other times, he would agree that two defense attorneys were absolutely essential, and that Walter was an indispensable member of the tandem. On other days, he wanted only me to handle his case. His unpredictability was one of the hallmarks of his illness, although sometimes to the point of exasperation, namely, mine.

Between July 1984 and the fall of 1987, I had received nearly 200 collect calls from Ross. Many conversations lasted well over an hour. These calls were in addition to our regular interaction throughout the innumerable court hearings.

Topics of our phone conversations usually included our defense strategy for upcoming hearings, Ross's care at the hospital, personal issues in his life, and his merely wanting to hear a friendly voice. There were times when two calls, separated by just a few days, concerned the exact same issue — the phenomenon of two different personalities wanting to discuss the identical subject and the second one not knowing that another had already spoken to me. One particularly exasperating

Chapter 33: Understanding the Many Sides of Ross Carlson

instance stood out and occurred shortly after we had received the hospital's reports in January 1987 that Ross was competent. Ross's call concerned information with which I was eminently familiar but which information Ross nevertheless believed was necessary to laboriously provide me in both minute written detail and a lengthy follow-up phone conversation.

Evidently, a second personality had seen Ross's voluminous notes with a notation "Remember to call David." The second personality, unaware that the author of the notes had already called me, repeated for more than an hour what he had painstakingly detailed first in the written letter and then repeated verbally only a couple of days previously: all of the events that had occurred between him and hospital doctors since his arrival at the state hospital as incompetent.

After the second call, which lasted about an hour and a half, ending around 7:00 p.m., I hung up, walked outside my office suite and down the hallway that led to the other suites. Upon noticing that all of the other offices had no lights on and seeing no one around, I began screaming at the top of my lungs. After finishing my primal cleansing, I returned to my office and reminded myself that dealing with an MPD sufferer required an enormous amount of patience. I knew that the better approach was to inform Ross we had already discussed the subject and I would be happy to summarize it again for him. In such instances, he would usually apologize for bothering me again and said he could find out from "the others" what we had discussed. Despite the more than two years of tutelage by someone as masterful as Dr. Newton, this occasion made me realize I was still a mere novice in dealing with MPD and that I should never have deluded myself into thinking I was anything more.

Encouraged by the appointment of Judge Kingsley, we had our sights set upon the second competency trial that was scheduled to begin September 21, 1987. Until then, Ross remained busy, trying to convince the state doctors he was competent. His conundrum, however, was that no one in his defense team bought into his ploy, and MPD's features were not something that one could turn off and on at a whim. If internal or external stressors or conditions caused him to dissociate, resulting in the emergence of different ego states, that phenomenon was going to occur in spite of what Holdin or whoever wanted.

On Tuesday, September 1, 1987, Ross phoned, informing me he was being transferred later that day to the Douglas County Jail. The move would make him more accessible to both sides in preparation for the upcoming competency hearing. After providing him with that week's list of scheduled doctor evaluations, Ross calmly said he'd call me after the last scheduled exam on Saturday. That Thursday, however, I received a surprise phone call just before noon. The voice was not that of my ordinarily placid client.

"Hey man, some bozo just dropped by yesterday, about 32, beard."

"Hello, Norman." I replied, remembering the voice of a street punk which I had first heard 3 ½ years ago during the Fairbairn taping. I immediately turned to a fresh page on my legal pad and said, "I don't think we've ever talked before. How you doing?" By this time, I had written the date and "PC — Ross 11:50, Norman" at the top of the first note page.

"I'll tell ya' how I'm doin'. This dodo grabbed my arm, and I swung at him, and I said 'Ain't no one touching me.' Then I said, 'What are you doin' down here?' And he said he hadn't read about the case. I said, 'What do you mean you haven't read about the case? Everyone's read about the case.' He said, 'What are you doin' down here?' And, I said, 'Man, I've been pullin' an eight.'"

"Did you explain to him what you meant by an eight?" I asked. My tape recorder was on a small end table an arm's length away. I was tempted to turn the tape recorder on and simultaneously press my phone's speaker button so I could record this call for our doctors' review. However, if I did, I knew I'd sound as if I were speaking in a tunnel. I elected to forego the maneuver, fearing it would spook Norman and destroy any trust between us.

"I told him, 'Man, I've already done an eight-year sentence. I've been locked up four years this month ... I get a day's credit for every day I do.'"

"Okay, what else did this doctor ask you?"

"He was trying to suck up to me. I told him how the state hospital and everyone in it sucks. He said he didn't like the hospital either, and

Chapter 33: Understanding the Many Sides of Ross Carlson

I told him, 'Hey man, you're just tryin' to snuggle up and kiss my ass, aren't ya?' He asked me about cooperating with my attorneys, and I told him, 'It's none of your goddamn business.' I told him I've had no trial yet, and he didn't even know what a trial on the merits was. He was tryin' to pull my chain."

"What else did he ask you?" I said as I pushed the "do not disturb" button on my phone. I was hoping to string out my conversation with Norman as long as possible and didn't want anyone buzzing me on the intercom with an invitation for lunch. Norman continued.

"He asked me about Judge Day and Judge Kingsley. I told him I didn't know a whole lot about Kingsley. He grabbed my arm. I pulled it away. He was a punk, man. His eyes lit up, and he said to me, 'Ha, big change!' He must have thought I was goin' to shank him. He got here around 10:00, 10:30 ... left around 11:00. They took my watch, so I have to guess by watching TV. He was tryin' to smooch me, but I wouldn't fall for his bullshit."

My first conversation with Norman lasted about 15 minutes, but it was significant because it demonstrated the trust that another of Ross's personalities reposed in me. After this call, there was only one other personality, Black, whom I wanted to meet. Fairbairn had met him briefly during his May 1984 videotaping. Rod and Marilyn Carlson may have also on the last day of their lives. I didn't know if I ever would.

At least with this phone call from Norman, I felt that I had earned the confidence of nearly all of the personalities. My patience had paid off. It was unfortunate the hospital had not exercised that same feature, especially since they were the professionals supposedly trained to do so. Judge Kingsley would hear much more about the hospital's gross ineptitude during the upcoming hearing.

CHAPTER 34

The Interminable State Diagnoses

The first time I had heard a state witness render a psychiatric opinion about Ross was when Drs. Norma Livingston, Scott Reichlin, and Alan Fine testified in 1984 before Judge Day. Simply stated, the opinions of those doctors were that,

(1) Ross did not suffer from MPD [Livingston]; (2) he was faking the disorder [Reichlin]; or (3) if he did have the illness, it was iatrogenically created by our doctors' inadvertent suggestions [Fine].

Although Judge Day had rejected each of those views, his finding that Ross suffered from MPD did not stop the onslaught of future state diagnoses. From July 1984, when Ross was admitted to the hospital, until September 1987, when the second competency trial was set to begin before Judge Kingsley, state evaluators made the following diagnoses of Ross's mental state: mixed personality disorder, atypical psychosis, paranoid personality disorder, retardation and depression, dissociative disorder with symptoms of MPD, mixed personality disorder with narcissistic features, adult antisocial personality disorder, and malingering. Nearly all of those opinions were rendered after the hospital's chief of psychiatry, Dr. Huffaker, and chief clinical psychologist, Dr. Trautt, both concluded in October 1984 that Ross suffered from MPD.

Six months after the Huffaker-Trautt findings, the hospital's records emphasized the haunting reminder that " ... treatment will take at least two years to restore him to competency." In his April 24, 1985, hospital note, Dr. Huffaker explained,

Chapter 34: The Interminable State Diagnoses

Until such time as Mr. Carlson reaches an integrated state, he will continue to be incompetent to proceed. ... In the long run, only through confronting himself through honest and open self-revelation, with skilled therapeutic help, can Mr. Carlson achieve integration of his personality, become competent to proceed, and have a realistic hope of good mental health in the future. The achievement of good mental health will be recognized by fusion of Mr. Carlson's various personality components, amelioration of his unhealthy tendency to split the world, ... and for him to be open, candid, and self-revealing about his past as well as inner feelings.

Instances of Ross's bizarre conduct, which, in part, formed the basis of Dr. Huffaker's recipe for success, were witnessed by other hospital personnel, such as Karen Patterson, a registered nurse. As Ross's first therapist from July 10, 1984, through approximately October 10, 1984, Ms. Patterson wasn't aware that Judge Day's court order even required treatment for MPD. That little detail made no difference to Ms. Patterson because she had no clue what MPD was anyway. The RN, however, was at least observant and an accurate record keeper. She detailed two significant incidents in the hospital records.

"Oh, yes, I remember this one," she said during my interview of her before the upcoming competency hearing. "On September 27, 1984, after approximately five minutes into our one-on-one, Ross's eyes suddenly began moving rapidly from side to side. He didn't speak for about 15 seconds, so I just sat still. He then sat up straight in his chair and with a puzzled expression said, 'Yes?' I had never seen anything like it before," Patterson ingenuously admitted.

"Did the behavior have any psychiatric significance to you?" I asked.

"What do you mean?" she replied.

"I mean did it suggest any psychiatric diagnosis? Were the movements or pause in the movements a feature of any psychiatric illness with which you were familiar?"

"I don't know. Like I said, I had never seen anything like it before."

I thought it best to move on but made a note to myself to be sure to repeat this line of questioning before Judge Kingsley. I then asked Patterson about an incident on October 2, 1984.

"That was when I approached Ross in the day hall for our one-on-one. He was dressed so unlike him — undershirt and blue jeans — plus, he was smoking a cigar. I had never seen him do that. We sat down for therapy, and he said he had nothing to talk about. By this time, I had known about Judge Day's findings. I asked Ross whom I was speaking to, and he answered, 'Ross Carlson.' He then moved his eyes from side to side for a few seconds, sat up in his chair, and looked directly at me. I again asked 'To whom am I speaking?' He replied, 'Ross Carlson — that's an unusual question to ask.' When I asked how long we had been talking together, he replied, 'Oh, about 20 minutes.' In actuality, we'd been together for about five minutes. He then stated he had an unusual taste in his mouth, 'like I've been smoking cigars.'"

I thanked Patterson for her time. Another "therapist" I interviewed before the hearing was Patterson's successor, Barbara Swerdfeger. A high school graduate in 1955, Ms. Swerdfeger began working at the state hospital in 1962. Soon after her hiring, she completed a nine-month training program as a psych tech. In 1965, she received three additional months of instruction, and since then had attended various workshops at the hospital. Evidently, that wealth of experience qualified her for assignment by the hospital as Ross's weekly therapist.

Swerdfeger had no experience with MPD, no knowledge of its diagnostic features, and no idea what MPD signs Ross manifested. "At one time, Dr. Trautt gave me some pamphlets regarding the illness, but I don't know where they are," she revealed after I asked her if she had ever reviewed any literature regarding the disorder. She, however, remembered a few unusual incidents involving Ross.

One occurred on November 5, 1984, when the night shift personnel attempted to obtain a urine specimen from Ross at 6:00 a.m. Ross's response of "fuck you" regarding the early wake-up call startled the staff. Around 9:00 a.m., another employee, Russell Serracino, approached Ross about his attitude and received a similar salutation. "Later that same day when Dr. Huffaker questioned Ross about his use of salty language that morning, he had no recollection of what the doctor was talking about," Swerdfeger said.

Chapter 34: The Interminable State Diagnoses

The next incident happened on March 3, 1985, when Ross was on his way to lunch. "His usual neatness had changed," Swerdfeger recalled. "At this time, he was wearing a T-shirt without sleeves, blue jeans, and his hair was uncharacteristically combed back. He was also wearing glasses. I spoke to him, but he didn't answer. Suddenly, I observed some very rapid and involuntary eye movements. Ross then continued on his way to lunch, but touched himself in a manner indicating he was surprised to see what he had worn that day. After lunch, he changed and seemed like his usual self."

The third occasion happened after the infamous May 28, 1985, pant-wetting episode. "When they asked him about it, he couldn't remember anything," Swerdfeger said.

The May 28, 1985, incident, which prompted the hospital's frantic call to me, involved the ignoble hospital tech, Jim Quintana, whom Kashaun had told us about. Quintana, a hospital employee for 11 years, recounted the episode to Judge Kingsley in open court.

"I was sitting in the dining room about two tables from Ross. Suddenly, he began staring into thin air. I hollered at him, but he didn't respond. After yelling a couple of more times, I walked over and said, 'Ross, Ross what's wrong?' He kept looking straight ahead. Then out of the blue, he poured water over his head. I began shaking him, again asking what was the matter. Finally, he shook his head back and forth and looked up at me. I said, 'Are you okay, Ross?' He answered, 'Nothing is the matter, why do you ask?' He then picked up his tray. I noticed that the seat of his chair was wet and that his pants were wet as well. Ross put his tray away, came back, and sat down."

After hearing Quintana's explanation, I couldn't tell if Ross's pants had gotten soiled from the water he had poured over his head and which spilled onto his chair, or if Ross had actually experienced incontinence. Quintana never bothered to tell Dr. Dawn McNiece, Ross's ward psychiatrist, the full story before she called me about the brain tumor scare. Quintana continued testifying about his observations.

Most recently, "Ross has been in an unusual state of depression," Quintana said. "His walk has become slower, his voice tones quieter, and he's been slouching in his chair."

Based on all of the above, Quintana nevertheless believed Ross was competent "based upon my intuition and gut feeling," the technician dead-panned. Judge Kingsley seemed to be clenching his teeth upon hearing Quintana's last utterance. I was sure tea leaves and tarot cards were also a part of Quintana's "expert" analysis. Fortunately, a measure of professionalism also existed at the hospital.

The hospital's records contained a brief note that Dr. Donald Cole had performed a mental status exam of Ross in July of 1987. The chart, however, contained no findings from that exam. There was no written report among the records. I understood why when I interviewed the doctor, a cheerful, friendly type who seemed oblivious to the hospital's animus toward Ross. The doctor's primary agenda was the responsible discharge of his medical responsibilities. I also led him through his testimony before Judge Kingsley.

After graduating in 1954 from Temple Medical School, Cole served a few years with the United States Army Medical Corp. He then returned to Temple for his psychiatric residency and where he taught for the next four years. He joined the staff at the Colorado state hospital in 1965, staying until 1972.

After several years in private practice, the doctor returned to the hospital about a year ago. During his two stints at the hospital, he had performed more than 100 court evaluations and had testified as an expert 30 to 40 times.

According to Dr. Cole, the state hospital was required to perform an annual mental status exam of its patients. When Cole checked the hospital's records during July of 1987, he noticed Ross's last evaluation had been conducted more than a year ago by a staff psychiatrist, Dr. Herbert Nagamoto. Therefore, Dr. Cole assumed the responsibility of examining Ross in order to meet the yearly reporting requirements. The doctor's initiative, however, was not fully appreciated.

Mike Chittenden, the clinical administrator of the ward, chided Cole insisting that the evaluation and attendant report were Greg Trautt's obligation. Dr. Cole disagreed, believing those duties belonged to the staff psychiatrist. Inexplicably, however, the doctor's findings never found their way onto Ross's chart. We made sure the findings found their way onto Judge Kingsley's notepad when Dr. Cole testified.

Chapter 34: The Interminable State Diagnoses

"Mr. Carlson looked discouraged and appeared tired," Dr. Cole began as he recounted his examination of Ross. "He held his head in a downward position with his chin almost resting on his chest. His eyes stared at the floor. During the exam, Mr. Carlson appeared utterly exasperated and hopeless."

"Did you make any significant findings during the exam?" I asked the doctor.

"The most startling finding occurred when I asked Mr. Carlson what is meant by 'Don't cry over spilled milk.' He responded that it meant 'Don't worry about it if you knock some over.' That is what a mental retard's response would be," the doctor explained. "You have to be pretty doggone sick to give an answer like that."

When Cole asked Ross to explain the meaning of "A stitch in time saves nine." Ross answered, "... saves nine what ... sorry, I don't know." "That's severe illness," Cole said.

Finally, when Ross admitted he had no sexual urges, Cole knew he had a patient sinking into an emotional abyss. "Vegetative depression" was the doctor's clinical finding.

I couldn't imagine why the hospital wouldn't want Cole's conclusions to see the light of day!

Another evaluation done at the hospital's behest was performed by a private practitioner, Dr. David Wahl. It was Dr. Wahl's examination on September 3, 1987, at the Douglas County Jail that precipitated the memorable call to me by Norman just before noon that day. Walter cross-examined Wahl.

While flirting with the diagnosis of MPD, Wahl described having observed a "significant fluctuation" in Ross's behavior during this evaluation. The doctor stated,

> *Initially, he presents himself as withdrawn, minimally communicative, and depressed young man who makes little to no eye contact. When stressful questions are asked, there is a significant change and Mr. Carlson becomes animated, angry, and anxious.*

Wahl found that Ross "... presents evidence of a dissociative disorder characterized by impairments in integrating identity and/

or consciousness." Therefore, after having only seen Ross for an hour, Wahl came within a millimeter of finding MPD. We obviously thought Wahl was brilliant. The prosecutors had no choice but to call Wahl as their witness during the hearing because, in spite of his observations of clear dissociation, he nevertheless felt Ross was competent. During the hearing, Bob Chappell then hoped to take the sting out of Wahl's observations of Ross's MPD symptoms by calling his last expert, another state-privately-retained psychiatrist, Dr. Kathy Morall.

Dr. Morall's principal diagnosis was adult antisocial disorder. Although an unflattering label, it nevertheless fell short of the more insidious diagnosis of antisocial personality disorder. However, in a devious slight-of-hand during her testimony, Morall changed her principal finding of "adult antisocial disorder" to the full-blown more pernicious "antisocial personality disorder" — in other words, a malingerer, a sociopath; someone without a conscience.

During my cross-examination of her, Morall admitted having never seen, diagnosed, or treated MPD. She had never even received any information about the disorder during medical school. She hadn't read the current literature regarding MPD, and wasn't aware of any texts that Ross could have studied before 1983 in order to fake the disorder.

The doctor's report contained a statement which read, "A review of the progress notes essentially indicated the lack of observation of behavior that would support dissociative episodes or loss of time." I showed her a stack of documents that contained 18 hospital progress notes, chronicling obvious dissociative episodes witnessed by numerous hospital personnel during Ross's stay, including Drs. Huffaker and Trautt, nurse Karen Patterson, psych tech Barbara Swerdfeger, and, of course, hospital tech Jim Quintana. I went through all of them one at a time, directing her to read the most compelling passages in each. Dr. Morall had to admit that every one of the 18 episodes was symptomatic of MPD.

Upon concluding my exam, I sat down and recalled my interview of Dr. Morall at a local Denver restaurant over a year ago. At that time, I had known the doctor from prior unrelated court cases and knew she had been hired by the state to evaluate Ross for the next competency hearing. During our meeting, she had commented,

Chapter 34: The Interminable State Diagnoses

"David, sometimes I just don't have enough time to get everything finished." The prosecutors probably wished she had taken the time in this case.

The matter was now in the hands of Judge Kingsley. His ruling would have to reflect his views of the state hospital's Baskin-Robbins' menu of diagnoses and their "treatment and care" of Ross. The judge announced a recess and left the bench.

CHAPTER 35

Enough is Enough

Within a half-hour Judge Kingsley returned to court, had his clerk distribute to each side copies of a two-page written opinion, and left the bench. While reading the first paragraph of the judge's Order, I could hardly contain my unabashed satisfaction over the judge's thorough condemnation of the hospital's arrogance. Although Judge Kingsley did not dismiss the case in order to pave the way for Ross's civil commitment, he did fire a blistering salvo at the hospital's wholesale treatment failures.

Adhering to the dictates of the state Supreme Court's decision in *Kort v. Carlson,* the judge declared that

> *following his commitment in July 1984, the Colorado State Hospital (CSH) staff failed to consider all relevant facts and exercise competent professional judgment and that by reason of such failure the defendant's meaningful treatment was denied.*

Kingsley next found that the hospital had **"*warehoused*"** Ross and ordered it to consult with our experts regarding MPD and to "work with us" to restore Ross's competency. Since the hospital had been able to find money for podiatrists and psychiatric consultants, the judge ordered it "to find funds to hire the necessary experts who would be able to treat and instruct CSH staff on how to treat the defendant." Judge Kingsley then warned the hospital that if it continued to avoid seeking the necessary outside expert help, he would appoint experts requested by us.

Chapter 35: Enough is Enough

We now had a second judge who found Ross was suffering from MPD and incompetent as a result of that illness. In the midst of Walter's and my restrained glee, the prosecution team hurried out of the courtroom with looks of shock, despair, and devastation. Although Ross appeared to be in his Steve mode, sitting calmly and taking copious notes as we read the judge's findings together, he also was his typical cynical self.

"Don't fool yourself, David," Ross said. "Nothing will change. The hospital will find a way around Kingsley's orders just like they did around Day's." I was sure Ross was wrong.

"Don't be so pessimistic, Ross. This one not only has teeth, but it's appeal proof. It mirrors the exact findings required by the Supreme Court. Things have to improve there. Just wait and see." As much as Walter and I tried to place an optimistic spin on the judge's order, Ross remained unconvinced. His final words as he was led away by the sheriffs were, "I appreciate your enthusiasm gentlemen, but Kingsley's order — they're just words on paper."

To provide Ross with a clean slate, the hospital moved him to a different ward where everything and everyone — room, staff, and treatment team — would be new and presumably uninfluenced by what had happened in the past. They promised to immediately hire qualified consultants to lead his treatment. Two months later, on December 13, 1987, I also opted for a new future.

On Saturday, December 12, 1987, Robin's then twelve-year-old daughter, Rachel Alyse, would celebrate her Bat Mitzvah. Our families and friends throughout the United States and Canada would descend upon Denver for the occasion. Our out-of-town guests had an added impetus to travel because on the next day, Robin and I would say, "I do!" to one another. One person, who couldn't attend that weekend's festivities, sent me a note of congratulations the day after my wedding.

December 14, 1987

Dear David,

I just heard. Congratulations! I'm happy for you. But doesn't the poor girl know what she is in for? Marrying a guy like you, stupid, old, fat, and dumpy looking. Poor Robin!

I thought I'd let you know that I felt slighted by not getting an invitation. I mean it's not like I wouldn't have rearranged my schedule and flown into town! Really David!

Sincerely,

Your most endearing client, or maybe just the most enduring. R.

After receiving Ross's letter, I spoke with him on the phone. I told him that he was on our list of invitees, but since he had been moved around so much, we didn't know where to send the invitation. The best we could do to celebrate our friendship was our usual exchange of holiday gifts.

He had mailed me a framed Brian Davis poster of a white Iris, against a black background, and I sent him Lee Iacocca's book. I hung the Davis picture in my home. By now, Ross had considered me more than just one of the passionate attorneys working on his case. I found myself unable to resist reaching out to him. He knew a lot about my family and that was okay.

By mid-December 1987, Ross had been living in his new permanent ward for nearly a month. Since the hospital had not begun any staff training or treatment by then, I contacted Pat Robb.

"David, as I told you a month ago, Dr. Kort had to prepare a special proposal to the legislature's joint budget committee for this case. Since the judge's order requires us to obtain the funds for consultants, that's what Dr. Kort has been doing. As soon as we hear anything, I'll let you know."

On December 22, 1987, Ross had called saying the hospital had told him that Dr. Walter Young, an MPD expert recommended by us, had been hired to conduct workshops and that another expert was on the way to begin treatment. There, however, was no established timetable. Ross sounded depressed.

I called Pat Robb for an update. "David, Dr. Mark Pecevich, our

Chapter 35: Enough is Enough

chief psychiatrist, is still negotiating with Walter Young, who wants to conduct a Saturday program. That will increase his fee to $2,500. One of our psychiatric consultants from the University of Colorado, Dr. Michael Weissberg, has also been contacted. Dr. Weissberg is responsible for selecting an independent panel of experts who will organize Ross's treatment plan. From that panel, Ross's therapist will be selected."

Another couple of months passed without any progress. I wrote Pat Robb again. A month later she called, but passed me off to Dr. Pecevich. I phoned him.

To my shock, the doctor informed me that Ross was not receiving any treatment even though in his words "the hospital has sufficient funds from last year's budget for whatever it needs." However, it was "senseless to have a workshop on MPD," Pecevich said, until the independent panel "evaluated Ross" and decided what was wrong with him.

"Evaluate Ross!" I cried out incredulously, feeling my heart racing and blood pressure skyrocketing, Pecevich's comments hit me up the side of the head like a two by four. I realized I had been deceived during the last few months about budget requests and negotiating with Dr. Young. It was all a bunch of utter and outrageous BS!

"Ross doesn't need to be evaluated anymore by the hospital," I continued, my voice remaining at a thundering decibel level similar to when I growled at newscaster Paul Day when he shoved a microphone to Ross's face nearly four years ago. "Two judges have already determined what's wrong with him. Your predecessor, Dr. Huffaker, and the head of your neuropsych testing, Greg Trautt, have both made the same diagnosis independent of one another. Judge Kingsley's order was to treat Ross for MPD, not evaluate him!"

"Mr. Savitz, don't you think it's a little inappropriate to have a judge make a medical diagnosis?" Pecevich countered dismissively. Who the fuck are you to question the judge's ruling! I felt like screaming into the receiver. Instead, I quickly calmed down, avoided an out-of-character obscenity, and responded firmly.

"Doctor, the judge did not render a medical diagnosis. He made judicial findings after listening to differing psychiatric opinions for several days. He issued a court order."

"We disagree. This is what we have decided to do," Pecevich replied.

"With whom is Dr. Weissberg consulting?"

"As far as I know, it's Dr. Orne and a couple of others."

Dr. Orne! That's all I needed to hear. My greatest fear had been realized. I was beside myself; my blood pressure was erupting again. The notorious, national MPD debunker would surely be retained to disembowel all of the good we had accomplished. Dr. Kluft's emphatic warning of four years ago, "Stay away from Orne!" was blasting in my ears. I quickly finished talking to Dr. Pecevich and uttered another expletive into the disconnected line. I immediately called Dr. Weissberg, whom I had never spoken to nor met. He had already left his office.

The following day, Dr. Weissberg returned my call and confirmed the independent panel's first step of evaluation. I elected to control my anger, especially since this was the first time I had dealt with this doctor. There was no reason to show Dr. Weissberg my bellicose side after 30 seconds into our first call. However, after we ended our conversation, I sat back in my chair and stewed.

I knew that a nurturing and positive therapeutic milieu could produce wonderful results for Ross. It was excruciatingly disappointing to realize this was never going to happen. We had been duped. Ross was right.

About five months had now passed since Judge Kingsley's order, which the hospital was saluting with its middle finger. Walter and were naive to think another court order would pull the hospital down to its knees. After all, the state hospital had disregarded Judge Day's order of July 10, 1984, appealed his decision requiring it to pay for Dr. Quinn's services, bounced the judge off the case for bogus reasons, and now was pulling down its trousers and mooning Judge Kingsley. We, however, would never wave the white flag.

I cleared away other files from my desk, and wrote Pat Robb a multi-page letter. I vented my anger and dispensed with any further cordiality. Among other things, I told her that Ross has been "probed, analyzed, and picked at *ad nauseam* by a plethora of experts. Enough is enough!" I told her that since the hospital has money to treat Ross, "stop dillydallying around" and get him treated.

Chapter 35: Enough is Enough

For the first time in the case, Pat Robb showed her true colors responding with vitriol of her own. She accused me of unprofessional conduct for faulting the hospital with wasting time.

Walter gladly rose to my defense, replying to Pat's April 1st letter with his own acid-tongued missive. He accused her of playing an April Fool's joke when she lashed out at me for charging the hospital with dragging its feet. Having gotten our respective shots in, it was now time for Walter and me to take meaningful action.

On April 7, 1988, we filed a motion with Judge Kingsley, informing him of the hospital's furtive scheme to undermine his rulings. We demanded a halt to the hospital's tactics and the immediate implementation of the judge's orders. The motion was set for hearing on April 25, 1988. Walter and I had thought the motions would stymie the possible involvement of Dr. Orne.

However, while working at my office on Saturday, April 16, 1988, I received a phone call at 1:00 in the afternoon that drastically changed the course of this case.

CHAPTER 36

Cyborgs & Dr. Martin Orne

The Saturday started off with my spending a quiet and productive morning catching up on a few lawsuits — ones that I had filed against two nursing homes for abusing elderly patients and another involving my defense of a lawyer who had been sued in a paternity action. Since I was the only one working in my suite, my solitude was guaranteed except by an occasional phone call. The last uneventful call occurred around 11:00 a.m. Then, around 1:00 p.m., I received the most bizarre call I had ever experienced in my nearly 20 years of practice.

"Please! Please!" cried the hysterical and sobbing, childlike voice. "They're trying to torture me! Doctors are trying to hurt me! Doctors are trying to eat my brains! David, you'll protect me?" The wailing was uncontrollable, the breathing rapid and heavy. I had never heard Ross sound so upset and scared.

"I'll protect you," I said, but having no clue what actually was happening. "Who is doing this?"

"I don't know ... trying to slide through back doors. Hit me with mallets. Eat my brain and torture me. They can do it."

"We will not let them do it," I said reassuringly, hoping to relax him and facilitate a switch from this childlike personality to an older and understandable alter, such as Steve.

"These people ... nothing stops them ... they keep coming." His sobbing and rapid breathing continued. I again asked whom he was talking about.

Chapter 36: Cyborgs & Dr. Martin Orne

"Doctors, mean men ... cyborgs trying to invade earth and steal secrets."

"Steal secrets from whom?" I asked quickly, but at the same time racking my brain in search for the right questions to ask and correct demeanor to present in order to cause Ross to switch out of his sci-fi delusions.

"Me ... trying to hurt earth, force secrets and torture me." Well, that question didn't work! "Something has to be done. I can't stop them. I need protection."

"We'll protect you," I said, again trying to relieve Ross's stress. If there was anything I had learned about MPD it was that internal and environmental stressors precipitate dissociations and that the best way to facilitate a switch to a more dominant alter was to assuage the individual's fears. "Where are you now?" I asked, hoping he was where I could talk to a staff person.

"Blue phone. Number 5. My building." Ross answered, now having finally stopped crying and beginning to settle down. I asked him who lived at the place from where he was calling, not understanding until much later that he was calling from the blue phone located in the ward hallway of his Building 5.

"Patients, people ... they kidnaped and put me away. Trying to slide through back door so you don't know. Walter said it wouldn't happen, but it always does. Robb and DA trying to get around Order ... do you understand?" Ross now began sounding a little older but still somewhat infantile. On the left-hand margin of my notes of our conversation, I wrote, "sounds like the character Benny in *LA Law*." Benny was a developmentally challenged adult who whined when stressed. I didn't interrupt Ross because I thought he was in the process of switching to an intelligible adult. He continued.

"Steal my things ... take my intelligent reports from me. Try to kidnap me. I didn't know what to do." That was not very intelligible; so much for wishful thinking!

"You did the right thing by calling me. Has anyone made any notes?" I asked, hoping he could read something one of the other alters had written.

"I couldn't write. I can't take much more, David."

Just in the Nick of Time

I told Ross I'd have one of our doctors call him. He asked for Quinn and as an alternative "Dr. Fair one," not recalling the name of Dr. Fairbairn, the one defense doctor to whom he had been the closest these last few years.

After assuring Ross someone would contact him, I began making phone calls while remembering Dr. Fisch's admonition of four years ago. At that time, when the doctor reported to Walter and me that he had received a phone call from Ross, who said he was being bombarded by the names of different personalities, I asked Fisch how bizarre did the disorder get. He responded, "You ain't seen nothing yet!" I believed, now, I was seeing it!

Since my unsuccessful efforts to reach our doctors were limited to leaving voice messages, I decided to call the state hospital. I asked the switchboard operator to have the ward psychiatrist speak to Ross because he appeared to be in such terrible distress. I was informed that only one psychiatrist worked at the hospital on Saturdays, but he was not located on Ross's ward. I remained on the line while the operator paged that doctor.

"Mr. Savitz," the operator said, "I've spoken to Dr. Neederhut, who said he doesn't know anything about the case. You'll have to call back on Monday and talk to Dr. Wiaduck, the ward psychiatrist."

In the slight chance the operator was playing a cruel joke, I suggested to her that a mental hospital might want to peek in at a patient who was weeping hysterically about cyborgs invading earth, stealing his secrets, and dining on his brains. My efforts to impart the urgency of Ross's psychotic meltdown fell on deaf ears. After another couple of minutes of placing me on hold, the operator returned to the line and reiterated that Dr. Neederhut wouldn't talk to me. I was incensed.

That night, I spoke with Dr. Fairbairn who had no luck in communicating with Ross. "David, he cut our conversation short. Said he couldn't trust me and wasn't certain who I was." In the meantime, I had spoken to the ward personnel, who agreed to keep an eye on Ross.

The next morning, Robin and I received an unexpected wake-up call around 8:15. It was a collect call from Ross. He no longer presented as paranoid and delusional but rather sounded quite depressed. This was akin to the presentation of the alter, Gray.

Chapter 36: Cyborgs & Dr. Martin Orne

"Yesterday, I was taken from my room to speak to Dr. Weissberg, Pecevich, and another man," Ross explained. "They called me a faker and said I had to cooperate. They videotaped me. I was scared, David. I don't know what I said."

"I'm sure you did fine, Ross. Let me speak to a staff member."

Bob Gonzales, a psych tech on the ward, then triggered my worst fear. "Dr. Orne was the third man," Gonzales revealed. Yesterday morning, Gonzales explained, Ross was taken to the administration building for an interview with Dr. Orne. Ross, however, said nothing during the interview, except he did drop to the floor and began screaming. Everything was videotaped. "The doctors are supposed to come back this morning for another session," Gonzales revealed. Having now had Ross's call of yesterday placed in context, I asked Gonzales to return him to the phone.

"David, stop these men, or Black will turn them into space dust. The cyborg is from Strunefield and has a funny voice. He is a giant" I had no clue what Ross was talking about, and Robin could see I was perplexed. I merely shrugged my shoulders at the sight of her facial curiosity. Ross continued.

"Black thinks they're hurting me. Since you can't help me, Black will have to. Neither Steve nor Norman can handle the cyborg. If you're small, you can hide from the big in the ventilator shaft. But if they catch you, they will put me in a cage, hit my head with a hammer, and eat my brains ... steal my secrets and take all my knowledge."

Somehow, a Sunday morning discussion about one-eyed beasts from the galactic empire did not portend for a relaxing day off. "I'll call Walter," I said.

"Walter is also a cyborg because he doesn't talk to me," Ross replied, effectively eliminating another vital member of the defense team from his communication. I promised once this episode was over to research cyborgs and discover why I didn't fit the mold.

"Can you or someone make notes?" I asked.

"I can't make notes," Ross answered. "All I can do is hide. It hurts so bad — my arms, stomach, neck, legs." I encouraged Ross to hang in there, and I would try my best to prevent Dr. Pecevich from snatching him up again.

I reached Walter and briefed him on the last two days. He wanted to speak to Ross himself. A half hour later, Walter called me back. Ross refused to speak to him, accusing Walter of being a cyborg. I respectfully assured Walter he was not.

I finally reached Pecevich at 10:40 a.m., directed him to cease and desist from coordinating any more Orne interviews and reminded him that Ross was represented by counsel, who were insisting upon being present for any such sessions. Further, I said, Ross was exercising his right to remain silent. I figured that the doctor would cower from my firm, legalistic rhetoric.

"Mr. Savitz, if you have a legal matter, take it up with Mrs. Robb. The hospital has contracted with consultants to independently evaluate Mr. Carlson, and that's what they're doing."

"Doctor, you have no authority to interview our client without our consent. If you're going to persist, we want one of our doctors present."

"Mr. Savitz, the consultants do not wish to have anyone else involved. The interviews will continue today and possibly tomorrow."

I couldn't believe the unmitigated gall of this guy. I repeated my protests, raising my voice, but characteristically Pecevich would not budge. He was totally unimpressed with my heated lawyering. Pecevich fended off my persuasive arguments (my perception, at least) as if he were deftly swatting away annoying flies. My only option was to try to convince Judge Kingsley of the impropriety of the Orne/Weissberg blitzkrieg.

At 5:30 that afternoon, Judge Kingsley, Pat Robb, Bob Chappell, Walter, and I conducted a hearing by telephone conference. It was the first time I had ever participated in a court proceeding on the phone while seated at my kitchen table and dressed in a warm-up outfit and running shoes.

I requested a restraining order to prevent the hospital from conducting any further evaluations of Ross. Pat Robb responded, stating the judge's latest order required the hospital to use funds to hire an outside expert to treat Ross. Dr. Orne, she said, was originally approached by the hospital in October 1984, but was not actually hired until after the judge's 1987 order.

"We have been ordered to provide treatment," Robb continued,

Chapter 36: Cyborgs & Dr. Martin Orne

"and we have found the best person, namely Dr. Orne, to advise us regarding that issue. The hospital's chief psychiatrist, Dr. Pecevich, is present during the interviews in the event Ross needs care."

The last comment was the biggest joke in the world. Pecevich was as interested in caring for Ross as his sympathetic colleague, Dr. Neederhut, had been that morning.

As a result of Robb's snowjob, the judge refused my main request. He allowed Orne to finish his interviews but ordered him to write a report regarding his findings and to provide us copies of the videotaped interviews.

I then called Ross, who was not happy with Kingsley's decision. "David, they said mean things. I tried not to say anything to them, but I don't know if I did."

I reassured him we were confident he did the right thing and that we were getting copies of the tapes to see for ourselves. "David, I'm so tired. I hurt so much." Ross then hung up without saying another word. I was left with having to wait for the Orne tapes.

CHAPTER 37

A Chair-Rocking Marathon

At 6:00 a.m. on Tuesday, May 3, I left my home in a hurry and headed directly to the office. Late yesterday, my secretary Leslie had left word on my home answering machine that the Orne tapes had been delivered to the office. Finally, I would learn about the events surrounding Ross's bizarre phone call and what, if anything, he had revealed to the Philadelphia debunker.

The night watchman of our office building was seated at his desk in the front lobby and looked at his watch as I said good morning. No, I said under my breath, most attorneys don't arrive at their office at 6:15 in the morning.

After exiting the elevator onto the sixth floor and walking toward our suite's double-glass doors, I could see that the interior of the suite was illuminated only by the lights of an awakening city. In an hour or so, the snow-capped Rocky Mountains would be visible to the west.

This morning, however, I would work in our east side, more isolated conference room. From there, the scenic attractions were small homes, various sized apartment buildings and Colorado's flat eastern plains. The setting assured no distractions.

I grabbed the two videotapes that lay on top of my desk and headed to the conference room. I pushed a chair a few feet from the monitor, propped my note pad on my lap, and inserted the first tape into the VCR.

The opening camera shot focused upon Ross and two other

Chapter 37: A Chair-Rocking Marathon

men seated at a long, rectangular-shaped table. Ross was positioned at the end of the table, while the two men sat at the elongated side and to Ross's right. Ross was slumping down in his chair, with his head lowered and his chin resting against his chest. He was seated just a few feet from the wall behind him.

Ross's eyes were hidden behind dark sunglasses, an appearance Dr. Fairbairn first brought to our attention more than two years ago. The glasses were ostensibly to protect Ross's sensitive eyes from the light. However, as a collateral benefit, they served as a two-way mirror — Ross could see out, but no one could see in.

Ross was dressed in jeans and a light-colored, fleece jacket that was zippered halfway up the front. Clutching a yellow-lined tablet close to his chest, his head was nearly buried in his jacket. He was sitting still.

A very heavyset man, seated approximately an arm's length from Ross, was staring at him. The second man, who was slightly built and further away from Ross, arose from the table and walked out of the camera's view. The first man, after several seconds of just looking at Ross, turned his head and faced the camera. Ross appeared either asleep or in a deep trance, thereby effectively ignoring his onlooker.

While seated, the first man, who appeared to be in his late 50s or early 60s, had his hands folded upon his enormously ample midriff. A receding hairline extended back to the middle of his head, where it met its swoop of thinning brown hair combed from left to right. Dark-colored, horn-rimmed glasses and a close-cropped mustache completed the man's imposing presence. He was smartly dressed in a light-colored suit with a white-pocket square neatly folded into the left breast pocket.

The slimmer man enjoyed a more youthful look, accented, in part, by his hair length reaching just below his ears. Dressed in a more academic style — a sport jacket, khaki trousers, and blue-patterned tie — he appeared to be in his early 40s.

The larger man spoke with a Central European accent — his voice reminding me of a former Austrian ski instructor. I recognized the heavier man from a few years ago when I watched the taped interviews between him and the diabolical Los Angeles Hillside

Strangler, Kenneth Bianchi. This gentleman was Dr. Martin Orne. The second individual, I assumed, was Dr. Michael Weissberg.

Dr. Orne instructed the cameraman to zoom in on Ross. "Let's see if we can capture his facial expressions since he's not choosing to communicate otherwise," the doctor said.

The picture now was just of Ross's upper torso and face. His military-style haircut and beard didn't look any different from when I saw him in court a week ago. I couldn't tell if his eyes were open or shut. However, he was mumbling something inaudible. He was slumping in his chair with the collar of his jacket turned up, nearly covering his ears. While cowering, he seemed as if he were trying to hide inside his jacket.

For several minutes, eerie silence filled the room. No one said anything or moved. The camera focused only on Ross who eventually stopped mumbling and sat more erect in his chair. That was his last movement for several more minutes. Dr. Orne finally broke the room's protracted tranquility in a kind voice.

"Do you want to take the opportunity to talk about things?" he asked. Ross's demeanor did not change. The doctor nevertheless continued speaking to his nonverbal charge.

"You must be as curious as I am. It's your life."

Ross remained non-responsive. His inquisitor tried another gentle approach. "We have things to discuss. Since you are comfortable right now, we'll leave you for a few minutes just the way you are. We'll be back."

After the doctors left the room, the camera continued filming Ross, who suddenly winced, resumed mumbling, and then fell silent. He remained that way for a few minutes, after which time the background noise of chairs and voices signaled the doctors' return to the room. Martin Orne spoke.

"This is Dr. Orne again. I think you're ready to wake up if you would like to take advantage of this opportunity. The state has spent a great deal for this evaluation. I doubt they will do it again. You would benefit from discussing matters so we can determine what really happened. You can stay uncooperative, but it is not a useful way of doing things."

Orne's cajoling was ignored. Ross's self-hypnotic trance

Chapter 37: A Chair-Rocking Marathon

guarded his mind like an impenetrable fortress — an undesirable intruder could not enter. The doctors decided to huddle again and left the room. During their absence, Ross remained motionless.

After returning to the room and unsuccessfully trying to prod a response from Ross, the doctors apparently resigned to strategize over the noon hour. Orne instructed the two attending staff members to take Ross back to the ward and return at 2:00 PM.

"Ok Ross, we'll go back now," a late-30s-looking Hispanic male, of medium-build said politely. Receiving no response, the staff member gently nudged Ross a few times while each time repeating his instruction. Ross did not awaken.

A second staff member, a bespectacled Anglo, who was slightly taller but about 50 pounds heavier than his co-worker, then appeared. He stood impatiently, intermittently shaking his head, as his co-worker unsuccessfully coaxed Ross from his slumber. The two employees then each grasped one of Ross's arms to stand him up.

Ross suddenly opened his eyes. He appeared frightened. He shook vigorously, releasing from his handlers' grasp, and began screaming, "Please! Please!"

Ross then fell to the floor, covered his head with his hands and wailed, "Don't eat my brains! Don't eat my brains!" Ross's legs were shackled, a restraint which had not been employed during any of his previous hospital evaluations.

Ross's bizarre phone call of two weeks ago that early Saturday afternoon was now more understandable. I was not unhappy that Ross had remained mute during this session, but I was also heart struck. After all, the Orne offensive had occurred on the heels of Ross having been hopelessly depressed most of that entire week. While so emotionally frail, Ross must have been consumed with fear that morning as he was led shackled from the comfort of his room to meet unannounced strangers in an unfamiliar location. Restrained and interrogated, he would have felt more like a prisoner than a patient. Is this really what the hospital had meant when it promised that meaningful psychiatric treatment was on the way? The two male workers, startled by Ross's agony on the floor, moved back from him. Shackled and laying in a fetal position, Ross continued clenching his notebook as he wept softly.

Dr. Pecevich appeared on screen for the first time and assured Ross that no one was going to hurt him. This naked pledge was obviously the full scope and extent of the doctor's care that Pat Robb promised during our phone hearing with the judge that Sunday afternoon. The doctor along with the two staff members lifted their limp, 145-pound patient to his feet. The staff members then proceeded to drag Ross from the room.

I had been watching this taped session for about two hours and needed a break. I had failed to rescue Ross after he had called that Saturday afternoon. Feelings of failure had resurfaced. Neglecting to respond to destitute cries was not what Savitzes were all about. I was treated much better than that as a child and saw my parents act as wonderful caretakers to so many others. It was my job to take care of my clients. They hired me to fix things, even impossible ones. I was disappointed in myself for not having rescued Ross the day he called and was very angry at Dr. Orne and his two underlings for having mistreated my client. Before finishing this tape, I walked to our suite's kitchen, said good morning to some friendly suitemates, and poured a cup of coffee.

By the time I returned to my task, the conference room was considerably brighter from the morning's sun. I closed the blinds and turned my attention to the balance of tape one. When Ross returned to the interview room, his demeanor had not changed. He resumed his trance-like, shrunken position while clutching his security blanket — his notebook. Dr. Orne placed a tape recorder on the table. He told Ross to say something if he objected to the recorder.

The slumbering rag doll remained silent. Orne spoke.

"Are you afraid of me?"

Ross surprisingly replied, but with a barely audible, "Yes."

"You aren't usually afraid of psychiatrists. I usually don't scare people," Orne said in a veiled attempt to appear comforting. Ross mumbled something inaudible.

"Do you know my name?" Orne asked.

"Cyborg," Ross answered.

"Silly pork?" the doctor incorrectly guessed, obviously not in step with the latest science-fiction rage.

Chapter 37: A Chair-Rocking Marathon

For the next hour, Orne attempted a variety of techniques, hoping to generate a complete sentence from his monosyllabic interviewee. The longest responses he elicited were, "Steal my mind" and "Eat my brains." Otherwise, the doctor spent the afternoon watching his forensic balloons fall to the ground like dying quail.

After finishing the first tape and needing a break, I briefed Leslie on its contents. She reacted with a pained expression of empathy. I told her everything would be okay. In all honesty, I wasn't sure.

The next morning, before returning to the office to watch tape two, I stopped with Robin for continental breakfast. She knew my custom when I came home from work; I nearly always left my business at the office. I rarely discussed my cases with her. She often discovered whom I represented by accounts in the media or phone conversations I had with other lawyers about a case. She had long understood that my role in the criminal justice system was to provide even the most malevolent client with the best representation possible. I would explain that, especially with respect to the most gruesome of cases, my job was similar to the surgeon operating on a serial killer with a brain tumor. Attorneys, like doctors, I would say, take an oath to serve every person no matter how heinous or unpopular his or her conduct. Robin knew that Ross's case was different.

She had well understood my compassion for Ross and belief in his illness. What worried her, however, was my stoicism from the emotional roller coaster of the last few weeks. She had remembered how distant I had become four years ago after I had witnessed the Fairbairn taping. I eventually told her what I had observed in those tapes because she had misinterpreted my distance as unhappiness with her. Now, she was concerned that I was again suppressing my feelings. "Honey, you know I have learned to be dispassionate. As sick as I was seeing Orne torment Ross, I can't allow that outrage to affect how I intend to interact with the doctor in the future. However, I am going to find every report, every publication, every court transcript, every possible utterance ever made by him about anything dealing with MPD. I'll be ready for him whenever he takes the witness stand."

With that, Robin and I kissed goodbye and she drove off to teach 3-year-olds at her preschool. I went to my office, pulled up

Just in the Nick of Time

my reserved seat and watched tape two. Sure enough, the opening scene showed the cyborg from Strunefield and his somnolent captive. Evidently, Dr. Orne had decided during the night's recess to become more aggressive.

"Open your eyes," the doctor commanded. "If you don't, I'll give you some smelling salts. I know you're awake; you're closing your eyes so you don't have to communicate with me." No one could accuse Orne of failing to grasp the obvious.

Receiving no response, the doctor threatened hypnosis. I didn't quite know how that was going to work because Ross was already in some other altered state. After informing Ross that he had 35 years of hypnosis experience, Orne tried several techniques to have Ross lift his hand, move his arms, or open his eyes. Orne would have had better success with a fossil. Frustrated, Orne announced a most controversial strategy. He would play our doctors' videotaped sessions with Ross. This tactic made me boil.

I had been told by Drs. Newton and Fisch that showing multiple images of his alters should be attempted only by a caring therapist and only after obtaining the patient's permission. For many MPD sufferers, seeing their other personalities on tape could trigger a psychotic reaction.

Orne turned on the monitor which had been set up a few feet from Ross. Deploying a counter stratagem, Ross rocked slowly back and forth in his chair and placed both hands over his eyes. Orne was peeved.

"Put your hands down. I want to show you a videotape of yourself with Dr. Newton." Orne then played the tape of Ross's interview with Fig.

Ross continued shielding his eyes. After several minutes of unsuccessfully convincing Ross to look at the tapes, Orne shut off the VCR. He then moved his chair within inches of Ross all the while talking about the personality Black. Orne grabbed Ross's right arm. Suddenly, Ross awakened. He quickly pulled his arm from Orne's grasp and menacingly raised his fist toward the doctor.

Instinctively, Orne pulled his body back and exclaimed, "Is this Black? Am I talking to Black?" Ross stared briefly at the doctor and then retreated to a trance-like state.

Chapter 37: A Chair-Rocking Marathon

Undaunted, Orne restarted the Newton tape. Ross's eyes opened, but his head was still down. He then coiled into a ball. He placed his hands across his chest and tried to nestle his head in between his arms. He was crying.

"I can't hear you," Orne announced.

Ross cried out, "David! David!" I clenched my lips and looked away from the monitor momentarily. I took a deep breath. Orne shut off the tape.

"Who's David?" Orne asked. "I haven't heard of him. Is he part of you?" Orne offered Ross a tissue, but the rolled-up ball of yarn refused the gesture. Orne placed the tissue on Ross's shoulder. Ross ignored it and resumed rocking back and forth in his chair. His hands over his weeping eyes and his legs visibly shaking, Ross continued to rock, at times picking up the pace. He was relentless — a chair-rocking marathoner. Orne was relegated to spectator status.

After several minutes, the doctor pleaded, "Can you stop this business you are doing?" Ross continued, at times rocking so hard and fast that his chair began banging against the wall behind him. Orne finally capitulated; he turned off the tape. Ross had rocked for about 45 minutes. The doctor stared at Ross who now sat motionless. The man of giant credentials and huge physicality had been checkmated by a 145-pound, strong-willed and fearless young man.

At Orne's direction, the two staff members approached Ross and attempted to lift him from the chair. They lost their grip, and Ross fell to the floor. The attendants had no choice — they again dragged Ross away. With that, the tape ended.

I turned off the VCR and just sat looking at the dark screen for several seconds. I opened the blinds, allowing the spring sun to re-enter the room. After straightening up the conference room, I returned to my office. I looked outside at the snow-capped mountain range and wondered if anyone was ever going to help this emotionally fractured young man.

PART 4

CHAPTER 38

Kingsley's Solution

Because the hospital was proceeding snail-like in its response to Judge Kingsley's October 1987 findings of Ross's incompetency, Walter thought we should pursue something more dramatic and quicker in order to put an end to Ross's case. Walter asked me to set up a meeting with Bob Chappell and his boss, Bob Gallagher, *the* district attorney, to see if the prosecution would agree to a finding of insanity. Such an agreement would involve a dismissal of the murder charges but Ross's commitment to the hospital where he would remain until restored to sanity. Based upon the opinions held by our experts of Ross's insanity, this was a reasonable disposition in our view.

If we elected to call Dr. John Glismann at a sanity trial, we knew the doctor believed that Ross suffered from a "severe narcissistic personality disorder" and was insane at the time of the murders. Glismann had explained to us that "Ross's view of himself and the high style in which he was expected to live were inflexible." Any attempt to interfere with that identity or lifestyle could not be tolerated by him, according to the doctor. Maintaining the standards of the Carlson family had to be accomplished at any cost. Ross's ability to reason and distinguish right from wrong, Glismann concluded, was so overwhelmed by this narcissistic force that he had no choice but to eliminate the meddlers with his lifestyle.

Although Walter and I had been heartened by Glismann's conclusion of insanity when we first met with him, we also thought

Chapter 38: Kingsley's Solution

a jury might believe that Glismann's analysis was developed while spending too much time alone in his small office. Now, however, after having been involved with Ross for nearly five years since Glismann's evaluation, we realized we may have been too presumptuous in dismissing the doctor's views, especially since he seemed to have described Justin to a tee.

Another of our experts, Dr. Richard Rewey, initially had diagnosed Ross with a severe borderline personality disorder with developing multiple personalities. However, after having seen the Fairbairn/Fisch/Newton videotapes of their interviews with Ross, hearing Dr. Newton's critique of these videotapes and discussions about his subsequent sessions with Ross, and then further evaluating Ross himself, Rewey was convinced that Ross suffered from MPD.

While being interviewed by Dr. Rewey during the winter of 1983-84, Ross explained the phenomenon of why the capable alters performed specific tasks (during the spring of 1984, while further explaining to Walter and me his configuration of personalities, Ross characterized the Justin group as "capable" of performing any number of different kinds of acts, the Ross young-ones as "incapable" of performing any tasks, and the Anti-Christ tandem as "destructive" in their capabilities). "It was like reading a bulletin board," Ross told Rewey. "We would read a note to do something and we learned not to question why. That's how we functioned." This dynamic, in part, formed an aspect of Rewey's belief that Ross was insane.

Dr. Fisch never wavered from his MPD diagnosis of February 1984. During a subsequent May 19, 1984, hypnotic interview with Ross, the doctor uncovered Ross's description of the murder scene in eerie similarity to what Ross had told Dr. Alan Fine nearly three months before. Dr. Fisch believed Ross's account was proof positive of his insanity.

In a chilling, emotionally-devoid matter-of-fact recitation, Ross told Fisch that moments before the homicides he was standing a short distance behind the murderer, who wore a black hood; the hood shielded the killer's face, Ross's parents were just a few feet in front of the murderer. They were holding hands. The killer was pointing his gun directly at the Carlsons. "The next thing I saw was the killer's face," Ross said. "It was me. Somehow, I got behind the killer again. He shot my parents. They fell dead. I walked over to them and looked down. Each of their faces was me."

Dr. Fisch viewed Ross's description of his murdering himself as "a classic dissociative experience" and falling squarely within the psycho-dynamics of someone suffering from MPD. When Dr. Fisch provided us his interpretation of the murder scene, I wondered what crossed Marilyn Carlson's mind as she looked into the barrel of her own mortality. Surely, she never could have imagined that her mother's curse, "I wish you were dead!" would be realized in such a horrific fashion.

Dr. Fisch's MPD diagnosis was joined in a month later by Dr. Fairbairn, although it took Fairbairn more than nine hours of talking to Ross before he realized he was not speaking to a complete person. After identifying the various personalities and their characteristics, Fairbairn related that when Blue or Gray was "out," the other personalities would be unaware or amnesic regarding the two's behavior during whatever period of time either was "out." Upon emerging after Blue or Gray had been "out," Justin would be aware only that "time had been lost." When Black or Norman had been "out," however, the emerging Justin would feel that "time had been stolen" from him. Ross's fractured mind rendered him insane, according to the doctor.

When Fairbairn questioned Ross about his different personalities, Ross listed the three tiers and nine separate names exactly as he had previously outlined them to me on February 24, 1984, in his Castle Rock jail cell.

Dr. Newton, in part, believed Ross was insane on the basis of his complex configuration of ego states. Newton thought Ross was incapable of knowing right from wrong because his mind was so fragmented by this constellation of alter personalities. In addition, there was no way of determining which alter had actually killed the Carlsons.

The prevailing judicial view in the country, which until now had only experienced a few cases nationwide where a criminal defendant diagnosed with MPD had raised an insanity defense, was that if the perpetrating alter could distinguish right from wrong, the defendant was sane. In Ross's case, however, we were never able to identify which personality pulled the trigger. In fact, we were prepared to argue that

Chapter 38: Kingsley's Solution

more than one alter may have been involved in the homicides — a conspiracy, if you will, among different alters. This position was borne out by Ross's "bulletin board" explanation to Dr. Rewey. As this explanation related to the killings, one personality would have been responsible for purchasing the revolver, another for driving Ross's truck to Tamarac, another for directing the Carlsons to the remote area, and yet a fourth acting as the gunman.

If we had to meet the supposition that either the narcissistic Justin or the protector Black pulled the trigger, thus making it irrelevant what other alters may have been involved in the overall planning and carrying out of the homicides, we were prepared to answer that assumption. If Justin were the killer, we would rely on our more enlightened appreciation for Dr. Glismann's brilliant theory of insanity. If Black were considered the trigger man, we would base our argument on Colorado's law that an individual had to be capable in distinguishing *moral* right from wrong versus *legal* right from wrong in order to be deemed sane. Although Black may have known it was against the law to kill another human being, he labored from the delusion that the younger alters were at risk of being killed or seriously injured by the Carlsons' abusive nature. He, therefore, felt the moral obligation to protect the young alters by eliminating their risk of destruction. We were prepared to discuss all of our arguments with the DA, if he asked.

On January 14, 1988, we met with Bob Gallagher, his chief deputy, John Jordan, and Bob Chappell in a conference room at their offices. Walter expressed our view that after two lengthy trials involving experts on both sides, two different judges had made identical findings regarding Ross's incompetency, the most important of which finding was that Ross suffered from MPD. And it was clear from our evidence that Ross suffered from that mental disease at the time of the murders. Therefore, a reasonable resolution of this case would be a stipulation to insanity. The meeting lasted about a half hour with the silver-haired Gallagher promising to get back to us. Neither Gallagher nor his deputies asked us to discuss why we believed Ross was insane.

On March 8, Bob Gallagher wrote Walter, declining our offer. Although Gallagher never mentioned Dr. Orne in his letter, it was obvious that the prosecution was going to rely on this MPD debunker once he became involved in the case. Six weeks later, after I had viewed Orne's interrogation of Ross, Walter and I filed a motion with Judge Kingsley to stop the foolishness of the so-called independent panel and to instead require the hospital to treat Ross's MPD.

On April 25, 1988, Walter and I appeared in court to argue our motion. By then, we were also scheduled to receive the Orne/Weissberg report, which would provide the first clue of Orne's detailed thinking about Ross.

Before we began the hearing, the judge's clerk walked into the courtroom and said Judge Kingsley wanted to see us in chambers. I informed Ross that I thought we'd be just a few minutes; I doubt he heard me.

When Ross first sat down with Walter and me in the courtroom that morning, he had looked depressed and was not very talkative. Given the events that had occurred since last October's resounding victory in the form of Kingsley's order, I was not surprised. Reports from the hospital revealed that Ross was in a bad state of depression because he was not receiving any MPD treatment and that no medications were helping. I was, however, taken aback by his deteriorating physical appearance. Neither Walter nor I had seen Ross during the last six months.

Instead of being clean shaven, Ross had grown a beard. Gone was his full head of blond hair, replaced now by a short, almost military-style cut. He seemed to have lost about 25 pounds since October. At 5' 10" and now maybe 145 pounds, this 23-year-old looked frail and middle-aged.

After about ten minutes, he reverted to a somnolent state and became non-communicative. Although he was dressed in a sport jacket, he no longer looked like he was going to shoot an ad for Esquire magazine. Instead, he resembled a 40-year-old, catatonic patient who had been dressed by hospital staff and was about to be wheeled out to the hospital lawn and left alone for an obligatory hour of Sunday fresh air. My heart sank at the sight of him. Ross sat motionless when Walter and I left the defense table to confer with the judge.

Judge Kingsley requested an overview of what was going to be heard that day. Pat Robb responded, advising the Orne report wasn't

Chapter 38: Kingsley's Solution

ready and wouldn't be available for another 30 days. She also complained about us having subpoenaed everyone under the sun connected with the hospital for this hearing. We, in turn, refused to release the hospital hierarchy from their subpoenas.

Bob Chappell thought the hearing should be continued until the report was ready, arguing that Orne and Weissberg actually could be devising a specific treatment plan for MPD. We thought the cure for cancer was a more likely event. Finally, after the attorneys finished their comments, the judge decided to speak his mind.

As was his custom, Judge Kingsley leaned forward in his chair. He placed his hands, palms down, in front of him. Looking at no one in particular, he gazed at the center of the conference table, his head tilted slightly to the right. Walter and I sat to the judge's right; Chappell, his investigator Bevis, and Pat Robb sat across from us. The judge's tone was both serious and sincere.

"May I just say something, and perhaps I shouldn't say this. I know — I will admit to being extremely naive. I listened very carefully to the testimony during last fall's hearing. The evidence seemed to be uncontradicted that if properly treated, there is about an 83 to 87 percent chance of a cure." The judge looked at me for affirmation as he made the last comment.

"It's certainly in the 80 percentile, your Honor," I stated.

"Well, that's what I had in mind. My feeling is this. There is no question in my mind that after hearing the testimony and looking at the pictures of the doctors' interviews with Mr. Carlson, that any fact-finding body would have found him insane at the time of the crime. If this issue of incompetency to proceed hadn't been raised four years ago, and instead Mr. Carlson was found insane, his treatment could have started, bing, bing, bing. Instead, we got hung up on this competency issue, and we're still hung up there."

"To carry my view a step further, the ideal situation in this case so far as everybody is concerned is to have this young man declared insane at the time of the alleged commission of the offense and get him treated."

With that, the judge sat back in his chair and quickly scanned both sides of the table. Walter and I exchanged looks with one another

259

of satisfaction. I felt that our four-year struggle had been vindicated by the judge's comments. I thought to myself, "Would the DA rethink his refusal to an agreement on insanity now that a wily, experienced judge had provided his objective assessment of the case?" I looked at both Chappell and Robb; each appeared unmoved by the judge's statements. Walter commented to the judge.

"Your Honor, you're very perceptive. And as the years go by, I have deeper and deeper respect for you. As an officer of the court — "

"Meaning he didn't start out with very much," Kingsley chimed in with a modest grin.

"It takes him some time, your Honor," I added to the momentary levity.

Walter then continued, informing the judge of our meeting in January with Bob Gallagher and the latter's rejection of our insanity proposal. "I didn't know about that," the judge remarked disappointedly.

Chappell and Pat Robb continued remaining mute during this discussion. They refused to add to Walter's comments about the unsuccessful results of our meeting with Gallagher. Since there didn't seem to be anything else to say about the matter and because it seemed reasonable to wait until the Orne/Weissberg report had been completed, we agreed to continue the hearing until the end of May and adjourn the proceedings until then.

When I returned to the courtroom, Ross's posture hadn't changed since I left him nearly two hours ago. He sat with his eyes closed, head tilted downward, and hands resting on the arms of the chair. I sat down inches from him and spoke softly.

"Ross, this is David. If you hear me, will you open your eyes so I can speak with you." I paused for a few seconds. He opened his eyes and faintly replied that he could hear. I told him about Kingsley's comments regarding insanity and explained why the hearing had to be continued. I asked him if he had any questions. In a barely audible reply, Ross mumbled, "David, they're going to hurt me again. Please don't make me go back to the hospital."

For a split second, I said nothing. I could no longer assure Ross he would be okay. I could no longer ask him to feel comforted by the

Chapter 38: Kingsley's Solution

legal representation of his two supposedly skillful attorneys. I could not admit that perhaps the law was a helpless guardian of his well-being. All I could do was pat him on the back and guarantee that Walter and I would not give up. "I'll speak to you soon, Ross," I said, while motioning for the sheriff to take him downstairs.

As I left the courtroom, I imagined having just spoken to a gregarious, cheerful, 23-year-old Ross and planning his future once he enjoyed better mental health. That image could have been the reality if only Ross had been treated since 1984 as the judge had envisioned. During the last four years, the world experienced the near completion of President Ronald Reagan's second term in office, the healthy development of millions of babies to graduating preschool children, and the approaching replacement of the workplace's typewriters with the new-fangled equipment called computers. Along those roads of progress, one verity remained constant — Ross Carlson would not receive treatment. With the Orne/Weissberg report and the May 26, 1988, hearing on the horizon, Ross's future remained even more unsettled.

CHAPTER 39

Psychotic Machines and the Firing of Walter

It was a forgone conclusion; Orne diagnosed Ross as antisocial personality disorder. Psychiatric labels aside, Orne was saying that Ross was malingering or faking the features of MPD. Orne explicated his opinions during his testimony at the May 26, 1988, hearing. Then, it became crystal clear that the appellation "independent panel" was a gross misnomer and that the state had been secreting Orne in the woods for some time.

The doctor revealed that he had been lying in bed with the prosecutors since 1984 — four years before Dr. Weissberg had formed his "panel" of two. During the late evening of June 21, 1984, Orne recalled, he received his first call regarding *Carlson*. The caller was Bob Chappell. Ross had just been found incompetent by Judge Day that morning. Would the doctor be willing to review the videotapes and police investigation, Chappell had asked. The doctor said, yes, and for that review charged the DA's office $3,000. He also told Chappell he would become more involved in the future, if necessary.

During my cross-examination of the doctor, he disclosed that Dr. Kathy Morall telephoned him in 1985, requesting his assistance in her evaluation of Ross. Orne, of course, agreed, resulting in her spending a three-day weekend in Philadelphia listening to Orne discuss "what was happening on those video tapes" of our doctors' interviews of Ross. Orne huddled with Dr. Morall for "25 hours, maybe a little more" during those three days. For his efforts, he was paid $6,000 in fees by the hospital, notwithstanding it had pled poverty when Judge

Chapter 39: Psychotic Machines and the Firing of Walter

Day ordered it to pay for Dr. Quinn's treatment of Ross during that same year. I glanced quickly at Walter whose looks of indignation were as palpable as these new revelations. The cash cow to Orne, however, did not stop with Kathy Morall.

For Orne's work last month "evaluating" Ross and conducting a follow-up workshop for hospital staff, the doctor had billed $2,500 per day for a total of $10,000. The hospital had balked at Dr. Walter Young's similar daily charge for his proposed MPD workshop, saying it was too much and, at the same time, concealing that it had agreed to pay that exact amount to Orne.

Orne's malingering diagnosis was based, in part, upon his view that MPD was merely a syndrome or constellation of symptoms and not a full-blown mental illness. Further, according to the doctor, a vast body of patients who initially did not possess the syndrome, developed it during suggestive treatment methods, which was the kind of criticism leveled by Dr. Alan Fine during the June 1984 competency hearing. There, Dr. Fine criticized the manner in which Dr. Fisch and Dr. Fairbairn conducted their earliest interviews of Ross, such as Fairbairn asking him "Who am I talking to?" and Fisch asking if either of his parents looked like Ross, or if he looked like them, when he shot them. Ross answered by saying, "They seem to look like me, and I look like them." Orne believed Dr. Fine was right on with his criticisms, explaining that the Fisch and Fairbairn techniques, although perhaps unwittingly employed, nevertheless created the belief of multiplicity in Ross's mind.

Dr. Orne also rebuked Ross's selective cooperation during the doctor's visit, which he explained as refusing to communicate with Orne during his attempted evaluation, becoming hysterical when returned to his ward by staff, and then shortly thereafter talking to me on the phone.

"There is no psychiatric entity where a patient is mute during an evaluation, later makes a telephone call and communicates normally, and then returns to the evaluation and is again mute," the doctor answered in response to Chappell's questioning. Admittedly, however, during my cross-examination, Orne agreed that Ross's informing me that someone was "eating my brains" could not be classified as a "normal conversation."

Ross's conduct that weekend sparked some telling questions from the judge, who jumped in during Chappell's examination. "Doctor, I looked at these tapes and there are two things I'd like to ask you about," Judge Kingsley said, peering at his notes and then returning to Orne. "One day, I noticed that Mr. Carlson walked into the interview room under his own power. However, at the end of a session, he had to be dragged out by the staff. Another time," the judge continued, "Ross's glasses had been removed, and he covered his eyes with his hands. When you tried to remove his hands, he resisted. Don't those two instances show he can hear or resist when he wants?" Orne, of course, agreed. I made a note to myself that we had to do a better job of explaining the dynamics of MPD to Kingsley.

Finally, Orne referenced a police interview with David Kachel, a classmate of Ross's, that was one of the documents provided to us in recent discovery. A detective questioned Kachel on September 22, 1987, more than four years after the homicides. Coincidentally, by then, stories about the second competency hearing had been splashed all over the media.

In his 1987 statement to the police, Kachel remembered talking to Ross in the fall of 1982 about the John Hinckley case. Kachel recalled Ross saying that "Hinckley should have tried to have people know him as another personality." Although Orne admitted never having spoken to Kachel, he surmised that Ross must have known about MPD before he murdered his parents in 1983.

Had Orne spoken to Kachel, he would have discovered his story had more cracks than the Liberty Bell. When we interviewed Kachel in 1988, about who (namely, Ross, Kachel, or another friend of theirs) actually raised the issue of a so-called other personality, whether the word "personality" was actually used during that conversation, and what was it about the conversation that stuck in Kachel's mind for more than five years after it occurred, Kachel drew a blank on each question.

Despite his opinion that Ross was a malingerer, Orne's views were directly opposite to those expressed by two of his esteemed and most trusted colleagues. Those contrary views, however, were never disclosed in the report Orne submitted for Judge Kingsley's

Chapter 39: Psychotic Machines and the Firing of Walter

consideration and were tucked under the mass of documents that filled the briefcase Orne brought into this hearing.

Before I began my examination, Orne voluntarily consented to my request to look at the documents in his briefcase since they related to his review of this case and authorship of his report. I handed the briefcase to Walter and then began questioning the doctor. During my exam, Walter excitedly waved me to the defense table. The judge allowed us a few moments to confer while everyone else in the courtroom remained at ease.

"You were right!" Walter whispered to me while squeezing my arm excitedly. "You have got to read these two reports," which he handed me, while pointing to specific passages in each. I immediately recognized the authors of the reports based on my pre-hearing research into everything Orne. The doctor had some explaining to do.

As he had done in *Bianchi*, Orne had asked internationally-known psychologists Edwin E. Wagner and W. Grant Dahlstrom, to conduct what is called "blind psychological testing." What this meant is that Orne sent Ross's Rorschach data to Wagner and his MMPI profiles to Dahlstrom. Neither doctor had any knowledge of the individual who took the tests or the legal or non-legal circumstances in which the individual was involved.

Both experts found no evidence of malingering in the documents they reviewed. Instead, they viewed Ross as "schizoid in his approach to reality" and evincing a "psychotic condition characterized by catatonic schizophrenic features." It is no wonder that Orne concealed this information from his report; these views presented even stronger evidence that Ross suffered from a major mental disease and break in reality. Such information, in turn, would have added to the compelling evidence of Ross's insanity. Orne sheepishly admitted that each of these colleagues was a renowned expert in his respective field. I chose to conclude my exam and save the additional ammo I possessed against Orne for his testimony during any potential future sanity trial.

When it now came time for Dr. Michael Weissberg to testify, Ross's behavior reflected just how paranoid and schizoid he could become. Before the doctor was called to the stand, Ross had already escaped into one of his trances. However, when Walter began his cross examination and pressing Weissberg about the evidence of child abuse uncovered by Dr. Fairbairn, that line of cross-examination suddenly aroused the Rip Van Winkle in our client. He broke his silence and began mumbling.

Since the first few minutes of Ross's utterances were unintelligible, I concentrated on Weissberg's testimony and continued taking notes. Suddenly, Ross spoke my name. I turned to him. "What is it Ross?" By now, his eyes had opened.

"Stop him. No more questions. He's one of them. Shut him down," Ross said firmly. He was breathing very heavily.

"What are you talking about? Shut who down?"

"Want **him** shut down," he emphasized, glancing at Walter, who was standing at the lectern.

"He has to examine this witness," I said emphatically, looking directly at Ross. "There will be a mid-morning recess pretty soon, and you can talk to Walter then."

"I don't want to," he replied equally assertively.

Once the judge announced the mid-morning recess, I approached Walter at the podium and clued him into Ross's latest demand. Walter noted in his outline where to begin when court resumed and walked with me to visit with Ross. The courtroom had cleared with the exception of one deputy sheriff. "Ross, how you doing?" Walter asked gently.

Ross abruptly pulled his chair away from the table and began crying. He refused to talk to Walter. I then knelt in front of Ross and tried unsuccessfully to have him speak to Walter. Ross merely lowered his head and cried while clutching his blue, hard covered notebook and expandable folder of files to his chest. Walter shook his head and walked back to the podium. When the recess was over, Walter resumed his questioning.

After a few minutes, Ross interrupted me again. "David, shut down the machine." I repeated that Walter had to continue. Ross then stared into space for a second or two. His eyes jerked spasmodically, and he slumped down into his chair. Within a few seconds, his eyes were closed. After about an hour, he re-awakened when the judge announced the lunch recess.

Chapter 39: Psychotic Machines and the Firing of Walter

"David, I want him shut down," Ross said, sounding very agitated. "If you don't shut him down, I will," Ross threatened. He backed off when I stated we'd visit with him during the noon recess. We waited about 10-15 minutes to allow the sheriff to get Ross settled and to enable us to discuss the strategies for Walter's continuing examination of Weissberg.

When we opened the door to the jail's visiting room during the recess, Ross was standing in the middle of the floor. He had removed his sport jacket, shirt, and tie. His tank top undershirt revealed his still very well-defined, upper torso. He greeted us with an icy stare and flushed face. His arms were at his sides. His fists were clenched. As we walked in, he gripped his fists tighter, displaying a road map of veins to his ample biceps. He said nothing, but his penetrating and fierce looks conveyed his message. In my five years with him, I had never seen him act this way.

Walter and I casually sat down at the table in the room, while Ross remained standing. He stood about five feet from us and to our left. Walter sat to my right.

"What do you want Ross?" I asked.

Ross looked at me and said, "I've received a note that he must be shut down." As he spoke, he pointed his right hand at Walter, but stayed fixated upon me.

"Ross, Walter is asking this doctor necessary questions."

Ross became more agitated and raised his voice. "That is not Walter; that is a machine and must be shut down."

Walter had heard enough. His self-restraint had been sufficiently tested. While remaining seated, he raised his head a notch and matching Ross's loudness, spoke directly to him. "This is an important witness. I'm trying to question him. You're interrupting David's notetaking and you're distracting me."

"Shut up!" Ross responded bitterly, while menacingly pointing his left index finger at Walter and glaring at him. "Do not talk to me. You are a machine. I want you stopped."

"What are you talking about? I..."

"I said shut up!" Ross interrupted, still fiercely pointing at Walter. "Do not talk. Just shut up!"

"Ross, please calm down," I interjected. "Let's discuss this. I know..."

"No discussion. You do it. Shut him down."

"Ross, this is the same Walter who's been with you since the case began."

"David, there is nothing to discuss. Do you hear me?" Ross's demeanor did not soften.

"Now listen, Ross..." Walter again attempted to get a word in.

"I told you to shut up!" Ross repeated. "I want your machine off of my case."

"I don't have to take this," Walter said, disgusted. "I'm leaving." With that, Walter left the room. I didn't blame him. The wiser part of me wanted to say, "Hey, wait for me!" However, my foolish part elected to remain.

"I'll stay," I said, masking my trepidation. I had often wondered how it would feel to finally meet Black: the persona who may have executed two schoolteachers. Now, I was finding out.

I reminded myself of the Fairbairn taping when Black had pointed at the doctor and told him to remove the restraints. Admittedly, I feared being alone with Ross in a room which suddenly seemed a lot smaller with Walter's absence. However, I was mindful of the advice shared with me by many experts: Try and meet all the personalities, even the violent ones. Don't back down from them. Show them respect like you would toward any of the others. Establish a rapport with all of the ego states.

I felt I couldn't leave the room, fearing my relationship with Ross would have been irreparably harmed. I remembered Justin's advice to Fairbairn. "If you want to get rid of Black, ask him to solve a simple mathematical problem." If necessary, I was ready to shout "3 times 3" faster than I could scream, "Guards, help!"

Ross and I sat inches away from each other at the table. He was to my left and at the end of the table. The door to the room was just a few feet behind me. The buzzer to ring the sheriff was on the wall to my right within an easy arm's reach.

I placed my hands on the table, leaned slightly forward, and looked directly into Ross's eyes. "Ross, I want you to try and relax," I said calmly. You hurt Walter's feelings. He..."

"David, I want that machine out of this courtroom," he interrupted angrily.

Chapter 39: Psychotic Machines and the Firing of Walter

"Ross, I will not tolerate you interrupting or raising your voice," I said confidently. "I've listened to you demean my friend and mentor and one of the best lawyers in the state. Now, please listen to me." Ross did. He relaxed and took a few deep breaths. Nevertheless, he was still adamant about wanting the "machine" fired from the case. He wanted me to assume sole responsibility for his defense. I told him I disagreed but would inform Judge Kingsley of his request.

"David, you can't do that, the judge is also a machine. He won't listen to you."

I continued talking reassuringly. Ross paused, stared away, and his eyes began to spasm. He then began weeping with his head bowed. I took a few deep breaths myself. He switched again; out came Steve, wondering where the time had gone and recognizing the salty taste in his mouth. I informed him that Walter had been doing a wonderful job on Weissberg and that we would finish the doctor's testimony after lunch. That occurred without further disruption, and the hearing eventually concluded late that day.

Arguing that it had complied with the Court's latest order requiring it to hire outside consultants and formulate a treatment plan, the hospital convinced Judge Kingsley that it could now restore Ross to competency. We wanted the Orne-Weissberg charade stopped and a treatment plan for MPD implemented. A month later, on June 27, 1988, the judge issued a surprising order, giving the hospital another chance and allowing it to treat Ross in accordance with its plan. The judge's reversal from his damning criticism of the hospital the previous fall was a stunner and catapulted Ross into a deep depression.

On June 30, 1988, I received a letter from Ross where he wrote, in part.

> *David, I didn't sleep as much as tossed and turned all last night. I had to force myself to eat what I could of breakfast. I really feel awful. I don't feel much like living, but I am going to try and work at it.*

As predicted, Kingsley's order nearly put Ross over the edge.

Just in the Nick of Time

A few days later, I received an envelope from him marked "Carlson's Last Will and Testament 6-30-88." His cover letter directed me to handle this document like the earlier will dated January 4, 1988, that he had sent me. I abided by his instructions. I placed the document in a locked cabinet, only to be opened in the event of his death. I needed to find a way to cheer him up.

CHAPTER 40

Adolescent Pen Pals

Robin and the girls knew how depressed Ross was feeling. He had been calling the house frequently at night since the Orne intrusion and Judge Kingsley's about-face. By then, Kristin was 11 ½ years old. Her heart was ten times the size of her age.

One weekday night before Kristin's bedtime, Robin and I were in the downstairs family room watching television. Kristin came to kiss us good night and asked if she could cheer Ross up by writing to him. Robin looked at me. "That's up to David," she said.

I thought long and hard before answering. It was one thing for me to be personally concerned with Ross. Did I want my family involved, especially a youngster Kristin's age?

Ross was not a female pen pal from another country whose interests were make-up and cute sixth-grade boys. In the minds of many, Ross was a cold-blooded killer who, after murdering his parents, had beseeched his psychiatrist to rescue him from jail and go for a car ride. On the other hand, I saw the good in Ross and had never feared him like Dr. Wilets did.

To Kristin, she had just remembered Ross as the sweet, handsome young man she had seen in court one day when Robin and the girls attended one of the case's hearings way before the Orne turn-of-events. Ross was so touched by the gesture, he wrote Robin and the girls a thank you note which Kristin kept by her night stand. "Boy, David, those girls obviously didn't come from you. They're beautiful — they look exactly like Robin."

Kristin resembled a Keene painting — a young girl with doe eyes and a delicate frame. Small for her age, her straight blond hair hung like a shawl to the middle of her back while her bangs fit like a curtain three-quarters down her forehead. She loved to smile, which turned her large brown eyes into circles of adolescent joy. However, anyone who felt the need to treat Kristin delicately because of her petite size and china-doll looks was mistaken.

She was a tough cookie who had fought through many feverish nights and a chronic bronchial cough since the age of two. Most kids would have demanded extra-large doses of TLC during any of her illnesses, but not Kristin. She was a fighter, possessed of an indomitable spirit. Kristin understood there was a very ill side to Ross, but she did not look beyond his emotional pain. She was the ideal friend — sensitive and nonjudgmental.

I concluded that any possible risks were minimal and outweighed by my compassion for my client. The communication, I decided, would give Ross a healthy outlet and afford him a temporary escape from his surroundings. Besides, I rationalized that Ross would be cured whenever he obtained his freedom. Thus, we would never be in harm's way.

"Sure, that's sweet of you to think of him," I finally said after thinking about it for a few minutes. "Go ahead. You write him. I'll send your letters in my envelopes so the hospital won't open the mail."

Kristin broke out in a wide smile. "Thank you," she said, while racing up the stairs. With that, Kristin Childs provided Ross an escape from his doldrums. The antidote became evident quickly.

"David, look what Ross sent me," Kristin said one day, showing me a homemade puzzle she had just received from Ross.

"That's great, Kristin. What are you supposed to do?"

"Well, David, you have to find the correct word for each of these questions. For example, 'how many states in the union?' You take the word 'fifty' and circle it. You do that until you get all the words."

Kristin was beaming at Ross's attention. After she returned the answers, including a letter of her own, Ross would reply with something else creative. Occasionally, he would send her comforting poems or letters of youthful advice. Their communication never related to his situation and seemed to alleviate some of his feelings of hopelessness.

Chapter 40: Adolescent Pen Pals

On August 11, 1988, the hospital presented Ross with a "carrot and stick" plan. This "ingenious" document was designed to force Ross to talk to the hospital cabal but included no psychotherapy of any kind. It was geared exclusively to address the most basic issues regarding competency. For example, he would have to answer the question, "Ross, what's the role of the judge?" If he answered correctly, he received a "prize."

The plan was simple — if Ross participated "meaningfully" in a hospital group session, he "merited" two hours to spend however he chose. By "demonstrating an understanding of the charges against him," which was one of the tests of competency, Ross would, for example, be entitled to read or use his computer in his room.

Further awards were earned by showing an understanding of possible case outcomes, such as prison or insanity, by participating in routine ward activities, such as recreation time or commissary attendance, or by responding to questions from staff members. "How are you Ross?" This farcical plan was presumably the collaborative effort of the hospital's best psychiatric minds and their consultants, Orne and Weissberg. Only a gnat could have failed this program.

The hospital's banal program also included one hour of individual "therapy" on Sunday morning. During that special hour, Ross talked to mental health worker, Bob Gonzales, the employee who had seen Ross wet his pants a few years ago, about the provocative subjects of skiing, aqua diving, books, and nature. In return for his participation in this "therapy," Ross earned ward or room privileges.

Whenever Ross opted for some real mental stimulation, he continued his communication with our girls. By this time of August 1988, nearly 14-year-old Rachel, had begun writing Ross.

Rachel was a striking teenager with a thick-blond mane of curls and the beginnings of a shapely figure. Robin and I worked hard to protect Rachel from the stares and budding testosterone of high school boys. From early infancy, Rachel exhibited maturity beyond her years. She was precocious at the age of nine months, already forming words, while most toddlers that young were just beginning to crawl. In December 1983, when I first met Rachel, the then nine-year-old sometimes acted as if she were Robin's caretaker. Now, more than four years later and mature well beyond the teenage world of her contemporaries, as she would often remind me, Rachel was an inquisitive child who was never content with a stock or evasive answer.

Rachel wouldn't buy the explanation that people sometimes became depressed without their understanding why and that medication was often the best way to treat depression. She wanted to know how the serotonin imbalance occurred and what chemical agents existed in Prozac. Ross's carrot and stick "therapist" would never have been able to handle Rachel, but it quickly became apparent that Ross also adored her.

Initially, Ross was curious in learning as much as he could about this new pen pal. The two comprised the perfect duo. They both were inveterate writers. Rachel loved asking questions, and Ross loved to give advice. Rachel kept Ross occupied for the next month or so until he had to concentrate on his goal for 1989. Then, he stopped writing the girls.

CHAPTER *41*

Ottsie's Disappointment & the Decision

Ross readily complied with the hospital's "carrot and stick" plan through the alter Holdin, who was also assigned the task of meeting with the state's new competency evaluators. By now, Holdin enjoyed complete mastery of the history of this case, could recite its particulars *ad nauseam* to any evaluator, and avoided making the one crucial mistake he had made before the second competency hearing, namely refusing to cooperate with our doctors. Instead, Holdin blandly answered all of their questions. Although Holdin succeeded in his tasks for nearly a year, it was usually the deliberative and mature Steve who spoke with me. And, during much of this time, another of Ross's alters, most likely Justin, undertook to communicate with Kristin and Rachel. Thus, the chameleon-like nature of Ross's illness remained intact, but for the unwary, it could prove profoundly disturbing.

On Tuesday morning, August 22, 1989, Ross and I appeared in court to obtain a date for Carlson III, the third competency trial. After we agreed upon the date of October 19, Ross began to leave the courtroom for the downstairs jail. Suddenly, someone yelled from the spectator section, "Ross! Ross! Hey, Ross!" Just then, a young man in his mid-20s approached us with a huge smile. His right hand extended, the excited individual said, "Ross, it's Ottsie Aichinger."

Ross stared at Aichinger for a few seconds, but declined to shake his hand. Ross passed me a quick glance and a mini shrug of the shoulders. He looked back at the young man and replied "I'm sorry. I don't know you." Aichinger appeared stunned, stood awkwardly silent for a couple of seconds, and dropped his hand to his side.

I pulled Ross away and told Mr. Aichinger we had to leave. I didn't know if this attempted greeting was a prosecutor's setup to test Ross's memory, or if Aichinger was someone from Ross's past eager to say hello. Ross was led away by the sheriffs, and I walked out of the courtroom.

I saw Aichinger visibly upset and talking to a woman who seemed to be trying to calm him down. I walked up to the two and introduced myself. Aichinger, dressed in a coat and tie, stood approximately 6' 2" and seemed to possess the build of an athlete. He shook my hand firmly. The female beside him wore her hair pulled back in a light-blond ponytail; she was dressed in tailored, linen suit, indicating the two were probably there for legitimate court business. The woman introduced herself as Janet Ward, Aichinger's attorney.

"My client is just a little shook," Ward said. "We're here to start a civil case, and he just happened to see an old friend and wanted to say, hello. Mr. Carlson didn't have a clue."

Realizing that Aichinger wasn't a government operative, I asked Ms. Ward for permission to speak with her client. Aichinger nodded eagerly.

"You seem upset," I said. "Can you tell me why?"

"Man, that was the scariest thing in my life," Aichinger said, shaking his head. "The guy looked right through me. We wrestled together for three years at Newton Junior High, '76 through '79. We were in the same weight class and practiced together every day during the season. We even had classes together." Aichinger explained that when the two then entered high school, they continued to see each other frequently. Ross would always come up to Ottsie and talk with him. The last time they saw one another was during the summer of 1983 when they would hang out at the local Rec Center all the time.

"Have you changed physically during the last six years to where Ross might not recognize you?" I asked.

"Sir, I've stayed practically the same since I last saw Ross. I recognized him immediately. There is absolutely no way he could have forgotten me. Maybe, it all makes sense now."

Chapter 41: Ottsie's Disappointment & the Decision

"What do you mean?"

"When we were in junior high, some of us thought he was peculiar — we joked that he had a split personality. Some days he'd act really young, and other days he'd seem so much older. He was always dressing like he was different ages. It was so strange..." Aichinger's voice trailed off, and he just looked straight ahead for several seconds. I thanked Aichinger and made a note with three huge asterisks to have him subpoenaed for any future sanity trial. This was Randy Staton revisited!

When I returned to the office that morning, there was a message from Walter. His investigator had uncovered another witness from Ross's past. The individual, Bill Patton, used to lift weights with Ross during their high school days. That alone was nothing new. Weightlifting merely fit the Stacey profile.

What made Patton special was that, according to him, Ross used to wear a black cape, talk like a delinquent, and smoke cigarettes when he came to the gym. This was a perfect caricature of Norman and additional evidence of the existence of other personalities long before the Carlson murders. Until this investigator's report, we had never known about Patton. He was obviously another witness we would call at a sanity trial, if we lost Carlson III. We knew Holdin's mission was to be declared competent in Carlson III, so he could leave the hospital. We also knew the prosecutors would be much better prepared for this third go-around.

Beginning on October 19, 1989, the prosecution team, led by Bob Chappell, flawlessly executed a two-pronged strategy developed by Dr. Weissberg for this competency hearing. First, the hospital's doctors focused on Ross's competency rather than becoming stuck on a diagnosis. For example, when Dr. Pecevich testified at Carlson III, he said he didn't have sufficient information to pigeonhole Ross with a specific disorder. Rather, he emphasized, "whatever illness, if any, Mr. Carlson suffers from, he is competent."

Secondly, Bob Chappell avoided the quicksand that had swallowed him during the previous two competency hearings. He refrained from testing our doctors' expertise in MPD. Instead, he asked our experts two basic questions: "Doctor, is there an objective test to determine if someone is telling the truth?" and "Since all the evidence regarding abuse has come from the defendant, other than your opinion, can you be sure Ross Carlson is telling the truth?" Both answers had to be, "No."

None of the state's well-crafted stratagems, however, seemed to perturb Ross. His behavior ranged from thoroughly disinterested to very active with interim bouts of protracted melancholy. About a week into Carlson III, Ross was grossly depressed and barely communicating with me. No doubt, the alter Gray had emerged. I would intermittently rub his back when I didn't have to focus on the court proceedings, but often gentle massages did no good.

On Thursday night, October 26, I received word from my office that Kelli Olson was traveling to Colorado that upcoming weekend. She was then planning to attend court on Monday, the 30th. If she had left a call-back number, I would have cautioned her against visiting because of Ross's severe depression. If that condition persisted throughout the hearing, he would not recognize even his staunchest supporters. That precise situation had already occurred with Ross's dear friends, Joe and Mary Guess.

When news of the Carlsons' murders was broadcasted by the local media in August of 1983, then 19-year-old Scott Cook asked his girlfriend, Mary Frances Guess, her younger teenage sister, Kathy, and the sisters' parents, Joe and Mary, if they would accompany him to visit his friend Ross at the University of Colorado Medical Center psych ward. The Guess family agreed. From that day on, Ross became Joe and Mary Guess's "adopted son."

As a stay-at-home mom, the brown-haired, brown-eyed Mary Guess visited Ross every three to four days while he was held at the Medical Center. The 43-year-old Joe Guess tried to arrange his design-engineering schedule so he could also visit as often as possible. Joe and Mary were criticized for befriending Ross, but they ignored their critics and reached out as their spirituality had taught them to do.

After Ross was arrested and transported to the Douglas County jail, the Guesses assumed the role of surrogate parents and visited him regularly until he was committed to the state hospital in July 1984. Ross turned the tables of kindness in April 1984 when Joe

Chapter 41: Ottsie's Disappointment & the Decision

was diagnosed with a brain tumor and required surgery. During the time from diagnosis to recovery, Ross would call Joe and provide him encouragement and optimism. It helped; the tumor was benign.

After Ross was committed to the state hospital, the Guesses arranged for a specific time for Ross to call them weekly. Therefore, at 7:00 every Thursday night, Joe and Mary could set their watch. Like Greenwich Mean Time, it was a collect call from Ross. The Guesses restricted their state-hospital-visits to only two occasions because Ross did not want Mary to see him in such a depressing environment.

One of Mary Guess's fondest memories of Ross was her April 1989 birthday, which did not fall on a Thursday. Ross surprised her by calling and speaking to her for more than two hours, as only Ross could do. "He just had such a thoughtful and considerate way about him," Mary recalled. "Here he was in this terrible place that wasn't doing anything for him, and he took the time to remember and think about me. He was just a special young man."

Throughout Ross's torturous experience in the state hospital, he never took advantage of the Guesses' loyalty. He always expressed a "thank you," and always remembered their generosity. For different Christmases, Ross would send Joe and Mary electronic equipment for their listening pleasure, including a dual cassette player and a CD player.

The one deed the Guesses performed, which elevated them to sainthood in Ross's eyes, was taking care of his small, gray Schnauzer, Muffin. In fact, one of the Guesses' visits to the state hospital concerned Muffin. It was one of the worst days of Ross's life.

The reverent way Ross spoke about his dog and the depth of his concern for that animal equaled and often exceeded the way he related to his special friends. Kelli Olson had thought it unusual that Ross could talk endlessly about Muffin but not a millisecond about his parents. After having taken care of Muffin for nearly four years, the Guesses had to inform Ross during the summer of 1987 that Muffin had become sick with mouth cancer.

Ross was crushed when he heard the news. "It was the first time I had heard him cry so uncontrollably," Mary Guess recalled. Ross authorized two surgeries to see if the disease could be successfully treated, but the procedures failed. The vet said that Muffin's end was imminent and that prolonging the dog's life would be at the cost of severe pain. Before Muffin was put to sleep, the Guesses drove to Pueblo so Ross and his pet could say goodbye.

During that fall day in 1987, Joe and Mary waited in the courtyard outside of Ross's building where a hospital guard escorted Ross. Although terribly frail, Muffin was so excited to see his dear master. Joe and Mary sat at a picnic table while watching the two play. When it was time to leave, tears streamed down Ross's face while he said farewell to his special friend.

Throughout their time with Ross, the Guesses saw him simply as compassionate and caring. The only time he ever acted differently was now in late October 1989 in Carlson III. When I informed Ross where the Guesses were seated in court, Ross looked at them with an empty, blank stare and told me "they look like nice people, David, but I don't know who they are." The Guesses did not take it personally but instead resolved to pray extra hard for Ross's well-being.

When Kelli then arrived in court on Monday, October 30, 1989, I informed Ross, "Someone special traveled a long way to see you. She's sitting on the aisle a few rows back. She's wearing a white blouse and dark skirt." There were only about a dozen other spectators in the courtroom, none of whom fit that description or location. Fortuitously, Ross seemed upbeat and very aware of the court proceedings. He turned around and looked directly at Kelli for a few seconds. She responded with a quick smile and a waist-high wave. Ross did not return the greeting. He turned to me and said, "Who is that, David?"

"Just an old friend who came to support you."

"She seems very nice. Tell her, thank you."

"Okay, I will."

During a recess, I thanked Kelli for coming, but had to explain that Ross was having one of those days where he had problems remembering.

"But he certainly would know me," Kelli assured me. "I visit him. I speak to him. He writes me all the time. We're very close."

"I'm sorry. Sometimes, he is not capable of remembering anyone."

Tears welled in Kelli's eyes as she shook her head unable to

Chapter 41: Ottsie's Disappointment & the Decision

fathom the severity of Ross's illness. She left the courthouse that day heartbroken. If only she had stayed until Thursday afternoon, November 2, the time for closing arguments. Then, Ross was in a great mood.

It was Walter's turn to argue our position, and Ross wanted a preview beforehand. Therefore, we met him downstairs in one of the jail's visiting rooms at noon on Thursday.

Alert and eager to assist, Ross opened his notebook and retrieved two sheets of white computer paper containing a meticulous outline of points he wanted Walter to cover. Ross's effort was well-conceived, contained a historical overview of the hospital's failure to treat, and concluded with a demand to the judge to dismiss the case. The judicial relief of dismissal was what we had requested a couple of years ago when it seemed that the hospital's refusal and inability to treat would cause Ross's indefinite hospitalization with no reasonable likelihood of his emergence from being warehoused. Dismissal of his criminal case would then allow for his civil commitment to a reputable hospital with competent and dedicated clinicians skilled to treat his disorder. He would remain at that hospital until he successfully treated and was able to re-enter society at little or no risk of harm to anyone.

"I would be happy to give the argument myself, Walter, but I'm sure you'll do an adequate job," Ross said with a wry smile as he handed Walter the outline. "Besides, it looks like I'm coming down with a cold."

We walked up to the courtroom and waited for Judge Kingsley to take the bench. He greeted us politely, but looked very serious. He leaned forward in his seat and spoke.

"I don't intend to slight any attorney," the judge said respectfully. "However, in my mind, it would not serve any purpose to have closing arguments."

Walter and I exchanged glances of resignation. Walter pushed his notes aside. I had my pen in hand and waited to record Kingsley's comments.

"Things have changed since my ruling in 1987," the judge explained. "The most significant event that occurred in the case since October 1987 was Dr. Orne's interview of Mr. Carlson. Mr. Carlson rocked in his chair for nearly 45 minutes without saying anything. Then, once he returned to his ward, he was able to call his attorney and speak for almost 30 minutes. Ever since that time, I've been suspicious of this young man."

I made comments on the left margin of my notes. "Kingsley mixed up two different sessions; obviously didn't hear a word of my testimony regarding how bizarre that call was."

The judge continued, speaking firmly without glancing at any notes. "More recently, the defendant's behavior with the hospital's doctors shows he controlled the interviews with all those people." Another of my margin comments followed — "Holdin succeeded!"

"Finally, I'm reminded of an old saying," the judge said as he looked out into the courtroom. "Fool me once, shame on you. Fool me twice, shame on me."

The judge concluded by finding Ross had been restored to competency and ordered us to return the next day at 9:00 a.m. to set the sanity hearing. He then adjourned court for the day, effectively ending his role in the case.

Chappell and his entourage quickly exited the courtroom, now able to hold their heads high. They did not gloat or snicker, obviously recalling that such demonstrations during previous hearings had backfired. They appeared relieved, having finally prevailed after three tries and more than five years of the case in limbo.

I looked at Ross who had finishing writing and said, "I'm sorry, Ross."

"That's fine, David. It was expected. Like you said months ago when the judge placed my treatment back into the hands of the hospital — something changed his mind. Now we know. I thought he understood MPD, but I guess he doesn't."

Always the confident optimist, Walter leaned over and said, "We'll crush 'em during the next trial. With the addition of Aichinger and Patton, we have overwhelming evidence of MPD before the homicides. Plus, in Newton, we have the best expert in the world."

"Well, I should be grateful to the judge for one thing — I'm free of the state hospital," Ross added. I elected not to remind him that he'd return there if we won the sanity case. Nor did I feel it was

Chapter 41: Ottsie's Disappointment & the Decision

necessary to mention how successful we had been so far in saving him from a lifetime of prison. Now, he was one step closer to that possibility.

Soon, Ross would meet a jury pool where 94% of its members, even before hearing one syllable of testimony, felt he was guilty and nearly 80% believed he should be found sane. Predictably, however, Ross was unconcerned.

The significance of Judge Kingsley's ruling, however, resonated with me. When the judge uttered the words "restored to competency," I immediately felt the pressure of Ross's future in my hands. Needing to plan for our next battle, Walter and I packed our briefcases and told Ross we'd see him tomorrow. Then, we'd appear before the trial judge, Judge Turelli, and set the date for the sanity trial.

CHAPTER 42

What's a Little Nosebleed?

On Friday, November 3, an old familiar face presided over court. Judge Turelli reclaimed his role as trial judge and set the sanity hearing for December 5, 1989. After our brief appearance before his Honor, Walter and I visited with Ross downstairs in the jail visiting room.

As he had looked in court, Ross appeared incredibly relaxed, wearing a blue buttoned-down shirt and tan slacks. His notebook was open with several computer printouts in front of him. "Gentlemen, I've taken the liberty to compile a list of people who Tony should interview," Ross said as he handed both Walter and me copies of his work product for delivery to our new investigator, Tony DiVirgilio.

"This looks great, Ross." Walter replied while reviewing the list. "I'll have Tony get right on it. David and I are going to meet this afternoon and..."

"Excuse me one minute, gentlemen," Ross said, abruptly interrupting the conversation. He then rose from his chair and walked the few feet to the bathroom. After a couple of minutes, he returned.

"I'm sorry, Walter. God, I never have nose bleeds," he said, seeming mildly distressed.

"Maybe it has something to do with that cold from a couple of days ago," I said, "although you don't sound stuffed up."

"I'm sure I'll be fine. Well, anyway Walter. After you and David put your great legal minds together, I'd appreciate one of you gentlemen updating me on your thinking."

Chapter 42: What's a Little Nosebleed?

"We always do, Ross," I said as Walter and I packed our briefcases and headed back to Denver.

On Saturday, November 4, after spending the day in my office and a couple of hours at the gym, I returned home for a rare night of bachelorhood. Robin had flown to Atlanta on Friday for a preschool teachers' conference, and her girls were spending the weekend with their dad in Denver. After having watched the 10 p.m. sports on each of the three local television channels, I was fast asleep. Well into the early morning hours, I was dreaming about John Elway touchdown passes during the upcoming afternoon's Broncos' game against the Steelers. My vision of jubilant end zone celebrations was suddenly interrupted by my phone. I couldn't imagine who might be calling so late.

Since I had spoken to Robin before going to bed, I figured it was perhaps one of those, "Hey, Dave, this is Jackie. Say, Dave ... the police ... they 'um sayin' they found a bunch of dope in my house. Now, Dave, you know I wouldn't be messin' with no dope after we walked on that last case. Can you come down to the jail and straighten' this whole thing out?" However, that was not the call.

"Dave, sorry to wake you up. This is Craig Smith, Arapahoe County deputy sheriff."

"Hi, Craig. What's up?" I asked, while rolling over onto my back and opening my eyes.

"Dave, we have transported Ross to Littleton Hospital. Earlier, we took him to Dr. Phillip Young in Castle Rock because he had been complaining about nose bleeds."

"I know. He mentioned that to Walter and me on Friday." By this time, I had turned on the light and was sitting against my headboard. The wristwatch on my nightstand read 2:45 a.m.

Craig explained that Dr. Young had drawn a sample of Ross's blood and called the jail last night with the preliminary results. He didn't like what he saw; there were indications of leukemia. The doctor instructed the sheriff's office to immediately transport Ross to the nearest hospital for more specific tests. However, Ross would not allow anyone at the hospital to touch him before he first talked to me. Craig Smith's news was shocking; I woke up very quickly. "Let me talk to Ross, Craig."

"Sure, but do you mind speaking to the doctor first? He thinks it's rather urgent that this testing is done as soon as possible." Craig then put Dr. Pajon on the phone, and the doctor provided me with some dispiriting news.

The doctor, speaking with a Latin American or Cuban accent, said that Ross probably had leukemia. He didn't know which kind, but it was one of two acute types — either the AML, acute myelogenous leukemia, or ALL, acute lymphocytic leukemia.

"We won't know for sure until tomorrow, but I suspect it is the latter," Pajon said.

In response to my question, the doctor cautioned about ALL, saying "the lymphoblastic type is very serious for Mr. Carlson's age group." He further emphasized that there was no time to delay. A rectal swab and treatment of antibiotics and blood transfusions had to occur immediately. If the procedures did not commence now, "septic shock and brain hemorrhaging could occur within 48 hours." Ross, the doctor said, would not allow any treatment until he first conferred with me.

"Let me speak to Mr. Carlson, please." By this time, I was wide awake and had begun rubbing my forehead. I waited for Ross to come to the phone and was determined not to sound despondent in wake of this grim news. After a few seconds, Ross was on the line.

"David, some bozo says I'm going to croak," Ross blurted out defiantly. "I'm not letting anyone touch me anally unless I know exactly what's going on."

"Ross, this doctor seemed very knowledgeable," I replied calmly. Plus, Dr. Young would not have considered your situation urgent if he wasn't absolutely sure. Remember how accurate he was years ago when he thought you had, what he called, a 'split personality.'"

"I understand, but I don't know this bozo. My legs are shackled to a bed, and they want me to cooperate while they stick me with needles and tubes ... no way! I don't trust any of these people. Would you mind coming down here?"

"Of course, I will, but please promise you'll allow them to perform some initial blood work before I get there." Ross agreed.

While traveling to Littleton at 3:15 a.m., I was accompanied by

Chapter 42: What's a Little Nosebleed?

the fear of a special person's imminent death and questions regarding my role in his possible demise.

For more than five years at the state hospital, Ross had tolerated horrific circumstances and never suffered a significant physical illness. Now, just two days after securing "freedom" from that hell hole, Ross was in a medical fight for his life. I remained positive during the 40-minute drive to Littleton Hospital but couldn't imagine a more macabre irony to this case. I also wondered — how did I become the guardian of my client's personal well-being?

Ross was not playing by the rules. In order to be his effective counselor, I could be passionate about his case but not too emotionally involved with him personally. Now, however, he was asking me to be his advocate on a much higher plane. He was asking me to participate in life and death decisions regarding his health. Those discussions were reserved for parents or family — not lawyers. Although Ross was adept at compartmentalizing his emotions, the innate childlike part of him had nevertheless wrapped his arms around me. He was asking me to protect his most important commodity — his life. As much as I had always tried to avoid becoming tangled in my clients' personal lives, I found myself unable to deprive Ross of my emotional involvement. I knew this young man was much more special than just a "client" and that I had allowed that transformation.

After traveling the deserted freeways that crossed southwest Denver, I arrived at Littleton Hospital around 4:00 a.m. This obviously was not the community's medical center for emergency trauma. There was no outside frenetic hustle and bustle; there were no emergency vehicles with flashing lights and sirens. Instead, the hospital entrance was peaceful and quiet. A middle-aged lady, attending the information desk, looked up from her magazine as I approached her station. She gave me directions to the intensive care unit, and then resumed her reading.

When I exited the elevator onto the second floor, Craig Smith was standing nearby in the ICU's lounge area. During the case, Walter and I had gotten to know this strapping deputy sheriff fairly well because he frequently was assigned to guard Ross when we had court hearings. Craig was mild-mannered and very personable, having often exchanged small talk with Walter and me during court recesses, or when we visited Ross at the jail. We were on a first-name basis.

This morning, Craig appeared quite concerned. After we shook hands, he introduced me to Dr. Pajon. The doctor had just walked from the unit into the ICU lounge area where Craig and I stood.

Dr. Eduardo R. Pajon, Jr. handed me his card, which described his specialty as "Medical Oncology/Hematology." The diminutive physician repeated his earlier admonitions and asked me to impress upon Ross the risks of delaying treatment. The doctor explained that when the nurses attempted to start the IVs of antibiotics and blood, Ross insisted they first remove his leg shackles. "Does Ross understand the course and risks of treatment?" I asked the doctor.

"Yes, I explained to him about the two different types of acute leukemia, and my belief that he probably has the ALL. I told him treatment would include chemotherapy for at least 30 to 60 days. I said for his age group there was a 50% chance of survival for the first year and a 20-25% chance to survive five years. A five-year survival usually indicates the leukemia has been cured."

Pajon said that Ross had accepted the diagnosis rather matter-of-factly and did not appear depressed. Why did that not surprise me? The doctor also said Ross wanted to read about the illness and to know the possible ramifications of not following the recommended treatment. I thanked the doctor for his concern and frankness and walked through the entry door of the ICU. The nursing station was to the immediate left and curved in front of the nine glass-enclosed rooms. In this L-shaped unit, rooms 1-6 were directly in front of the nurses' desks while the rooms furthest away, 7-9, comprised the shorter leg of the L. Each of the rooms was much larger than the more standard hospital room, thus affording ample space for specialized equipment and personnel. Ross occupied room 1, which was about 30 feet past the nurses' station.

As I walked the relatively short distance, before arriving at his room, I reminded myself to stay calm but firm. Dr. Pajon's leukemia discussion had scared me, but I would try not to show Ross alarm or fear. I would instead speak optimistically and rationally. This is what I was good at, and it was also what Ross had always expected of me. I

Chapter 42: What's a Little Nosebleed?

would tell him that once he beat this illness, we would then concentrate on his case. As I approached his room, I wondered if I really had been awakened this morning, or if this was just another dream.

CHAPTER 43

The Demons of Life-Saving Treatment

I could see Ross lying in bed and staring at the ceiling as I walked down the ICU corridor. Upon entering his room, he turned toward me and managed a faint smile. Deputy Sherriff, Ben Riggans, was seated by his side.

When I passed the foot of his bed, a vivid reminder of his criminal predicament briefly overshadowed his medical emergency. Ross's ankles were secured by manacles attached to a metal chain which snaked through the bed's bottom frame. Deputy Riggans, dressed in sheriffs' garb of slate-blue slacks and short-sleeved shirt, stood as I entered the room. The deputy's weapon was, of course, holstered; his handcuffs were fastened to his wide, dark belt.

I greeted the thinly built Riggans, and he politely responded, "Hello, sir." He stood and backed away several more feet to afford Ross and me some privacy. I walked in front of Riggans and stopped at the head of the bed, purposefully shielding Ross from the deputy's view.

Although a blanket covered Ross to his chest, I could see he was wearing the hospital-issued, white cotton gown with the cloth ties at the neck. His hands were resting by his side; a hospital identification band bounded his left wrist. Present but idle were monitoring equipment mounted above his bed and IV bags arranged on stands several feet to his right.

Ross looked pale, almost wax-like, but maintained his smile as I stood before him. I returned the smile and placed my left hand on

Chapter 43: The Demons of Life-Saving Treatment

top of his. His hand felt warm. I leaned toward him and quietly asked him how he was feeling.

"I feel fine, David," he said, surprisingly alert and upbeat. "I apologize for not standing up to greet you, but as you can see, they have me anchored to the bed." Even though Ross's nature was to deflect somber moments with humor, I was nevertheless momentarily caught off guard by his glibness.

"I can see that. We'll save the handshake for when you're finally released from the hospital with a clean bill of health."

"I'm not sure about that, David."

"Ross, it'll happen if you let them treat you. You gave them blood; next is your accepting these IVs."

"David, I told them — if you want me to cooperate, don't keep me shackled like a dog. Fat chance I'd run away with two armed deputies hovering over me and tubes in my arms."

"Ross, I told Smitty to contact Hugh Thompson so we can talk about these restraints, but time is critical."

"If that's the case, they'll get back to you. In any event, you know I won't let anyone touch me anally."

Ross's comment presumed I knew about episodes of apparent abuse which his defense team had never learned. Although we had hoped treatment might reveal such details, his statement suggested that serious demons remained tucked away in his mind. I assured him that the desired medical procedure was benign and would be performed discretely in a very sterile environment. Since he refused to budge, I told him I'd work on the restraints' issue that morning. He sought to placate me. "I'm sorry they had to call you at this god-awful hour. Tell Robin not to be mad at me."

"No problem ... I had to get up anyway to answer the phone." Robin would have kicked me for such a stupid joke. Ross, however, indulged me with an accepting grin.

I left Littleton Hospital bewildered, unable to imagine what awful things would cause him to delay treatment under such dire circumstances. Ross had looked more vulnerable than I had ever seen him. Although he could control the course of his treatment, he had no power over the course of his illness. During our short visit, he seemed to experience a human emptiness that none of us ever hope to confront but is sometimes inevitable with matters beyond our control. Knowing Ross's fundamentalist upbringing, I wondered if Ross subconsciously felt he was being asked to pay the ultimate penitence to his parents. At this point, I frankly didn't know anything except that Ross was sick and he was asking for my help.

I arrived home at about 5:00 a.m. tired, and with my universe thrown into disorder. For the last six years I had plowed my soul into Ross's case, trying to save him from a life of prison. How did that objective all of a sudden change to one of saving him from a potentially fatal medical condition? I was supposed to be working on the intricacies of the insanity defense not the distinctions between myelogenous and lymphocytic leukemia. When I signed up for this case, there was no fine print saying I would have to deal with Ross's morbidity when he reached the age of 25.

About 20 years ago, I had lost a friend who died in his mid-20s from leukemia. Hank was too sweet a guy to have succumbed so early in life. Surely medical science, I thought, must have made enormous strides since then to combat this illness. I needed to confer with a doctor who would confirm my optimism.

Since only the newspaper-delivery boy and clerk at the nearby 7-11 would be awake at this hour, I decided to get some more sleep. Tossing and turning for the next two hours accomplished nothing more than advancing the morning from darkness to light. I spent the next excruciatingly slow hour reading the Sunday paper while intermittently looking at the clock. I decided that 8:15 a.m. on Sunday was a civilized time to call people.

Shocked with the news, Dr. Fairbairn and Walter agreed to visit Ross as soon as possible. Tomorrow, Walter would ask his nurse paralegal to gather medical articles about leukemia.

After talking to Walter, I became deluged with calls from the media. Evidently, the sheriff's office released a bulletin. My standard comment was that Ross has been admitted to the hospital for some diagnostic blood work, and we were awaiting the outcome of those tests.

I skipped going to the Broncos game. Robin arrived home

Chapter 43: The Demons of Life-Saving Treatment

around 4:00 p.m. and, after learning why I was home, did her best to sound optimistic. However, her look of concern coupled with Dr. Pajon's earlier survival rate discussion emphasized the frightening news. Around 5:15 p.m., Dr. Fairbairn called, having just returned from the hospital. I was hoping to receive leukemia lesson 101.

"Ross has been cooperating by receiving platelets, antibiotics, and blood," the doctor explained.

"What are platelets?" I asked, revealing I probably had slept during that lecture in my college biology course.

"They're minute cells in the blood," the doctor began. "They react to trauma by causing clotting. In leukemia, there are a low number of platelets, which places a patient at risk of bleeding into himself without detection. That's why hemorrhaging is such a grave risk with this illness. Blood and platelets have to be transfused now in order to increase the healthy white blood cells. Ross's white blood count was a very low 100; a normal person's is around 5000. The white cells are the ones which fight off infection and act as the body's immune system. Antibiotics fight off any potential infection which may already be in the blood. If Ross develops a cold or other infection, he is in critical danger because his immune system is so weak. Infection is another one of the most serious complications of this disease."

Fairbairn's information was helpful and provided further relief since it confirmed that my earlier pleas to Hugh Thompson regarding the shackles had succeeded. Hugh had worked out a compromise with Ross where the deputies removed the metal restraints and instead attached leather straps between his ankles. Fairbairn also said that because Littleton Hospital didn't enjoy the best expertise in the metro area for treating leukemia, Ross would be transferred to University of Colorado Medical Center immediately.

On Monday afternoon, November 6, Ross called me around 1:00 from CU's Medical Center. "David, I met with two doctors who are in charge of my care. The lead doctor is Dr. Paul Seligman. A younger woman follows him around; she was described as a fellow in hematology. Her name is Dr. Karen Kelly. They wanted me to sign consent forms for two procedures, but I told them I needed to first talk with you."

"What do they want to do?"

"They said if I have the lymphocytic form, I have a 30% chance of surviving five years. David, for a 30% shot, I may forego any procedures."

"You've got to be kidding? Why do you so undervalue your life? You've got to fight, Ross. I'm not bored with you, yet. What's involved?"

"Extracting bone marrow. I told Dr. Seligman you would call him to discuss these tests. He's returning to my room around 3:30. And one more thing." Now what? I asked myself. "The University police intend to use a two-point restraint, shackling both my left ankle and right wrist. Same old problem, David. I'm not going to receive treatment hog tied." Ross, having now assured me I was not dreaming Sunday morning about the conflict between manacles and platelets, was resolute to be treated with dignity. I couldn't blame him. Later that afternoon, Walter and I spoke with Dr. Seligman.

"Your client needs to be treated NOW," the doctor emphasized, aghast at Ross's preoccupation with the restraints' issue. "This illness is extremely life threatening."

We assured the doctor we'd act to expedite treatment and asked about the bone-marrow-core biopsy and aspiration procedures he wanted performed. I was ready for leukemia lesson 102 after having read several articles about the disease that morning. Seligman was eager to provide the lesson.

"Leukemia is where the bone marrow produces an abundance of immature young, white blood cells. The manufacture of these so-called cancerous cells proliferates to where they eat the red blood cells whose function is to carry oxygen to the brain and other organs of the body. With leukemia, these immature cancerous cells take over the blood system, destroying the red blood cells and rendering the healthy white cells useless. The marrow which produces these killer cells is located within certain bones in the chest, thigh, and pelvic areas. Unless the flow of these cells is stopped, they'll destroy the entire body. This is why the disease can be so fatal."

"How do you stop the manufacture of those cells?" I asked. Described by Ross as being short like Dr. Fisch, Seligman stood tall in wisdom and patience like our esteemed psychologist. The oncologist continued his explanation.

Chapter 43: The Demons of Life-Saving Treatment

"Like other forms of cancer, chemotherapy is the treatment. When introduced into the body, the chemo kills the immature white blood cells. However, there's a problem. The chemo can't distinguish between the good red and white blood cells and the destructive white ones. Therefore, it destroys both the good and the bad. The trick is to have the chemo exterminate enough bad white cells and through other medications and blood transfusions produce sufficient red blood cells to make for a healthy body."

"What will you learn from the bone marrow?"

"By studying the marrow, we can identify the specific type of leukemia and learn the extent of the leukemic-cell infiltration. The precise drug protocol is determined by this identification. The procedure is very painful. We anesthetize the pelvic area, insert the needle, and then push it deep into the bone in order to remove the marrow. If for some reason aspiration is unsuccessful, we perform the biopsy."

"I understand there are acute and chronic forms of leukemia. What are some of the meaningful differences between the two?" I must have sounded like an inquisitive first-year med student to Seligman. However, I knew Ross would read the literature Walter's nurse had copied. Even though Ross trusted me, he still wanted some control over his destiny. Dr. Seligman did not mind the questions.

"Acute leukemia is more insidious because of its rapid onset. That type results in the loss of blood through a particular orifice. Symptoms of weakness or vomiting means the immature white blood cells have proliferated in great numbers and have begun attacking the bone, blood, organs, and tissue. By the time the patient is symptomatic, the disease has already spread."

Hearing that foreboding comment, I responded, "So when Ross was complaining of a cold last week and experiencing nose bleeds on Friday, the leukemia, presumably the acute form, had already started assaulting his system?"

"Correct. Now, with chronic leukemia, the signs are more gradual, allowing earlier detection and easier management of the disease. Chronic also refers to a higher level of maturity of the abnormal white blood cells."

"So, if he does have the acute form, treatment has to begin quickly," I responded to the obvious but also because I wanted confirmation.

"That's correct. That's why it's absolutely necessary your client undergoes these first two procedures right away." We agreed to tell Ross what we had just learned.

Because the University security had not yet applied the second restraint, Ross willingly pursued the aspiration that day. Around 6:30 the next evening, Ross called me at my office. "David, the diagnosis is ALL," he said very matter-of-factly. "My blood count is about 200 now. Although it's much higher than it was a day or two ago, my normal count should be around 5,000."

"When do they want to begin the medications?"

"They want to start the chemo tomorrow. They said my hair will fall out."

"You can have some of mine."

"David, you can't afford to give up any of yours."

"Okay, so I'll buy you a wig. What else did they say?"

"They want me to eat a lot. However, the food must be cooked well to avoid any bacteria. I can't have any salads or fruit."

"Well, I remember you used to like pepperoni pizza. I'll bring a pie over, but I'm not serving it with crystal and china."

"You do have a good memory for your age, David. Do I get any wine?"

"How about some Manischewitz sweet-concord grape? I have a bottle left over from Passover?"

"You're cute. How about a grape Mr. Misty?" I had no clue what he was talking about; I confessed my ignorance. "Come on, David. Kristin and Rachel would be shocked that you weren't hip to Mr. Misty. It's only the best slushy drink around ... made only by Dairy Queen."

"Of course, I knew that. One large Mr. Misty ... done. Do you have any restrictions regarding visitors, watching tv, or having a VCR in your room?"

"Not that I know of."

"What are your favorite kinds of shows? I'll bring over some tapes."

Chapter 43: The Demons of Life-Saving Treatment

"Comedies."

"You got it."

"I'm going to beat this, David."

"Of course, you are. Do you think I would purchase this great dinner and temporarily part with the Best of Eddie Murphy if I didn't think you could?"

"Assuming a good response to the chemo, I have a 50-50 chance of surviving at least three years."

"That's a slam dunk."

"I hate to belabor this, David, but I'll go along with the arrangement worked out with Hugh Thompson, but not both restraints. Two of his deputies, McCarty and Mahne, take turns guarding me. Plus, the hospital has its own security. My chances of pulling off an escape with that kind of manpower and while undergoing chemotherapy are pretty nonexistent."

I told Ross I would resolve the restraint issue quickly. My telephone conversation the next morning, November 8, with Dr. Karen Kelly underscored that necessity.

The doctor advised that although she'd like to start Ross's chemotherapy that day, she couldn't do so because of complications, making him more susceptible to renal failure. Ross's platelets were also low, and their count could drop even further as a result of the chemo. The first 48 to 72 hours of treatment would be crucial. I asked what Ross should expect regarding his body's reaction to the chemo.

"Most people can tolerate the regimen he will be on. For the first 15 days, he will feel tired, run down, and feverish. Then he'll begin to experience nausea, vomiting, and perhaps blurred vision. Days 17-20 will be rough because additional medications will become part of the protocol. He will lose his hair because we are introducing drugs that will kill his cells. We won't be able to tell for at least three weeks if he's responding positively. Some people take five to six weeks."

With such a sterling outlook for the next few weeks, no one could blame Ross for wanting treatment done with respect. Since we already had a court appearance scheduled for tomorrow, I drafted a motion for Judge Turelli's intervention. Walter and I visited Ross that afternoon at 2:30 to discuss tomorrow's court appearance.

Ross's private room, on the sixth floor, was situated at the end of a long corridor on ward six east. It was probably about 150 feet from the closest elevator. An exit door for the floor was about 50 feet from his room.

When we walked into Ross's room, we were greeted first by an omnipresent deputy sheriff. The burly-looking man, who seemed in his late-30s and was about 5'10" tall, arose from his chair which was at the foot of Ross's bed and directly across from the entry door. The door was about 15 feet from the bed. One large window was located to the left of the bed. As was the case at Littleton Hospital, this deputy was armed and positioned to afford himself the best view of visitors. He left the room, allowing Walter and me complete privacy with Ross.

I was surprised to see the extent of Ross's shackles, believing the earlier compromise reached with Hugh Thompson at Littleton would apply also to CU's Medical Center. Instead, the restraints were much more restrictive.

Ross's left ankle was bound by a thick, metal shackle which contained a steel loop at the end. Metal links ran through the loop and around the bed frame and were secured by a metal lock. Ross's right wrist was similarly restrained and secured to the bed post. A long, metal-link chain was threaded along the bottom bed frame, allowing him considerable movement within the bed. Ross was willing to compromise.

"Gentlemen, the ankle manacle is fine. However, the one around my wrist has to go," he said. "It's a painful reminder of my childhood. I'm not sure of the circumstances, but I've been told (i.e, his reference to communication by another alter personality) that wrist shackles are bad and, if continued, will result in my being killed by another," Ross explained. Walter and I listened without commenting.

I assumed the sixth-floor staff and patients were quite content knowing an accused double-murderer residing down the hall was well restrained. However, my only concern was Ross. Delayed treatment brought him one step closer to his mortality. Even if there were gruesome childhood memories interfering with his will to survive, I wasn't going to give up. As an MPD sufferer, Ross's antipathy to an anal swab or having his wrists restrained was perfectly understandable.

I had a dear friend who suffered from protracted periods of

Chapter 43: The Demons of Life-Saving Treatment

depression; she became rigid whenever anyone greeted her with a hug. One of my adult female, MPD clients slept with a light on. Another such sufferer would begin hyperventilating whenever she saw a red shirt or blouse. All of those people had a substantial history of sexual abuse. As a result of therapy, each one of them knew the reason behind their fright. I did not know the source of Ross's fears, and believed he also lacked that knowledge. There was something else troubling him.

"How else can we help, Ross? You look preoccupied."

"Up until last week, David, I actually saw some brightness in my future. In spite of Kingsley's ruling and my knowledge that Dr. Newton was retiring, I thought my life had hope. With this diagnosis, my dreams have been dashed," Ross admitted with uncharacteristic openness.

"Don't lose faith, Ross," Walter said.

"I'm not sure I can be that optimistic, Walter. Things never have seemed to work out for me. Kelli and I have planned a future together, and I want to do something regarding child abuse. I don't see that happening now," Ross said dejectedly.

Walter and I again listened. It was extremely unusual for Ross to reveal himself. During the last ten minutes, Ross's emotions had ranged from firmness and resolve to introspection and depression. We hadn't seen this complex side of him since the emergence of "Ross" during the Fairbairn taping. Perhaps, we too were seeing Ross. We remained silent, wanting him to continue.

"If I've committed what the district attorney has charged me with, then I believe man has to atone for the bad things he has done. If I can share my experiences with people who have also been victims of abuse that may help others along the way," Ross concluded. I promised that within a few days, I would talk to the Kempe Center. Ross was grateful.

The next day, I would appear before Judge Turelli to vacate the upcoming court dates and to argue the issue of the restraints. I spoke to the hospital's chief of security, Phil Jones, early that following morning before court.

"Chief Jones, I must confess I'm stunned by your insensitivity to Ross's medical condition and disregard of the consequences of him not receiving immediate care."

"Like I said, Mr. Savitz, I can't be concerned about what might happen if he refuses treatment. I have to look out for the safety of the hospital staff and community at large. We have a written policy regarding the nature of the restraints, and I'm not diverting from that."

"I assume you'll divert if you're ordered to do so by a court."

"I will consider court orders."

"I suspect you'll **abide** by a court order," I emphasized. "I'll advise the judge appropriately."

Judge Turelli shook his head in disbelief as I explained Ross was as secure as Ft. Knox. He'd be lucky to crawl out of bed once treatment began. Without hesitation, the judge ordered the hospital to explain forthwith why the handcuffs should not be removed.

The next morning, Friday, November 10, the hospital's attorney phoned me. The hospital's security would remove the wrist restraint. Dr. Kelly arranged for the chemo to begin that day.

I was now optimistic regarding Ross's treatment and determined to provide him the best opportunity for success. I paid him a surprise visit on Saturday afternoon, November 11.

CHAPTER 44

Dancing with Ginger and a Colt 45

Heads turned, followed quickly by smiling faces as I hurried down the hallway of floor six east. I don't think the hospital staff ever saw someone carrying so much. My left hand clutched a grocery-size, brown-paper bag that was half full of tapes and books. Underneath my left arm and cupped within my palm, I secured an 18" square by 2" wide cardboard box. The item inside was still warm. In my right hand, I held a large colorful, plastic cup filled with a tasty liquid. Tied loosely around the cup were several long strings connected to circular objects flailing in the air.

I declined requests of assistance because "if I let go of something, everything else will fall to the floor." A nurse happily opened the door to Ross's room. Denny, the 6' 1", lean, western-looking, deputy sheriff on duty at the time, must have thought he was in the middle of a party. As soon as Ross saw me, he broke out into a huge grin.

"David, you didn't forget. Thank you!"

"Ross, Kelly and Seligman are in charge of platelets and chemo. I'm in charge of food and fun. Enjoy!

This is Pizza Hut's most scrumptious pepperoni pizza. Here is your purple slush, or as we drink aficionados refer to it, a Mr. Misty. I'll tie these balloons to your bed post. The tapes are Eddie Murphy classics, and the books have extra-large print which you need because of your advancing age. Besides, I want you to be well fed and in a good mood when Kelli arrives this weekend."

"Thanks, David. I figure this may be the last weekend I'll have hair and feel decent enough to spend time with her."

"You two guys enjoy yourselves. I'll check on you after Kelli leaves."

On Saturday night, Kelli caught the red-eye flight from Phoenix and arrived in Denver at 4:00 a.m. on Sunday. Her stay would be brief; she was scheduled to leave the next night at 9:00.

During their day and a half together Kelli and Ross laughed, watched videos, ate well-cooked frozen food, and danced with Ginger.

The slender, middle-aged Ginger Buckley was the head nurse of the oncology unit, but Ross had eyes for another by the same name. Ross had baptized his IV appendage on wheels with the name, Ginger. Whenever Ross left his bed, he always had to take his partner-on-rollers with him. Occasionally he would dazzle Ginger with one or more classical dance steps made famous by Fred Astaire. Fred and Ginger were the ballroom attraction in Room 6310.

Amidst all of this good-natured fun, however, one thing was missing — the opportunity for Ross and Kelli to be alone. A deputy sheriff — either Mike in the morning or Denny at night — was always present. On Sunday night, Ross and Kelli, while whispering in front of Denny, talked about their last day together.

"Tomorrow is going to be our last chance," Ross said.

"I know, but Denny is not going to leave us alone in a million years," Kelli replied pessimistically.

"I'll handle that. Just make a run to the drugstore tomorrow before you get here."

The next morning, Monday, November 13, Kelli figured she would go through the motions. She was staying at the Landmark Inn on South Colorado Boulevard. Across the street was a Target department store.

Kelli walked into the store, and during one of the most embarrassing moments of her life, completed her purchase. With her recent acquisition tucked hidden in a little bag, she walked back to her hotel, hopped a cab, and arrived at Ross's bedside. She nodded and smiled. Ross was delighted. They had the remainder of the day to find a quiet moment together. Ross's treatment, however, proved to be an obstacle.

Chapter 44: Dancing with Ginger and a Colt 45

Before lunch, a nurse informed Ross he would be receiving platelets later in the afternoon. Pain and grogginess were common aftereffects of that treatment.

As anticipated, the fluids did knock Ross out for a few hours. He was awakened around 6:30 for dinner, which he quickly consumed. Then in an earshot of Denny, Ross asked Kelli, "Would you mind accompanying me to the bathroom and help remove this tape?"

Kelli knew Ross wanted to seize this last opportunity. Her mind flashed back to 1983, the last time they had been intimate. She wanted to be with Ross, but it wasn't like before. There was no wining and dining. No soft music. No dark lights. She realized there might never be another chance. She whispered to Ross, "I'm really scared," while gesturing her head sharply to the right in Denny's direction.

"Don't worry," Ross replied. "He sees nothing and knows nothing. He's very cool."

Ross then spoke to Denny. "Denny, she's going to help me get this tape off."

"Okay," Denny replied, briefly looking up from his magazine and then returning to reading.

Ross arose from his bed and escorted Ginger into the bathroom with Kelli walking by his side. He closed the door behind them. The time was around 7:00 p.m., Kelli would have to leave in about an hour to make her 9:00 flight.

The two stood face-to-face, smiling at each other. Kelli began giggling; she was nervous. Ross untied his hospital gown from the back, allowing it to slip off his arms and fall onto the floor. Ginger was still at his side. While undressing, Kelli asked Ross to turn on the bathtub to muffle their sounds. Ross complied and then helped Kelli onto the sink counter.

He held her gently at the sides of her shoulders, pulled her upper body toward him and the two began kissing. Kelli put her arms around Ross's back as they embraced. He slid his arms down her back and began moving her lower torso to the edge of the counter. Kelli moved her right hand to Ross's groin area, found what she had been seeking, and began stroking it tenderly until it responded.

Kelli arched her back slightly and raised her legs, allowing Ross passage. Ross performed slowly while holding Kelli's buttocks in place. Kelli looked at her lover and then closed her eyes. Ross did likewise, joining his soulmate in a flood of affection that had eluded them for so long. Their muted moans were echoes of the intimate chorus they had shared more than six years ago. Tears glistened in Kelli's eyes as she held Ross tighter and tighter, unsure if there would be future moments together. She whispered in Ross's ear.

"Promise me I'm not going to wake up. Don't tell me this is really another one of your love letters."

Ross promised her everything was real and that the two had been reunited in love. "I thought you had forgotten about me," he said.

"Ross, no matter what happens, I will always love you."

Ross looked into her eyes and just before kissing her said, "You are the most important person in my life."

Suddenly, after about fifteen minutes together, they heard a nurse enter the room. Ross stopped moving. He and Kelli both listened.

They heard Denny say, "He's in there getting cleaned up."

The nurse knocked on the door and said, "What are you doing in there?"

"I'm trying to get cleaned up," Ross replied. Kelli put her hand over her mouth, fearing an outburst of laughter or hysterical screaming.

The nurse responded. "Do you want me to come in there and change your tubes, or do you want to put a towel around yourself and come out here?"

"Can you please return in about five minutes? I'll come out there."

Kelli quickly grabbed her clothes, stepped in the shower, and closed the curtain. Ross draped a towel around his waist and wiped away his perspiration with a moist washcloth. Within a few minutes, the nurse returned. Ross exited the bathroom and was attended to. After thanking the nurse and watching her leave the room, Ross immediately returned to Kelli. They resumed where they had left off.

After another 15 minutes, it was getting close to 8:00. The two shared one last kiss and one last "I love you." Ross walked back into the room and returned to his bed. Kelli followed within a few

Chapter 44: Dancing with Ginger and a Colt 45

minutes. She kissed Ross, said goodbye to Denny and left. When she arrived at the airport, she couldn't leave without speaking to Ross one more time.

"I can still feel you."

"I'm glad. I'll always be with you."

"Tell Denny, thank you."

"I will."

Kelli flew home with a permanent glow and warm heart while remembering Room 6310. During the next few days, however, the room returned to its traditional medicinal venue.

On Thursday, November 16, I visited Ross at 3:30 in the afternoon. The doctors wanted to perform a spinal tap, but Ross wanted my input first. He complained that his jaw was hurting because of the medications, making it more difficult for him to eat firm foods. He looked thinner and paler than the day before Kelli had arrived. His speech was now more labored.

The tap was designed to determine if the leukemia had penetrated into his spinal fluid and brain. Because his platelet count had reached a good level, it was a favorable time to perform the procedure. Dr. Seligman, and his taller associate, the 5' 9", honey-blond haired Dr. Becky Helton, were anxiously awaiting the go ahead. With my encouragement Ross agreed to undergo the tap, providing I remained in the room. Naturally, I agreed.

Since the procedure required an invasion of the spinal column at Ross's lower back, that area had to first be anaesthetized. Following Dr. Helton's instructions, Ross lay on his side with his chin touching his chest and knees drawn up — an adult fetal position. A nurse assistant steadied Ross for the cleansing and injection.

Dr. Helton cleaned Ross's lower back with an antiseptic, avoiding any contamination of her gloves or needles with the solution. As a further precaution, the doctor wore her long hair in a bun. The injection was next.

The doctor carefully inserted the sturdy needle in the middle of Ross's spine, aiming slightly cranially. While securing the needle with her left hand against Ross's back to avoid dislodgement, the anesthetic solution was injected slowly and carefully. Ross was awake during the entire procedure. At the first hint of pain, the doctor would terminate the injection. Satisfied that the lower spinal column and surrounding ligaments were sufficiently blocked, Dr. Helton inserted another needle into the same lumbar area. She aspirated a sufficient amount of spinal fluid for lab analysis.

Ross tolerated the 20- to 25-minute procedure without any complications. He had closed his eyes throughout, employing one of his "spacing" techniques. His breathing seemed relaxed and he uttered nary a sound. When informed the tap had been completed, Ross opened his eyes. His face looked flushed, but otherwise he appeared fine. He thanked me for staying by his side.

The nurse made certain Ross was comfortable while she gathered her tools and supplies. The medical team then left. Ross continued lying on his side, and I remained standing by him. He wanted to chat, in spite of me not wanting him to expend unnecessary energy. He tried to be his old humorous self even though his speech was slightly slurred.

"I watched Eddie Murphy in Concert on Sunday with Kelli and Denny. Denny liked it, but I think Kelli thought it was a little raw."

"Why didn't you watch *Slap Shot?* She would have liked that."

"I wanted to make sure Denny liked it." I would later learn why.

Ross then asked me to retrieve a card that was standing on his nightstand. It was a get-well card from a woman in Arvada, Colorado who described herself as an MPD sufferer. She was praying for Ross.

Just then, Ross began talking more slowly and haltingly. His eyes started to droop. Within seconds, he was sound asleep. I left around 5:15 and went to my health club.

As I began pedaling the stationary bike, I reflected upon Dr. Helton's comments as she was administering to Ross. "He's a pretty strong young man." "Yes, I know that," I replied. In order to avoid welling up, I turned on my Walkman and began reading the newspaper while pedaling.

The next morning, Friday, November 17, deputy sheriff Mike Anderson called my office.

"Mr. Savitz, Ross wants to speak with you." There was a slight pause. I could hear Anderson telling Ross I was on the phone.

Ross was in obvious pain. "David ... David ... I don't feel good."

Chapter 44: Dancing with Ginger and a Colt 45

"Ross, take it easy. Don't strain yourself."

"David ... can't breathe ... feel bad." Ross sounded in great discomfort. It pained me to hear him struggle so. "David ... I had a lousy night. I needed to talk to someone friendly."

"Ross, I'm glad you called me. I'm sure the medication is working. Pretty soon you're going to feel a lot better."

"David, would you have Fairbairn call me?"

"I sure will. Have Mike take the phone and try to get some more rest." After contacting Dr. Fairbairn, I spent the next several hours working on other matters. At 2:30 that afternoon, I received a call from Dr. Seligman with whom I had now established a very cordial relationship.

The thin, bespectacled physician appeared no taller than about 5'5" and in his mid-40s. However, whatever Seligman lacked in height, he had gained in professional stature at such a young age. From what I had learned by talking to my other physician friends at the hospital, particularly Dr. Marvin Schwarz, Seligman was a superior hematologist/oncologist.

I liked Dr. Seligman because he was thoughtful, considerate, and never mentioned Ross's criminal situation. The doctor was strictly concerned with Ross's care and bristled whenever a delay was encountered with treatment. Seligman well knew the urgency of Ross's situation and strove to ensure that no measure was overlooked for his patient's success. If Dr. Seligman were calling, it was important.

"David, Ross does not want to take his vincristine, which is part of his chemotherapy. It's administered through an IV, but Ross said he can't breathe."

"I know. I spoke to him this morning. Speaking was difficult for him."

"The thing is, this is essential medication. Dr. Fairbairn stopped by around noon, but I wasn't here. I'll call him at 3:00 to determine his assessment. However, would you please stop by tomorrow and encourage Ross to follow our treatment schedule?" I agreed to. The next morning, Saturday, November 18, I called Ross around 11:30.

"David, I didn't sleep well last night. I'm in a lot of pain. I'm having difficulty breathing. I'm going to die."

"Ross, you will not die if you take your medications. If you don't promise me you'll take this vincristine, I'm going to come over there and administer it myself."

"David, you don't know how."

"I'll learn by the time I get to your room. See, I don't want you to die, but you will if you don't follow your doctors' orders."

"Okay, David. I'll tell the nurse I'll accept the chemo today."

"You better because I'm coming over around noon, and I want to see an empty IV." At 12:30, I visited Ross bringing with me a Mr. Misty, several balloons, and a package of lifesavers. Ross was eating his lunch slowly and said his jaw felt a little better. He mentioned having "lost a lot of time." I assured him he hadn't missed anything important. After he finished his lunch, he laid back in his bed. He turned toward me and asked me for a favor.

"David, you have a bunch of tapes with Newton's voice on it. Will you bring me those, or better yet, will you make me a tape of your voice? You relax me."

"The Newton-Savitz tapes will be here tomorrow."

That evening, Robin and I went to a friend's 50th birthday party which was held at the Western Art Museum in downtown Denver. The occasion was the closest I'd ever come to dressing western style — jeans, a white shirt, and brown Florsheim boots stretched my creativity. Throughout the night, we and the other guests two-stepped, ate barbecue, and laughed. The evening allowed me to divert my thoughts and enjoy good friends. However, once the party ended and Robin and I drove home, my mind turned to other things.

Although I was able to picture dancing at my milestone bash in four years (minus the Western theme), I also knew Ross had to survive another twenty-five years before reaching the half-century mark. I had difficulty envisioning his celebration.

The next night, Sunday, November 19, while I was watching television downstairs, Robin yelled from upstairs for me to pick up the phone. It was around 8:45.

"David, I'm sorry to bother you at home."

"That's okay, Ross. Do you feel all right? You don't sound too good."

Chapter 44: Dancing with Ginger and a Colt 45

"I'm okay," he said, although his speech sounded quite strained. "David, I want you to have the codes to my floppy disks."

"What codes?"

"In order to retrieve the data on most of my disks, you have to plug in certain letters and symbols and then a password. I want to give you all of that." I knew how Ross prized his computer and the extraordinary steps he had taken to maintain the secrecy of his work. His eagerness to disclose this information gave me an uncomfortable feeling.

"Why? You're going to be fine, Ross."

"David, I've felt bad today from the drugs. My stomach feels lousy, and I'm losing my ability to use my hands. If anything happens to me, I want you to have my disks. You need to know how to get into them." The more Ross spoke, the worse I felt. I wanted to fight his pessimism but thought that might make him worse so I agreed to take down the information.

"Okay, Ross, I have paper and a pen."

"Inside the black footlocker at Walter's are two smoke-glassed cases containing my disks. One of those boxes is marked 'personal/private/confidential,'" Ross explained, speaking slowly and deliberately.

"Okay, go ahead."

"After you insert the disk in the C drive, you hit CD, back slash, confide. It'll ask you for a password. You type 'Rossraggmuffin.' You then open up the disks by typing 'wp, back slash, library, back slash, lib, and the numbers 8025719.'" Because I was computer illiterate and didn't know the lingo, I wrote down everything verbatim.

"Is that it?" I asked, knowing my secretary Leslie would understand the information if I recorded everything accurately.

"If you didn't get all of this, look at my copy of the leather-bound King James' bible here at the hospital. The index page under the Genesis heading contains certain codes. They can be extrapolated. One last thing, David."

"Go ahead."

"The Will I sent you ... I made provisions for the Guesses, the Kellers, Olson, and my idea for SCAT."

"That's the *Stop Child Abuse Today* concept that you had discussed with Walter and me."

"Correct. The rest is for you, David."

"Ross, please don't talk like that. You're feeling the chemo, which is what the doctors explained to you would happen. Try and get a good rest, and I'll stop by tomorrow."

"Okay, David. Good night."

"Good night, Ross."

I sat on my couch for a few minutes, reviewing the data to ensure I recorded it right. I went upstairs and told Robin about the call. I tried to act as if everything were okay. She looked at me with a pleasant smile, but I knew she wasn't fooled. We went to sleep after watching the 10:00 news. Around midnight, our phone rang.

"David, this is Ginger Buckley, the nurse administrator on Ross's ward. Sorry to wake you."

"That's okay. What's wrong?"

"Ross tried to commit suicide earlier tonight."

"Jesus! What happened?"

"He removed a gun from the holster of the female guard on duty. He placed the nozzle in his mouth saying he wanted to die. The guard managed to grab a hold of the trigger and began screaming for help. An intern rushed into the room, pulled Ross's hand away and subdued him."

"When did this happen?"

"About 9:30 tonight. Ross is currently in a four-point restraint. Dr. Weissberg said you should be called. We've called Dr. Fairbairn also."

"Is there anything I can do?"

"Not now. We just wanted to let you know."

"I appreciate your calling." Ginger assured me the hospital would provide me with an update in the morning. As I lay in bed with my arm around Robin, I was struck by the near-perfect symmetry of Ross's intended last conversation with me. He had entered my life as a result of his use of a 22 revolver. He wanted to leave me at the end of a Colt 45.

CHAPTER 45

Goodbye, My Friend

At 8:00 the next morning, I met Dr. Julie Sutarik at the physicians' station of the oncology ward. I knew the petite intern was on duty last night and had assisted in thwarting Ross's suicide attempt. I was concerned about her and wanted to learn more details about the incident.

"I was attending to a patient about four doors down from Mr. Carlson when I heard the guard screaming," Sutarik calmly explained, her flushed face, however, revealing the tense circumstances surrounding Ross's despair. "When I arrived at Mr. Carlson's room, I saw him and the guard sitting on the floor. Ross had the barrel of the gun in his mouth and was saying 'I want to die. I'm going to die anyway.' Fortunately, the guard, who wasn't much bigger than me, had her finger on the trigger. Before entering the room completely, I yelled for more help. Then, I ran behind Ross and tried to get his hands off the gun. Within a couple of minutes, two residents came into the room."

Sutarik described how she, Dr. Gwen Hewitt, who was taller and at least 20 pounds heavier than Sutarik, and Dr. Tom Trouillot, who was fortunately a physical match for Ross, positioned themselves to Ross's side away from the line of fire and managed to free his grip. Within seconds, the female guard had pulled the gun away from Ross. Doctors Hewitt and Trouillot then held Ross down until the university police arrived.

Ross, shackled now with four-point restraints, was again, unwilling to participate in treatment. Dr. Sutarik urged me to convince Ross of the "critical importance" of today's procedures. I was surprised that anyone at the hospital still gave a damn about him. He had compromised the judge's and security people's trust, and I was running out of rabbits.

Why would anyone heed my pleas anymore? If Ross didn't care about himself, why should anyone else? I felt like racing down the hallway, bursting into his room, and excoriating him for acting as his own executioner. I wanted to ask him why we should be concerned with his welfare when he was trying to throw it in the sewer? I took a few deep breaths instead.

After six years with Ross, I knew he could exasperate Job. It was too common that one minute the 25-year-old could dazzle you with his intellect and maturity, and within the next breath disappoint you with inanity and stupidity. One moment, he could be charming, and then in the blink of an eye, brutish. I knew not to be personally offended by his unpredictable, chameleon-like behavior, which for one who suffered from MPD was actually a predictable feature of his existence. I didn't expect anyone at the hospital to understand Ross like I believed I did and could not be surprised if others weren't as forgiving of his behavior.

Since his diagnosis, he had certainly given me enough hints that he viewed his situation as hopeless, but I never thought he'd try to kill himself. Since I wasn't in his shoes, I undoubtedly couldn't imagine how gloomy he saw his life. So, I planned to approach Ross as I usually did — empathic and nonjudgmental. Before I was able to walk to his room, Dr. Seligman and five of his staff were waiting at Ginger Buckley's office to speak to me first. The mood was somber.

"David, we need to get Ross treated," Dr. Seligman implored. "We're not concerned about his legal situation, just his care. You're the only one he'll listen to. We need you to convince him to give us more blood. He must take platelets, antibiotics, and his chemo. We need to treat his abdominal pain with magnesium citrate and a nasal tube. A rectal tube had been recommended, but we know not to broach that subject with him." Seligman explained why Ross was having such severe abdominal pain.

"Patients taking this form of chemotherapy will often suffer what we call a paralytic ileus. Essentially, the drugs cause the nerves in

Chapter 45: Goodbye, My Friend

the bowel to constrict, causing a blockage. If the large bowel doesn't move, it will not squeeze out the stool, and the bowel will then become distended. In a rare patient, there will be so much distention that a small perforation of the bowel will result, leading to severe infection."

Because any infection was dangerous, the solution was to treat the blockage with medications, including morphine for the pain. Last night, the staff wanted Ross to walk around his room, hoping the movement would open his bowel a little. That's when he surprised the guard.

"Well, you know he's going to resist treatment the way he's shackled," I said.

"We know that. That's where you come in. He has to be treated for this problem, but we no longer have the luxury of moving him around. His having to lie down, places more pressure on his abdomen." I could sense Seligman was building up to something. "Because of that complication," the doctor continued, "Ross had to be evaluated surgically. Our gastroenterology department has already been involved. However, the treatment now has to be more invasive, especially in areas where Ross was extremely resistant." I got it.

"And all you want from me is to convince Ross to accept treatment into each of his orifices while horizontal."

"That's correct." I thanked the doctor and his staff for their update, concern, and, most of all, their eternal optimism regarding my upcoming meeting with Ross. As I left Seligman and staff for Ross's room, I was sure I must have dozed off during a law school practicum when the orifice lecture was given to aspiring trial lawyers.

Nevertheless, while walking down the hospital corridor, I did find some comfort in the decision I had made at Penn State 25 years ago when I elected psychology as my major. All I had to figure out now was how I, as a lawyer, could convince a client, who was charged with murder, suffering from an unusual mental illness, undergoing treatment for a violent form of leukemia, and probably having experienced different forms of childhood sexual abuse, that he should permit doctors to stick tubes up his nose and anus so his bowel wouldn't perforate and cause him to die of an infection. Knowing we probably covered this precise issue in undergrad psych and now having received a refresher course from Seligman and his team, I felt much better as I entered Ross's room.

An unarmed, male deputy sheriff was seated at the foot of the bed. He walked out of the room and stood outside the open door, affording me a private visit. Each of Ross's wrists and ankles were individually shackled to the bed.

Usually when I visited, Ross would sit upright in his bed and engage me in light banter. This morning, he was on his back and appeared distressed. His customary glib greeting was absent. He looked like a very ill patient. I nevertheless wanted to know what happened last night.

"Spiders got into my body through my behind," he explained with labored speech. "Spiders trying to kill me. I put the gun in my mouth to kill the spiders," he said while grimacing.

"What would have happened to you if you had done that?"

"Nothing. I was just going to kill the spiders. I couldn't do it, David, because I wasn't strong enough."

"Do you recall talking to me on the phone last night?"

"No, what about?"

"Do you remember what you did that resulted in all of these restraints?"

"I know I must have been bad."

"You scared a lot of people last night."

"I'm sorry. I didn't hurt anyone did I?"

"You didn't but..."

"I don't want to hurt anyone."

". . . a lot of people are concerned for their safety as well as yours."

"Tell them I'm sorry. David, the drugs are making me scared and causing a lot of pain."

"I know, and the doctors want to treat that with special medication and a nasal tube. They assure me these will reduce your abdominal pain. Plus, they need to schedule your chemo and platelets. Can I tell them to make the necessary arrangements?"

"I don't know," Ross said in discomfort. After staying with Ross for about an hour, it was apparent he wanted a fuller understanding of his medical situation and that he had stabilized. Because Dr. Fairbairn agreed to visit the hospital later that morning and provide Ross with the

Chapter 45: Goodbye, My Friend

explanation he wanted, I felt it was okay and return to my office. Early in the afternoon, I spoke to Fairbairn.

Although he felt he had made headway with Ross, he sounded noticeably perturbed with Dr. Seligman. "He didn't seem as interested in understanding Ross's psychiatric illness as he was in having us encourage Ross to accept treatment," Fairbairn said while referring to Seligman. "I thought he should know that one of the secondary side effects of prednisone is to cause hallucinations. That might explain Ross's explanation about the spiders."

Although I didn't feel a need to trumpet Dr. Seligman's cause, the last thing I needed was a rift between two doctors important to Ross's treatment. I knew Seligman felt Ross was mentally "crazy," but I also understood he could care less about the particular psychiatric nuances that drove his patient's behavior. Dr. Seligman had candidly admitted to me he realized Ross "did not interpret or process thoughts like the average person." However, at this juncture, he just wanted to ensure that everyone was on the same page regarding Ross's care. After thanking Dr. Fairbairn, I made plans to visit Ross later that afternoon and bring him a gift.

By now, my stepdaughter Kristin was 12 ½ and her same caring self. She had made Ross a 2 ½-foot-square calendar for the month of November. The chemotherapy had a tendency to make Ross groggy and blur his vision. When I entered Ross's room around 2:00, he was sitting up watching television. He looked much better than he did yesterday although his speech still sounded strained. "For some reason, David, it's a little bit more difficult to talk today. My jaw feels as if it has been injured."

"It could be because you stuck the barrel of a 45 in your mouth."

"Oh, I remember you telling me that."

"What I'd like you to swallow now instead are your medications and food. You need to concentrate on getting healthy and maintaining your strength."

"I'll try David."

"Good. I have to go back to the office. Before I go, I'll stand the calendar on this air vent. Can you see the numbers?"

"Yes, it's Tuesday, November 21."

"Correct, in two days it will be Thanksgiving, and you'll be eating Turkey. I'll check with you tomorrow. Kristin is working on the calendar for December."

The next morning, Wednesday, November 22, Ginger Buckley called me at my office around 8:30, and informed me that Ross had been uncomfortable since 4:00 this morning. His abdominal pain had not gotten better, and he had pulled the NG tube out of his mouth five times. "Staff understands it's an uncomfortable device," Buckley admitted, "but they're trying to remove the build-up of fluids in his stomach. His temperature is 40 degrees Celsius which is about 104 degrees Fahrenheit. He's been covered with a cooling blanket to reduce his temperature. That will in turn guard against him becoming dehydrated and reduce his stomach distress." After hanging up, I assumed Buckley's report concerned just one more complication that would soon be remedied.

Around 11:00 a.m., Ross called in obvious misery. "David ... David ... I . . ." He was breathing very heavily and quickly.

"Ross, try to take it easy. Try to relax. I'm here."

"David, . . .I . . ., I can't ... can't."

"Ross, I'm not going anywhere. Just try and relax. I spoke to Ginger Buckley earlier this morning. She told me you're in discomfort, particularly your stomach, and that a tube has been inserted down your throat to remove fluids." There was a pause on Ross's end of the line for several seconds. He then resumed talking.

"David, the hospital security doesn't allow me to use the bathroom," he explained, now sounding much more relaxed. "They finally brought in a portable toilet this morning, and I was able to go gobs and gobs. It relieved a lot of pressure. Then they took me downstairs for x-rays, and I went volumes again. I feel a lot better."

"That's good, Ross," wondering if I really had to know the intimate details of my client's bowel evacuations. I finally figured what the hell. If he wanted to share these personal experiences, I would add it as a plus to our balance sheet of bonding.

"What's been the problem with the tube?"

"With both my wrists and ankles shackled, I get scared with

Chapter 45: Goodbye, My Friend

that tube down my throat. So, I take it out. If I weren't so tied up, I could deal better with it."

"I don't think now is the best time to fight them about the restraints. Just do the best you can. No one is going to hurt you."

"Okay, I'll try. I have to go now. Thanks David."

"You're welcome. Talk to you later." Since Ross sounded much better and more upbeat, I figured he was going to have a good day. Sensing an opportunity for some exercise, I spent the noon hour at the Sporting Club.

When I returned to the office, there was a note from Leslie which read "Deputy Roberts called. Ross not doing well; asking for you. I called Roberts back. He said about a half hour ago, Ross became delirious; is having breathing problems. Doctors have been working on him since. Please call ASAP."

Within fifteen minutes, I was in Ross's room. It was a disquieting scene. Ross was sitting up wearing an oxygen mask. When I entered, Ross immediately fixed on me and took a deep breath. He motioned for me to come by his side. Standing to the left of Ross's bed were Dr. Rebecca Helton, a male intern from Iran, Ginger Buckley, and two nurses. Watching off to the side were two deputy sheriffs, one of whom was Dwayne Roberts. I walked to Ross and grasped his hand, which he had held out for me. Dr. Helton spoke.

"Ross has developed an acute respiratory problem. This is often encountered with chemotherapy. We're using portable oxygen to help him, but he needs to be transferred to the ICU which is better suited to handle this complication. He won't go without discussing it with you."

Dr. Helton talked with uncharacteristic concern. This was not the face of the same doctor who, a week before, had calmly explained the spinal tap procedure. I knew Ross had felt the doctor's anxiety. Ross tugged at my hand to come closer. He pulled the mask away from his mouth so he could speak softly to me.

"David, they're trying to kill me. Don't let them kill me, David."

"Ross, I guarantee you that is not the case. They're trying to help you."

Just then, Dr. Brian Morrison came into the room. He was a fellow in critical care medicine and worked directly under my good friend, Dr. Marvin Schwarz, the ICU's attending physician. Morrison was a tall, strapping man with ruggedly handsome looks. He appeared to be in his mid-30s.

Morrison asked to examine Ross's lungs. After Ross managed a few deep breaths, the doctor turned to me and firmly said, "Your client has to be transferred to the ICU now." Ross looked at me. I nodded in agreement, assuring him he would be under the care of a great physician, Dr. Schwarz.

Ross squeezed my hand and said, "You're an extraordinary man. Please stay with me." Rarely, had Ross ever sounded so needy and been so complimentary. I promised I would not leave him.

A few minutes later, Dr. Fairbairn walked into the room and was quickly briefed by Dr. Helton. Bob then spoke to Ross, concurring with the wisdom of the necessary transfer. At approximately 2:40, a very frightened young man was wheeled to the ICU. Accompanying Ross were the portable oxygen equipment, a cadre of medical personnel, two deputy sheriffs, and his lawyer.

When we entered the ICU, no one spoke in terms of Ross being in grave danger. Rather, the unit's administrator, Barbara Geeslehardt, informed me that the next 24 to 48 hours were critical because Ross's respiratory problem had to be stabilized.

As I walked into the ICU, I observed six individual rooms located on the right and left sides of the unit. Each room had a sliding glass door in the front. The nurses' station was located in the center of the unit, providing a visual of every patient. Ross was wheeled into a room toward the far end of the right side. Two chairs were positioned in front of the nurses' area and just to the right of Ross's location. A sheriff sat in one of the chairs. From time to time, I sat in the other.

A small lounge was located outside the ICU. Through the open door of the unit, visitors could see the nursing station and the rooms closest to the lounge. One could not see into Ross's room from the lounge.

Around 3:00 p.m., a tube was inserted through Ross's mouth into his trachea. This intubation was an essential procedure in respiratory failure and designed to assist Ross's breathing. Shortly after that, Dr. Morrison entered the ICU and told me, "He's very sick."

Chapter 45: Goodbye, My Friend

"Define sick," I said.

"I'm not sure he'll survive."

Morrison's use of the term "very sick" was like a lawyer telling a client that a jury's verdict of death was "very unfavorable." I wasn't interested in talking to a rookie doctor prone to understatement. As a result, I told Morrison I wanted to speak to Marvin Schwarz. That was arranged immediately.

I had been friends with Marvin for about 12 years. During that time, we had jogged, played racquetball, gone to basketball games, and had dinner together several times a month. When he ran, he tilted his head severely to the right. When I first witnessed his jogging style, I thought he was a human leaning tower of Pisa. I was afraid he'd fall over. He never did.

A former major in the Army Medical Corps, he was built rock solid and weighed about 190 pounds. His muscular build was earned from working out feverishly on Nautilus equipment. He had a thin moustache and combed his hair straight back, ala Pat Riley. Riley probably could have beaten Marvin in a game of HORSE, but I'd bet on Marvin any day in hand-to-hand combat.

Marvin was one of the country's foremost pulmonary and emergency care academicians, having consulted in his specialties nationally and internationally. At times impatient with lay people, he would often yelp like a crazed professor if I dared ask him a medical question during a run. He always answered because I would tell him that his ranting violated Denver's noise ordinance, and it would cost him a grand for me to represent him.

During the mid-1980s, I employed him as an expert witness in a physician malpractice case. After Marvin gave his deposition, the attorney for the defendant-doctor settled for policy limits.

Marvin was not the type to mince words. From the ICU, it was a five-minute walk within the medical center to Marvin's office. When I arrived there, Marvin was studying x-rays on a view box. Instead of displaying his hyper-maniacal-jogging demeanor, today he was professional and solemn.

"Hi David. Let me show you," Marvin said with Dr. Morrison and others looking on. "These are Ross's x-rays of just a couple of hours ago. This white area covering the lungs shows bleeding into the lungs. This is caused by his leukemia and chemotherapy which results in dangerously low platelet levels. It's extremely difficult to give him adequate oxygen because of this severe hemorrhaging. However, we're going to do everything we can to correct the problem. If we can't, he will not survive."

I now understood. Ross was fighting for his life. I thanked Marvin and walked back to the ICU. There, Robin and Leslie were waiting in the lounge. Evidently, the look on my face revealed the grim circumstances. The two ladies took turns hugging me and said they would stay in the lounge in case I needed them. Leslie gave me my phone messages. The press and well-wishers had been calling for an update. I walked back into the ICU.

At 3:45 p.m., Dr. Seligman came in and said there were "very serious complications." He looked deeply concerned. I knew he didn't want Ross to die.

At 4:15 p.m., Dr. Seligman returned in the company of Dr. Helton. They had just reviewed more current x-rays with Marvin. Paul Seligman looked at me disconsolately and said, "Ross is on life support. If he isn't able to breathe on his own, he will not survive."

"Will he last until tomorrow morning?"

"I think so. We can always get someone through the night."

I walked into Ross's room. He was lying still with tubes in his mouth, oxygen lines through his nose, and IVs of blood, platelets, and antibiotics. Several pieces of monitoring equipment were reporting his vital signs. No one had yet pulled the plug. Under my breath, I said, "Come on, Ross, hang in there. Hang in there. Don't die."

I sat in one of the chairs outside his room and observed nurses taking turns attending to Ross. Suddenly, when one of the nurses attempted to adjust the tube in Ross's mouth, he jerked violently like he had been electrocuted. His entire body shook vigorously for a few seconds, during which time he expelled a huge amount of blood. Upon observing this, other staff scurried into Ross's room to clean and comfort their dying charge.

At 5:50 p.m., Dr. Brian Morrison advised me that "Ross is probably going to die tonight. He just had a grand mal seizure.

Chapter 45: Goodbye, My Friend

He's showing blood in his arms which may indicate bleeding into his brain." I turned around and headed toward the lounge. As I did, Dr. Michael Weissberg, whom I hadn't seen since he testified in Carlson III, entered the unit. He approached me and kindly inquired how I was doing.

"I don't think I ever realized how close I was to this young man. It's almost like losing a son."

"I'll stick around if you need me for anything," Michael offered.

I told Robin and Leslie things did not look good, and I was going to stay a little longer. I assured Robin I would be home shortly and told Leslie I would call with any news. For the next hour or so, I walked back and forth between the lounge and the ICU.

At 7:00 p.m., Dr. Rebecca Helton walked into the lounge and said, "He's in a semi-coma and may not survive the night. I should call his grandparents and inform them of the situation. They'll have to decide how long he should remain on life support."

I looked at Becky Helton for what seemed like an eternity, although it was probably just a few seconds. From the time of Craig Smith's first phone call at 2:45 a.m. on Sunday, November 5, until now — 7:00 p.m., Wednesday, November 22 — I was the only person who had been consulted regarding Ross's care. My job had been to ensure that Ross had the best chance to live. Evidently, my role had now ended.

The job of determining when to pronounce Ross dead was deemed the prerogative of his next of kin. For a split second, I was tempted to tell Dr. Helton, "Well, that's me." However, in the next breath, I knew this was not my decision. I gave Dr. Helton the phone numbers for Ross's grandparents and returned to the ICU.

At 8:00 p.m., a nurse on the night shift walked into Ross's room. I was standing there looking at the still figure of my 25-year-old client, resting peacefully. The entire unit was quiet. The guard was seated reading a magazine.

"Ross, open your eyes," the nurse said. Ross could not.

"Ross, squeeze my hand," she said. Ross could not.

The nurse went through the remaining check list of movements, while moving from one side of Ross's bed to the other, pulling on his toes and raising his fingers. Ross remained lifeless throughout this exercise.

I had fulfilled my promise. I blew a kiss and said, "Goodbye my friend."

CHAPTER 46

Remembering Special People

The next day, November 23, was Thanksgiving. That morning, Marvin called my home at 7:00. I was lying awake in bed.

"David, Ross is still on life support," Marvin said, "but he has deteriorated significantly. His chances of survival are nil. You're going to have to call the grandparents and tell them to contact me. We need to know how long they want the systems connected." Although I had expected this news, my heart sank nevertheless. The premature end of Ross's life from a dastardly illness of such short duration was a result in his case that I could have never imagined. But I was also losing someone whom I really cared about and whose life I thought I could successfully turn around so he could experience some joy in it. That goal was now unattainable. I immediately phoned Ross's maternal grandmother, Mrs. Hill, and informed her of the situation. She said she would contact other family members for a joint decision.

Within a half hour, Mrs. Hill called, saying the family had decided to allow "nature to take its course" and discontinue Ross from the machines. After the autopsy, Ross's body would then be returned to Minneapolis for internment alongside Rod and Marilyn Carlson.

At 8:45 a.m., Marvin phoned again. By this time, I was in the kitchen with Robin and the girls. We were all helping to prepare that afternoon's turkey dinner. It was all we could do to distract us from our sadness. I had anticipated this second call.

"David, Ross just died while on life support. His blood pressure fell, and his heart stopped beating. I'm sorry."

"Thanks, Marvin."

"Do you want to come down and view the body?"

I thought for a few seconds. "No, but thanks for asking. I prefer to remember how he looked when he was alive and well."

A pall of grief overcame Robin and the girls as I hung up the receiver. They surrounded and hugged me as I stood stoically in the middle of the kitchen, looking out the window at nothing in particular. The swiftness of Ross's death from the time he was diagnosed on November 4 — just 19 days ago — until today was too numbing to do anything but just stare into space. I wiped the glisten from my eyes, and, as promised, phoned a number of people with the news. I had been unable to reach Kelli Olson, but at 1:30 that afternoon, she called me in tears.

She had received a call this morning from Walter's staff informing her Ross was gravely ill. She bolted out the door, raced to the Phoenix airport, and caught a flight around 10:00. She didn't learn of Ross's death until she arrived in Denver.

"I didn't know Ross had died when I left my house. I figured if someone could tell him I was coming, he would stay alive until then," she explained while sobbing. "The plane was over booked, and there were so many people trying to fly standby. I began crying hysterically that my fiancé was dying and might not last through the day. Finally, an agent at the counter said, 'We'll get you on this plane.' I never got a chance to tell Ross a final goodbye and that I will always love him."

"When Ross died, he knew how much you loved him, Kelli."

After arranging to see Kelli tomorrow afternoon, I spent the balance of the holiday at home with family and friends. During dinner, I looked into my friends' eyes as they talked about their lives and family. I tried to be an attentive and engaging host, but all I saw were visions of a handsome 19-year-old in a county-issued orange jumpsuit, a framed poster of a white Iris, and a congratulatory note on my wedding. The next day, I had made arrangements to open and read Ross's will in front of a select few people.

At 10:45 Friday morning, November 24, Walter Gerash, Paul Vranesic, the grandparents' lawyer, and Kathy Allen from the United Bank of Denver sat in my office to learn of Ross's last wishes.

Chapter 46: Remembering Special People

I showed Walter, Kathy and Paul the 4" x 10," plain white envelope that I had received from Ross in early July 1988. The front of the envelope contained a white label which said "Carlson's Last Will and Testament 6-30-88."

I opened the envelope and removed one piece of folded, white paper. The heading read, **CARLSON'S LAST WILL AND TESTAMENT**. The document contained seven paragraphs, the date of 6/30/88, the signature *Ross M. Carlson*, and a two-sentence postscript.

Ross named me as the administrator of his estate, and he made four separate bequests.

First, he bequeathed me his papers, files, work product, computer, and computer software. He directed me to produce that material for publication, if there was such a market. I was to receive my hourly fee and expenses for that effort and 5% of any publisher derived assets. He hoped I would use those latter funds for my stepdaughter Kristin's education.

I was touched by my nomination as personal representative and smiled at the bequest of publishing his story. It was just like Ross — he knew I loved to write, and now he was challenging me creatively to write a book.

His second beneficiary was Kelli. She was to receive 15% of his current assets, 15% of any additional funds from all sources, and any other of his possessions.

The two special couples in Ross's life, Joe and Mary Guess and Jack and Maryann Keller, were mentioned next. Each couple was to receive 10% of Ross's current assets and 10% of any additional funds from all other sources.

The remaining 35% of funds from all sources were to go in trust to an organization that helped abused and neglected children. I was to select the worthy charity. If there were assets, I would have chosen the University of Colorado's Kempe Children's Center for the Prevention and Treatment of Child Abuse and Neglect.

Finally, a special account was to be established with a Minneapolis florist. Each Friday, a single yellow carnation was to be left at the grave of Marilyn Carlson.

Ross's postscript was a special thank you to the six people to whom he bequeathed his worldly bounty. Although heartfelt and sincere, Ross's intentions for the most part would have to go unfulfilled. He died with few tangible assets, and I ensured Kelli that she could select whatever she wanted from Ross's things.

Jack and Maryann Keller were touched by Ross's last wishes. While Jack served as Ross's conservator for nearly 2 ½ years, he graciously gave of his time, never seeking the limelight or any compensation for his work.

Ross's fondness for Joe and Mary Guess was even less unexpected. He knew he had become the Guess's "adopted son" throughout his ordeal. Emotion overcame Joe and Mary when I informed them of their special place in Ross's will.

By law, the balance of the money in the Rod and Marilyn Carlson trust went to Ross's grandparents. Ross's only personal possessions consisted of his clothing, stereo equipment and tapes, computer and disks, and miscellaneous files and documents. One such document was a letter addressed to Kelli which Ross had included in the larger envelope that had also contained his will.

Kelli selected those personal items which comforted her and graciously gave the Guess family one of Ross's stereos. I retained Ross's computer, disks, papers, and work product.

Ross's sudden death did not leave the people who cared about him any opportunity to bid him farewell and to comfort one another. That void, however, was soon filled by a thoughtful phone call.

CHAPTER 47

Bring Him Home

Two days before Ross's death and before any of us imagined that such an outcome was remotely imminent, I had received an unexpected phone call from Pastor Richard Groh of the Denver First Church of the Nazarene. Coincidentally, the Carlson family had attended that church during the mid-1970s long before Reverend Groh had become one of its spiritual leaders. Unaware of the Carlson family's previous connection to the church, Pastor Groh had nevertheless read about Ross's illness, was aware that Ross had no family in the area and had offered to provide him any needed care and support. At the time, Ross was too consumed with treatment issues to address the pastor's act of kindness.

However, sensing the absence of closure among Ross's friends after his death, Pastor Groh called me again, this time the day after Thanksgiving, and volunteered to have a memorial service at his church. After a quick canvass of Walter and others, I gladly accepted the pastor's offer. On Tuesday, November 28, about 75 people gathered in the church's chapel to pay tribute to Ross.

Kelli finally had the opportunity to tell the world about the seven-year relationship with her "soulmate." Their meaning for one another was captured in the letter I had given to Kelli after Ross had died. Because that letter had been included with Ross's will, I knew it had been written after I had called him on June 27, 1988, with the news of Judge Kingsley's 180-degree turnaround ruling favoring the hospital.

Kelli tearfully read Ross's parting words entitled "Farewell," which he had addressed to "Dear Silk," his affectionate name for her.

The letter, in part, said, "I suppose you could say that the majority of my life has been composed mostly of confusion and pain. If you are reading this, it is because I am no longer in this state of torment."

"In this fickle world that has vacillated so much in what is demanded from me, you were the one constant. You always loved with passion and without reservation. That is what I regret leaving behind. But I hurt and I am so tired. I desperately need some peace. A peace that I can't seem to find here. You will be sad. Time in her kindness will take the sting away."

Up until now, Kelli had done her best to read Ross's parting words. However, as she came to the next passage, she had to pause. Her pain flowed down her cheeks. Members in the audience shared her pain. After a few moments, she read on.

"Make a new beginning and try to remember me fondly. I am glad that our lives touched, and I hope that some good came of it. You have said that you love me, and I will never know how much. But your love for me could burn with no more intensity than mine does for you."

As Kelli walked from the podium, she clutched Ross's letter so no one could pry it loose. It was now the only part of him that she could cling to. She resumed her seat and slumped into the comforting arms of a friend.

The mourners' attention was now directed to Joe Guess as the slightly-built man with reddish-blond hair stepped to the stage. His once-slurred speech now fully recovered from his 1984 surgery, Joe spoke in a soft, clear voice.

"Two years ago, Ross's dog, Muffin, died," Joe said. "Upon learning of Muffin's death, Ross wrote a poem, which, I believe, could easily have been written about Ross. It reads,

> Goodbye old friend.
> You deserved much better than me.
> Your strength, courage, and intelligence
> Were your trade marks.
> In a world of hatred and pain, your heart was pure.
> You gave solace and comfort.

Chapter 47: Bring Him Home

You gave so much and asked for so little.
Sleep ..."

Joe suddenly stopped. He had been doing so well. He sniffed, brushed his moistened eye with the back of his hand, and continued,

... Sleep well Old Friend, roam free in your new pastures.
I pray you remember me fondly.

Joe then took a few deep breaths and finished with a reference to the scriptures. "I have long been concerned about the pastures Ross might face, for, as it is said in Isaiah, 'All we like sheep have gone astray.' But God has given me a calm reassurance of Ross's spiritual well-being as well as his total control of the situation that we don't understand. So now I am confident that, in spite of the ravages of evil, in spite of the vagrancies of fate, but by the love and mercies of God, freed from the pain and sorrow of earth, Rod, Marilyn, and Ross Carlson are finally reunited in love, and they share a happiness they have never known."

As Joe walked to his seat and into the embrace of his wife and two daughters, I caught his eye and conveyed a heartfelt smile. Walter spoke next.

Walter mentioned that when he first met Ross, he saw "a tortured soul." "I saw the beautiful face of a clock," he stated lyrically, "but I quickly noticed that the time piece and ticking were all wrong." Unfortunately, Ross's torment continued as the "bureaucracy of the hospital stonewalled his treatment." Walter believed that the terrible ordeal Ross had to endure within the justice system, especially at the state hospital, ravaged both his mind and body, resulting in his tragic death. As Walter left the podium, I walked to it while removing my notes from my inside suit pocket.

My upcoming eulogy was not scheduled to be the next speech I was supposed to make on behalf of Ross. That "next" speech was supposed to be in the form of a closing argument I would make at his sanity trial where I would outline the tortured life this young man led and the broken mind that resulted. There, I would seek to muster my skills as an advocate in order to persuade a jury to find Ross insane for the murder of his parents and thereby commit him to an indefinite period of mental health treatment until he was restored to sanity. There, I would talk about the productive life that was ahead for Ross Carlson once his mind, splintered from unspeakable acts of cruelty, again became whole. I never envisioned being called upon to deliver an encomium as the "next" speech for my 25-year-old client.

"I will not forget Ross Carlson very easily," I began. "He has imprinted my soul and impacted my life."

"Many lawyers," I said, "believe it is unwise to become involved in the personal life of a client, believing it may cloud the lawyer's objectivity. However, I believe that certain cases cry out for a lawyer's compassion. The plight of Ross Carlson had beckoned my humanity. Ross extended his hand in many different ways, and I grasped it quickly and tightly."

"All of us have in some way been profoundly touched by this young man during his short lifetime. What was it about Ross that attracted such warmth and emotion from so many different kinds of people?"

I mentioned his marvelous sense of humor and how when I visited him during the last few weeks in hospital room 6310, he often excused himself so he could dance for minutes on end with Ginger. I revealed that Ross often referred to the Colorado State Hospital's doctors as broken thermometers. Whatever Ross's temperature was, the state's doctors always said it was 98.6. I mentioned Ross's empathic nature and how he engaged my two stepdaughters as pen pals and offered them insights into adolescence. I talked about how considerate and thoughtful he was. "David, if this is an inconvenient time, I'll call you back," he uttered with frequency and sincerity. There were thank you notes to my secretary and birthday cards and presents to those special in his life.

"With such a large inventory of special qualities, it is easy to understand why this young man was so easy to befriend," I

Chapter 47: Bring Him Home

stated. "Like any meaningful relationship between two people, the significance of that alliance does not become realized until it is close to the end or at the end."

"I so much wanted Ross to survive his last illness. I pleaded with him to accept treatment even though it caused him pain. It hurt me to see him endure procedure after procedure, but this young man was too special. I wasn't going to lose him to leukemia without a joint fight."

"During his last day, he and I exchanged terms of endearment while holding each other's hands. When I left him for the last time and during the days since, one of my favorite songs has played over and over in my mind. The song is called *Bring Him Home*; it comes from the Broadway musical *Les Misérables*."

I explained that the scene in which the song occurs involves the main character, the elderly Jean Valjean, and a young man, named Marius. At the end of a bloody battle during the French revolution, Jean Valjean managed to escape and carry with him the severely-wounded Marius. In a desolate Parisian city, Jean Valjean cradled Marius in his arms, and cried out for the Almighty to spare Marius's life. Marius, you see, was engaged to marry Jean Valjean's daughter, Cosette. Ross Carlson had an entire life of dreams ahead of him.

Jean Valjean's plea is the song *Bring Him Home*, which I then played to the audience.

BRING HIM HOME
God on High
Hear my prayer
In my need
You have always been there.

He is young
He's afraid
Let him rest
Heaven blessed.

*He's like the son I might have known
If God had granted me a son
The summers die
One by one
How soon they fly
On and on
And I am old
And will be gone.*

*Bring him peace
Bring him joy
He is young
He is only a boy*

*You can take
You can give
Let him be
Let him live.*

*If I die, let me die
Let him live, Bring him home,
Bring him home,
Bring him home.*

"The Almighty heard Jean Valjean's words. Marius survived and married Cozette. As Ross lay in bed ravaged by his disease, God on high also heard my thoughts. Ross Carlson is finally experiencing peace and joy," I ended.

Later that day, I jogged along the Highline Canal and thought about Ross. I played the *Les Mis* tape as I ran. While continuing my solo journey along the canal, I reflected upon Ross's death and wondered why, of all days, it occurred on Thanksgiving. My pragmatic side would say it was mere happenstance, but others, I recognized, might draw a more spiritual significance.

Many individuals believed divine intervention resolved Ross's dilemma of needing treatment but having such disdain for the state

Chapter 47: Bring Him Home

hospital. Others felt the state was spared the expense of housing Ross in prison and that a double murderer motivated by greed had received a just punishment. Still, there were people who mourned Ross's passing and believed his death unjustly deprived a severely ill youth any semblance of a decent life.

Although the taking of another's life is normally unjustified, the law, however, provides exceptions under certain circumstances. Ross's defense team believed his fractured mind rendered him insane for the murders of his parents. Even the University Hospital medical staff, who cared for Ross during his last illness, aptly recognized within such a short period of time that he processed information differently than anyone whom they had ever met. Ross would often say, "I live my life like a bulletin board — I read what I'm supposed to do and where I have to go. I may not remember how everything gets done, but somehow it all does." I dare say most of us do not think like that. However, a broken and abused mind often does.

Perplexing to some is whether Ross's last wish of a weekly carnation for his mother eliminated her as a suspect of parental abuse. More confusing still is — if that hypothesis were true, why did Ross then kill both parents? The solution of a tandem death would not have been a difficult one for Ross, even if only Rod Carlson and not his wife was the abuser.

Ross viewed his parents as an inseparable unit which not even he could separate. He always felt like an outsider within his own family — looking in, but never feeling a part. If Rod Carlson had to be eliminated, so did Marilyn, his partner in marriage, who oft times may have looked the other way. Ross would never have received his mother's love if he had deprived her of Rod.

Ross's death left many unanswered questions, including who actually abused him and in what ways. Treatment of Ross's illness would have answered many of these mysteries. However, treatment never occurred.

Ross had endured five and a half regrettable years at the state hospital. In spite of that shameful experience, not once during that time did he suffer a serious physical illness.

Two days after Ross had been found competent, he was

diagnosed with leukemia. If he had not contracted the disease, the outcome of his upcoming trials destined him for a life in prison or at least fifteen or more years at the state hospital. For him, the latter of those alternatives was worse. One of the features of Ross's personality, the capable Justin Nicholas Time, was to emerge "just in time" to thoughtfully protect the other personalities from any harm. It was Justin who decided not to buy the dynamite in 1982 because the explosives were designed to blow up the Carlson home with Ross inside. It was Justin, skilled in karate, who defended the helpless "incapable" alters from school bullies and other bad actors.

I cannot help but wonder if it were Justin who emerged "just in the nick of time" to save the other personalities from a life behind bars or from the more unacceptable confinement at the state hospital. How timely for the solution to have occurred on a day of family gathering, Thanksgiving. For it was on that day that Ross Carlson may have achieved in death what he had never accomplished in life — peace with his parents.

Chapter 47: Bring Him Home

```
Carlson's Last Will
and Testament 6-30-88
```

Outside of the envelope typed by Ross that contained the Last Will and Testament of June 30, 1988 he sent to David Savitz

CARLSON'S LAST WILL AND TESTAMENT

To Jack and Maryann Keller, I request that 10% of my current assets and 10% of all future funds derived from any and all sources be distributed to them in trust over seen by Mr. Savitz.

The remaining 35% of funds that may be derived in the future, I wish to have put in trust overseen by Mr. Savitz and for the interest from that trust donated to a group that works for the care and protection of abused children. This group receiving these funds will be chosen by Mr. Savitz on the merit of their performance of meeting the needs of the children.

Of the remaining funds that may be left, I wish that an account be opened with a Minneapolis florist and that a single yellow carnation be left each friday at the grave of Marilyn Carlson.

Date: 6-30-88   Signature: [signature]

Ross's excerpted typed comments and signature of his Last Will and Testament dated June 30, 1988

EPILOGUE

Much has happened in my life — both professionally and personally — since Thanksgiving 1989, the day Ross Carlson died. During the 1990s, I represented other persons afflicted with MPD. Every one of those cases, however, was civil in nature.

One involved a malpractice suit on behalf of a woman against her former treating psychologist; Dr. Fisch referred this client to me. While treating my client, who sold life insurance, the psychologist frequently discussed problems he was encountering with the insurance policies he had purchased from her. My client became very confused during therapy. She didn't know whether to talk about the parent who had abused her as a kid or her shrink who was now abusing her as an adult. The psychologist settled before trial.

In another case, I represented a man in his late 20s who had been repeatedly sodomized by his small-town pastor while the client had been an altar boy. The youngster then became horrifically victimized for many years by a satanic cult of which the pastor was a member. The client, whose dominant personality was gay, had more than 20 personalities, including some who were female. One of the younger personalities loved showing me how *she* played with a little stuffed puppy which the client carried in *his* knapsack. The client's mind was so fragmented that I recommended long-term therapy versus pursuit of a costly and emotionally wrenching lawsuit.

A third client was a very attractive and coquettish woman in her early-30s who was in the midst of a divorce. Normally, I loathed practicing in the domestic relations area, but took the case because of the young lady's illness. During her testimony at the permanent orders hearing, the client switched to a young girl who cried out for me to save her from the bad man. The bad man was my adversary who, in the midst of his cross-examination, caused my client to switch to a weeping child. He looked at me apologetically while I was seated at the plaintiff's table and said "Help me!" With the judge's permission, I approached the

Epilogue : Bring Him Home

witness stand and gently calmed down my client. Soon, she reverted to her main personality. After awarding my client maintenance and long-term mental health treatment, the judge, a widower, called me to the bench and whispered half-kiddingly, "David, when this case is over, will you fix me up with the older one?" In the next breath, he admitted he had always been skeptical about the disorder, but firmly believed in its legitimacy after hearing expert testimony from Dr. Fisch and seeing the client's transformation into different personalities before his own eyes.

Besides these three sufferers, there were others, including a woman in 2007 who was seeking the return of custody of her two teenage children and another lady in 2009 who suffered injuries in an automobile collision. The latter female was another referral from Dr. Fisch. My experience with each of these individuals provided eerie similarities to my experience with Ross.

All of these other clients had several personalities with different names, ages, and features. Each of the clients had been victimized by child abuse — always repeated acts and always sexual in nature. Each client possessed a dominant alter who seemingly dealt with me a majority of the time, and each had a depressing personality and one or two younger alters. Every client's behavior was consistently unpredictable. All of the clients trusted me, and every one of them tugged at my heart.

I wanted each to feel better and become whole. I was upset they had been brutalized as a defenseless child by a very mean adult, and I fervently wanted to prevent that conduct from recurring. Those are the feelings which brought me to the Kempe Children's Center and its fundraising arm, the Kempe Children's Foundation, the community passion in my life. The Center is the facility which Ross and I discussed during the later stages of his case but which I first heard about during Thanksgiving weekend of 1986 in a case totally unrelated to Ross's, which at that time had been ongoing for more than three years.

On November 28, 1986, the day after Thanksgiving, I was working in my office and minding my own business when the phone rang. That summer the Colorado Supreme Court had overturned Judge Day's ruling that appointed Dr. Barry Quinn to treat Ross and for the hospital to pay the doctor's fees. As a result of the Supreme Court's ruling, Ross was languishing without therapy. He had developed a new personality Holdin to deal with the state hospital so he could appear competent. However, this particular call had nothing to do with Ross. The speaker's tone was very subdued.

"Dave, Judge Carelli."

Immediately, I knew a joyless call from a district court judge on a holiday weekend did not have the feel of a Hallmark greeting card. I had known the judge for many years and sensed from his serious tone that idle banter was not on his mind. He came right to the point. "I'm glad I caught you in, Dave, because I'd like you to do the court a favor."

I knew I was in for some major trouble. A judge asking for a favor ran neck-and-neck with a mother asking, "So why haven't you visited me lately?" I decided to hear the inevitable.

"How can I help judge?"

"Dave, I have a case in my courtroom where I've already appointed a lawyer, but he has asked to withdraw. Says he can't handle it. I need an experienced lawyer."

"What kind of case, your Honor?"

"It's a child-abuse death case."

I knew it! It was something horrific!

"A three-year-old boy was allegedly beaten to death by his parents. The public defender represents the mother, and I'd like you to represent the father."

The words "three-year-old beaten to death" evoked an awful feeling. I had become emotionally detached from the deaths of Rod and Marilyn Carlson but became dispirited upon now learning of the fate of such a young child.

I kicked myself in the rear for having come to work that Friday. A part of me wanted to say, "Judge, why don't we both hang up and act as if this call never occurred." However, I respected my ethical responsibility to accept even the most unsavory and heinous kinds of cases and obliged the judge. The next month, I met with the coroner and learned of Anthony Wright's last few months on earth.

Anthony had visible bruises, lacerations, and external marks of different sizes and colorations on nearly every part of his body — skull, lip, chest, stomach, penis, quadriceps, back, buttocks, and hamstrings. He died of a combination of a subdural hematoma (bleeding into the

Epilogue : Bring Him Home

brain) and internal abdominal carnage. The probable instrumentalities of the non-deadly injuries included a metal hanger, stick, belt, wire paint brush, hand, and fist. The lethal injuries were likely caused by an iron-piggy-bank smash to the skull and a brutal kick with leather shoes to the stomach.

Notwithstanding the gruesome nature of Anthony's death, I vowed to represent his father with all the fervor and zeal I could muster. I would try to show he was a non-player or minor participant in the conduct and that the child's mother was the main perpetrator. However, if convicted, I would ask for a short prison term because the father had been abused as a child and was merely repeating a cycle from which he did not know any better. Those were my obligations. The constitution demanded no less.

In preparation for trial, I spoke with many local child abuse experts. Most impressive were those affiliated with the University of Colorado's Kempe Children's Center. The bad news was that the Kempe Center's witnesses were scheduled to testify for the prosecution. The good news was I discovered a potential resource for the Carlson case and an eventual worthwhile civic endeavor.

While simultaneously representing Ross Carlson and Anthony Wright's father, I had seen the worst possible outcomes from two different families. The fatal results in both situations were tragic but preventable. Anthony Wright's father received 28 years in prison for his conduct; the mother received 18 years, her break for testifying for the prosecution. Ross's situation was, of course, resolved by a much higher power. Both of those cases combined as the springboard for my charitable work for the Kempe Children's Foundation. After Ross died, I knew I wanted to help try to reduce the incidence of child abuse.[2]

Since 1992 and for a total of twenty-five years, I served in different capacities as a board member of the Kempe Children's Foundation. During that time, I spoke to thousands of people about the nature and ills of child abuse, including high school and college students, teachers of all grades, legal, medical, and religious groups, and various community, statewide, and national organizations. I have talked to as few as five

---

2. In the spirit of Ross's bequest in his Last Will and Testament, a portion of the proceeds from this book's sales will be donated to Kempe in his name.

people and to as many as 500. No audience was ever too small.

During one occasion in April of 1992, I spoke to several teenagers who were participating in a diversionary program through the Denver juvenile court system. A 14-year-old boy slipped me a piece of note paper; it read "Wuy do you thank most fimly are violent?" I told him most families aren't. He never knew that.

By now, that teenage boy has reached adulthood. Hopefully, he has discovered I was right.

Other people connected to the Carlson case with whom I have remained close have continued their journeys in their respective careers or experienced peaceful closure. As of the time of this publication, Walter Gerash is 94 years old and has long retired from the practice of law. Dr. Ralph Fisch passed away a few years ago, but until his death continued treating all forms of dissociative behavior, and continued to flatter me with his referrals. Both Judge Day and Judge Kingsley have passed away after distinguished careers on the bench.

Michael Weissberg and I have become good friends over the years. When Ross was receiving his leukemic treatment at The University of Colorado Medical Center, Michael offered to see him and comforted me upon observing my vigil. Michael and I have shared opposite ends of the podium in several forums discussing this case. To this day, we respectfully disagree about Ross Carlson, even though Michael continues to be wrong. We have enormous respect for each other's professional skills and refer cases to one another. Michael served as my expert consultant when I sued one of his colleagues for psychiatric malpractice during the late-1990s. He published a book about the *Carlson* case, entitled *The Last Deadly Sin of Ross Michael Carlson*, and encouraged me to write mine. As the inspiration for this book, I wish I could tell Michael that it is has been published. I know he'd be pleased. Regrettably, he has been suffering from Alzheimer's disease for more than a year and would not be able to comprehend my thanks or remember who I am. I am saddened by his illness.

In 1993, Robin and I moved to the foothills outside of Denver amidst a forest of Evergreens and herds of deer. We became empty nesters a few years later when Rachel and then Kristin moved onto college. Both young women have been carving out productive lives for themselves, Rachel in the real estate world in Denver, and Kristin, as a

Epilogue : Bring Him Home

teacher in southwestern Colorado. She is the mother of our adorable grandchildren, Piper Sue, born in May 2006, and Kash Cooper, born in February 2009.

My son Curtis has flourished in the business world in the Dallas, Texas area and has been married to a southern belle, Renee Savitz, since 1988. They are the proud parents of my adult grandchildren, Cameron, born in September 1993, and Madison, born in December 1994. Madison was married on October 7, 2018. About two years later, on November 20, 2020, she and her husband Bill presented Robin and me with our first great grandchild, Zane Zizzis Savitz Ioannides.

As much as we all savor new and healthy lives, we are constantly reminded of the inevitability of the converse. On April 14, 1995, my father died at the age of 80. Thirteen years later, on January 2, 2008, my mother followed at age 89. It was my parents' model of benevolence that has provided me with the tools to reach out to others, including, of course, Ross.

In March 2001, I was profoundly touched by another exceptional person who had been involved in the Carlson case. Then, Dr. Newton, with whom I had developed a very special relationship since Ross's death, called me. I assumed it was either to inform me he was about to visit Denver or to cajole Robin and me to make another trip to Bozeman and meet his new wife, Patti. Instead, it was to say he had just been diagnosed with terminal leukemia. At his age of 83, Fig had elected to forego any treatment, refusing to endure the agony of chemotherapy just to live another few months. He was calling to say goodbye and to thank me for having been such a good friend. He estimated he had perhaps a couple of weeks to live. On March 20, I flew to Bozeman and spent that night and the next morning reminiscing with Fig. I did most of the talking; he could barely speak. He was so tired and weak. Two days later, Patti Newton called to say that Fig had stayed alive just to see me one last time. He died early that morning.

Was it purely coincidence or something more profound that two of the most disparate figures in the Ross Carlson case died of leukemia — one at age 25 and the other at age 83? I do not know. However, I thank them both for teaching me so much about this illness. I dedicate this book to them.

APPENDIX A

From Paracelsus to the Hillside Strangler

Although Paracelsus is believed to have described the first case of MPD in 1646,[3] the illness did not become well known by the public until the last half of the twentieth century. During that period, the mental disorder was chronicled in the widely read stories of **The Three Faces of Eve**[4] and **Sybil**.[5] Before 1980, MPD was not formally recognized by the psychiatric community as a discrete mental illness but only as a symptom of hysterical neurosis.[6] However, in 1980, the American Psychiatric Association's *Diagnostic and Statistical Manual of Mental Disorders (DSM-III)* listed MPD as a diagnostic entity under the category, dissociative disorders. At that time, the illness was thought to be very rare in the general population,[7] in part, because MPD exhibits a multitude of symptoms among many personality states, thus making it difficult to diagnose and differentiate from other psychiatric syndromes.[8] In addition, other psychiatric disorders, such as atypical psychosis, major depression,

---

3. Bliss, E. L. (1980), Multiple Personalities: A report of 14 cases with implications for schizophrenia and hysteria. *Archives of General Psychiatry*, 37: 1388-97; and Putnam, F.W. (1989), A History and Definitional Criteria. *Diagnosis and Treatment of Multiple Personality Disorder*, New York: The Guilford Press, 28.
4. Thigpen, C.H., and Cleckley, H: New York, McGraw Hill, 1957.
5. Schreiber, F.R.: Chicago, Henry Regency Company, 1973.
6. Coons, P.M. (1984), The Differential Diagnosis of Multiple Personality. *Psychiatric Clinics of North America*, 7(1), 51.
7. Braun, B.C. (1984), Foreword. *Psychiatric Clinics of North America*, 7(1), 1.
8. Coons, P.M. (1984), 51.

Appendix A: From Paracelsus to the Hillside Strangler

and various psychosexual and personality disorders, may often coexist with MPD.[9] That earlier belief may have been unfounded, resulting in the past under-diagnosis of MPD and clinical decision to diagnose many patients as schizophrenic, which was a much more popular diagnosis at the time.[10] Adding to the confusion is that the term "split personality" has often been used to describe schizophrenia because during some phase of that illness the individual would experience delusions, hallucinations, or a disturbance in affect and form of thought. The fanciful term of "split personality," however, is often mistaken for but should not be confused with multiple personalities, which, as shown in this book, has much different diagnostic criteria.

Another diagnostic hurdle to MPD is that many sufferers of that illness would be unaware or indifferent to lapses of time.[11] If they became aware and mentioned it, they feared being called "crazy," thus they did not report the amnesia.[12] Still others suffering from the disorder did so with personality states which either choose to keep their existence hidden, or were powerful enough to suppress weaker states from emerging.[13]

Since the primary cause of MPD is child sexual abuse, many patients were threatened with severe bodily harm or death if they revealed the dark secrets of their bedroom.[14] As a result, many

---

9. Coons, P.M.(1984), 52.
10. Coons, P.M. (1984), 51.
11. Coons, P.M. (1984), 52.
12. Coons, P.M. (1984), 52.
13. Kluft, R.P. (1985), The Natural History of MPD. *Childhood Antecedents of Multiple Personality*, American Psychiatric Press, Inc., 205-06. A special note of thanks is extended to R. Richard P. Kluft. Ever since Dr. Cornelia Wilbur referred me to this esteemed psychiatrist from Pennsylvania, Dr. Kluft became my closest behind-the-scenes consultant throughout the course of Carlson. During that period, the doctor was one of the country's foremost experts in MPD, wrote prolifically about the illness, and, although I would have gladly done so, never asked for a cent in spite of the numerous times I accessed his expertise. Richard Kluft was merely a dedicated professional.
14. Wilbur, C.B. (1985), The Effect of Child Abuse on the Psyche. *Childhood Antecedents of Multiple Personality*, American Psychiatric Press, Inc., 21-35.

sufferers led a life of repression and denial and hid their disorder.[15] Lastly, many clinicians doubted MPD's authenticity because of its dramatic presentation.[16]

During the mid-1980s, an abundance of literature was published devoted exclusively to the understanding, diagnosis, and treatment of MPD.[17] Particularly meaningful from this literature was the collective assessment by clinicians that an average of 6.8 years elapsed between the time patients entered therapy with symptoms compatible with the illness until the time they received an accurate diagnosis.[18] During that time, the patients received an average of 3.6 erroneous diagnoses.[19] It was not surprising that the American Psychiatric Association then reexamined the incidences of the disorder in the general population.

In 1987, the revised edition of the *Diagnostic and Statistical Manual of Mental Disorders (DSM-III-R)* no longer considered the prevalence of MPD as so rare as had been earlier thought. By 1988, it was estimated there was at least a quarter of a million sufferers in the continental United States.[20] Since that time, there was a sharp increase in reported cases in the United States. Some believed the 1980s' increase had been due to improved awareness among mental health professionals, while others believed the illness had been over diagnosed in persons who were highly suggestible to the inadvertent cues of their therapist.[21]

In the *DSM-IV*, published in 1994, the name of the illness was changed to Dissociative Identity Disorder or DID. The name change evolved both to dispel the notion that there are actually different "persons" inhabiting the patient's body and to more accurately reflect the pathological disturbance of identity created psychodynamically. Since the events regarding Ross Carlson predated 1994, his illness has

---

15. Wilbur, C.B. (1985), 21-35.
16. Coons, P.M. (1984), 51.
17. Braun, B.G. (1984), 1; and Coons, P.M. (1988), Introduction. *Dissociative Disorders 1988. Proceedings of the Fifth International Conference on Multiple Personality/Dissociative States*, Chicago: Rush-Presbyterian-St. Lukes Medical Center, xv-xvi.
18. Kluft, R.P. (1987), An Update on Multiple Personality Disorder. *Hospital and Community Psychiatry*, 38(4), 365.
19. Kluft, R.P. (1987), 365.
20. Kluft, R.P. (1988), Resolved Multiple Personality Disorder as a True Disease Entity. APA Annual Meeting, Montreal, Canada, May 10, 1988.
21. Kluft, R.P. (1987), 363-65.

Appendix A: From Paracelsus to the Hillside Strangler

typically been referred to throughout this book as MPD or multiple personality disorder.

The recognition of MPD as a mental illness that would excuse criminal responsibility did not occur until Billy Milligan, the Ohio rapist, was declared insane in 1978.[22] The Los Angeles Hillside Strangler, Kenneth Bianchi, tried to use that defense in 1979 but was unsuccessful.[23] In December 1983, Ross Carlson entered a plea of not guilty by reason of insanity to two counts of first degree murder, also on the basis of MPD, which is the most serious of the four types of dissociative disorders.[24]

The psychological doctrine of association is that memories are brought to our consciousness or awareness through the connection of ideas.[25] Things which could not be remembered but existed separately in our subconscious are deemed "dissociated."[26] The various types of dissociation can be conceptualized as lying on a continuum from the minor adaptive behaviors of everyday life — such as daydreaming, meditating, or the classical adolescent "tuning out"[27] — to the major pathological forms, such as multiple personality disorder, the most maladaptive of them all.[28]

---

22. Savitz, D.B. (1990), The Legal Defense of Persons with the Diagnosis of Multiple Personality Disorder. *Dissociation*, III(4), 195. Thanks to Dr. Kluft, who was one of the editors of this journal, I was afforded the opportunity to make my first contribution to the psychiatric literature.
23. Savitz, D.B. (1990), 195.
24. Because so much of this story occurred from 1984 through 1989, the psychiatric manual referenced during the balance of this chapter will be the 1987 *DSM-III-R* (American Psychiatric Association, (1987), *Diagnostic and Statistical Manual of Mental Disorders, (3rd ed. — revised)*, Washington, D.C.: Author).
25. Frischholz, E.J. (1985), The Relationship Between Dissociation, Hypnosis, and Child Abuse in the Development of MPD. *Childhood Antecedents of Multiple Personality*. American Psychiatric Press, Inc., 101.
26. Frischholz, E.J. (1985), 101.
27. Trial lawyers often utilize the adult form of "tuning out," for example, when a witness we're examining unexpectedly blurts out a statement harmful to our case. Instead of showing our displeasure with the comment, or emoting in some other manner that our case has been adversely affected, we respond nonchalantly as if the comment were the most innocuous utterance ever made in a court of law.
28. Putnam, F.W. (1989), 6.

Three principles can be used to characterize most conditions of pathological dissociation. The first is that the individual undergoing a dissociative reaction experiences an alteration in his or her sense of identity.[29] Secondly, there will be a disturbance in the individual's memory for events occurring during a period of dissociation.[30] And thirdly, the vast majority of dissociative disorders are traumatically induced.[31]

The dissociative disorders recognized in the *DSM-5* are: (1) Dissociative Identity Disorder; (2) Dissociative Amnesia; (3) Depersonalization/Derealization Disorder; (4) Other Specified Dissociative Disorder; and (5) Unspecified Dissociative Disorder. If interested, the reader can explore the differences in these disorders by consulting the *DSM-5*.

---

29. Putnam, F.W. (1989), 6.
30. Putnam, F.W. (1989), 7.
31. Putnam, F.W. (1989), 7.